Melodrama and Meaning

MELODRAMA
AND
MEANING
*History, Culture, and
the Films of Douglas Sirk*

Barbara Klinger

Indiana University Press

Bloomington and Indianapolis

The paper used in this publication meets the minimum requirements of American
National Standard for Information Sciences—Permanence of Paper for Printed
Library Materials, ANSI Z39.48-1984.

Manufactured in the United States of America

Library of Congress Cataloging-in-Publication Data

Klinger, Barbara, date
Melodrama and meaning : history, culture, and the films of Douglas
Sirk / Barbara Klinger.
p. cm.
Filmography: p.
Includes bibliographical references and index.
ISBN 0-253-33199-4 (alk. paper).—ISBN
0-253-20875-0 (pbk. : alk. paper)
1. Sirk, Douglas, 1900–1987—Criticism and interpretation.
2. Melodrama in motion pictures. I. Title.
PN1998.3.S57K55   1994
791.43'0233'092—dc20   93-27574

1 2 3 4 5 99 98 97 96 95 94

For Richard and Matthew

Contents

Acknowledgments   *ix*

Introduction   The Many Faces of Melodrama   *xi*

1

The "Progressive" Auteur, Melodrama, and Canonicity   *1*

2

Selling Melodrama: Sex, Affluence, and *Written on the Wind*   *36*

3

Tastemaking: Reviews, Popular Canons, and Soap Operas   *69*

4

Star Gossip: Rock Hudson and the Burdens of Masculinity   *97*

5

Mass Camp and the Old Hollywood Melodrama Today   *132*

Conclusion   Cinema, Ideology, History   *157*

Notes   *163*

Filmography   *181*

Bibliography   *182*

Index   *194*

Acknowledgments

I AM INDEBTED TO a great many people who contributed to the progress and completion of this book. For their powers of criticism and encouragement at the very earliest stages of my research, I wholeheartedly thank D. N. Rodowick and J. Dudley Andrew. More recently, James Naremore, Claudia Gorbman, Dana Polan, and Mike Budd read versions of the manuscript, providing insights and revision suggestions that I found instrumental in sharpening arguments and clarifying the organization of various chapters. For their extensive time and energy, I am deeply grateful. Christine Gledhill generously provided me with some additional bibliography from the BFI card catalogues that helped me realize the depth and breadth of academic writing on Sirk. Laura Mulvey offered a fascinating account of British intellectual life in the 1960s and 1970s, only a small part of which I was able to include, but which nonetheless provided a significant framework for thinking about early writings on Sirk.

Without the support of Indiana University, I would have been without the time and often the inspiration for writing. The comparative literature program granted me a leave to get started on the manuscript. The Office of Research and the University Graduate School awarded me a summer faculty fellowship in 1990 so that I could devote that time to writing. In addition, the Dean of the Faculties Office funded a year-long Multidisciplinary Faculty Seminar on Cultural Studies that R. Christopher Anderson and I coorganized in 1990–91. Through my exposure to different fields interested in cultural history in the course of this seminar, I substantially rethought my manuscript to make its arguments more historically responsive. For their part in this aspect of revision, I thank Chris Anderson, James Naremore, Casey Blake, Patrick Brantlinger, Kathryn Flannery, Richard Bauman, and Beverly Stoeltje.

I have also benefited greatly from the students at Indiana. John Berks and Millie Manglis helped with various editorial aspects of the manuscript. The students in my seminar on the 1950s and in my American film class provided such stimulating discussions of the postwar era that my own work on the period was significantly energized. Tom Amettis patiently photographed many of the illustrations in the book.

Valuable contextual information came from film archives in Los Angeles and New York. Ned Comstock at the Doheny Library's special collections at the University of Southern California led me to an impressive collection of materials from Universal-International regarding the studio's advertising policies during the 1950s and its specific campaign for *Written on the Wind*. The Margaret Herrick Library at The Academy of Motion Picture Arts and Sciences in Los Angeles held the trailer transcripts for all of Sirk's melodramas, as well as bountiful clippings from fan magazines on Rock Hudson. At the University of California Los Angeles, I viewed several of Hudson's films from the 1960s, as well as episodes of the 1950s television game show, "Strike It Rich." In New York, the Museum of Modern Art and the New York Public Library had press books and clippings on the films' stars that proved very useful for conceptualizing how studio and media practices contribute to film meaning.

Finally, Richard Miller gave me the kind of boundless support, sharp editorial insight, and repartee I needed to get through the Sturm und Drang of writing. For his ability to transform the most serious of moods into the silliest, Matthew Miller deserves an equally special place in these acknowledgments.

Introduction

The Many Faces of Melodrama

If you wish to observe the process of combustion, you have
to put the object into an atmospheric medium.

V. N. Vološinov[1]

URING THE LAST forty years Douglas Sirk and his family melodramas have
achieved an almost legendary status in film studies. While French critics
had written enthusiastically about Sirk as early as the 1950s, he gained what
would become his lasting critical reputation in the field in subsequent decades.
From the 1970s forward, British and U.S. Marxists and feminists defined Sirk as
a significant political auteur and subversive master of melodrama.

Much of the academic left's attraction to Sirk stemmed from his situation as
a European intellectual working within the formulaic system of Hollywood filmmaking. Born in Germany of Danish parents in 1900, Sirk (an Americanization
of "Sierck") was educated at German universities in law, philosophy, painting,
and art history. He had extensive training in theater, overseeing productions of
the works of such renowned dramatists as Sophocles, William Shakespeare, August Strindberg, and Bertolt Brecht. He also served an apprenticeship in cinema
at the prestigious German film studio UFA. Due to the increasingly inhospitable
climate of Germany, Sirk left the country in 1937, eventually immigrating to Hollywood to work at Warner Bros., Columbia, and finally Universal-International.
It was at this last studio that he made his most highly regarded melodramas:
Magnificent Obsession (1954), *All That Heaven Allows* (1955), *Written on the
Wind* (1957), *Tarnished Angels* (1958), and *Imitation of Life* (1959).[2] Sirk's biographical credentials and interviews established him as an artist familiar with
sophisticated theories of representation and capable of articulating the social significance of his films. In Sirk, critics found a filmmaker who, in addition to embodying one of the major axioms of the auteur theory concerning the ability of
gifted directors to create films of substance within conventional Hollywood
genres, seemed dedicated to critiquing the bourgeoisie.

Sirk's political auteurism in the early 1970s had almost immediate consequences for the study of melodrama. Inspired by Sirk's reflective observations on his filmmaking, Thomas Elsaesser wrote an influential essay that invented a category of films called the "sophisticated family melodramas" of the 1940s and 1950s, largely comprised of the works of Sirk, Nicholas Ray, and Vincente Minnelli. This label defined the potential of some melodramas to surpass the genre's cathartic aims and reactionary tendencies to achieve aesthetic complexity and social commentary. Thus, the sophisticated family melodrama realized the genre's historical capability to act as a revolutionary form during times of cultural struggle.[3] From this critical perspective, the vivid critiques of the family as a social institution, the anguished sexual malaise, and the excessively symptomatic style in Ray's *Bigger Than Life* (1956), Minnelli's *Home from the Hill* (1960), and Sirk's *Written on the Wind* appeared ingeniously transgressive of the repressive Eisenhower era with its vision of the complacent nuclear family. Sirk, the most self-consciously Brechtian of these directors, emerged from Elsaesser's essay as a filmmaker whose oeuvre demonstrated how melodrama, often considered a trivial genre, could achieve the status of a serious artistic and cultural form.

Numerous critics have since noted Sirk's responsibility for the attention that melodrama subsequently received in film, television, and popular cultural studies. Pointing out that Marxist appreciation of this director as a political auteur led scholars to seriously consider melodrama as a genre worthy of analysis for the first time, Christine Gledhill writes, "Through discovery of Sirk, a genre came into view."[4] Such accounts portray Sirk criticism as instrumental in creating academic respect for the genre, as well as in founding perspectives on melodrama's subversive relationship to the dominant ideology. As the "father," in this sense, of melodrama theory and criticism, it is not surprising that Sirk continues to hold a prominent place in contemporary work on the genre.[5]

While still clearly invested in Sirk's importance to auteur and genre criticism, this book attempts to reconsider substantially the legend of Sirk and his sophisticated family melodramas as it has been passed down through several generations of academic theorists and critics. Specifically, I want to explore how historical analysis challenges our ideas about this director and his films. My reasons for wanting to subject these films to historical revision are twofold. First, political analysis of Sirk's melodramas has tended to be regulated mainly by biography and form; that is, by Sirk's avowed intentions to critique America as realized in the internal structures of his films. This study seeks to provide a stronger historical dimension to questions of the relationship of auteur, genre, and ideology, arguing that such a dimension is crucial to recognizing the role external social and historical factors play in negotiating the cultural politics of a body of films. Second, the process of placing Sirk's films in social and historical context raises a more general issue. What determines a film's meaning and ideological significance? Its internal features? Its viewers? The discursive environments in which it appears? My analysis will address the particular contributions these environments make to understanding how film meanings are created and changed over time. Historicizing Sirk's films thus has larger implications for understanding the impact of cultural forces on interpretation, giving us insight into the intricate relations between texts and their contexts.

Like the work of Jane Tompkins on Hawthorne, Charles Maland on Chaplin, and Robert Kapsis on Hitchcock, I offer an authorial case study that questions conceptions of artistic reputation as constituted by the merits of an oeuvre.[6] I examine the process of "reputation building" that took place in relation to Sirk; that is, how his creative identity and the meaning of his melodramas were *constructed* by such factors as his publicized intentions, the practices of critical institutions, the media, and social and political circumstances. Departing from the idea that works alone reveal the genius of their authors, this approach helps us grasp the dialogic relation between artistic reputations and history—the dynamic circumstances under which an author's status and the status of her or his works are established, sustained, transformed, unappreciated, or even vilified. Thus, part of this book will explore the dependence of Sirk's authorship on historical developments, as well as key factors within academic and journalistic institutions that defined his melodramas from the 1950s through the 1980s.

As the "father" of melodrama studies, Sirk also provides an opportunity to reconsider melodrama's relation to culture, ideology, and history. Since the influential work of *Screen*, Thomas Elsaesser, and Peter Brooks in the 1970s, examinations of film melodrama have rarely lacked attention to this relation. In approaches devoted primarily to textual analysis, critics have continually interpreted individual films as responses to times of national and social crisis, from the moral dilemmas of post-revolutionary France, to the class conflicts and forbidding sexual mores of the Victorian era, to the repressiveness of the postwar, Eisenhower years.

Yet textualists often have not sought to interrogate fully melodrama's historical dimensions, but to establish the aesthetic and political codes of its form. Close analysis has tended to privilege the text itself, "only mak[ing] use of melodrama's history as it contributes to defining the melodramatic mode," as Peter Brooks has said in describing the parameters of his own study.[7] In interpretations focused primarily on identifying the narrative and stylistic traits of a genre, history frequently serves as a backdrop against which the vivid formal responses of the individual text are staged. When history assumes this secondary function, eras can appear as monolithic (that is, the repressive Eisenhower years), rather than as times exhibiting complex and contradictory attitudes toward such issues as the family and sexuality. Similarly, we may gain little information about the social networks that make melodramas so popular and meaningful for their audiences, networks that substantially help to negotiate a genre's ideological meaning in specific settings.

More recently, research by Lea Jacobs, Jeanne Allen, Maria LaPlace, and others has considered the effect such contexts have on melodrama by examining the original circumstances in which various kinds of melodramas were produced and received. These writers clarify the roles played by social institutions and cultural discourses in shaping the genre's significance in particular circumstances, discussing the impact of such factors as censorship, consumer culture, and star images on melodrama's form and appeal to historical audiences.[8] Attempts to thus contextualize melodrama depict history as a discursive field that acts on the genre to negotiate the structure and signification of its most intimate internal features. In this sense, film form is inextricably bound to the historical agencies that define the conditions of cinema's cultural existence. Moreover, by giving us insight into past identities specific melodramas may have had, historians also present us with a sense of their "lived ideologies," ideological values attained as a result of particular social contingencies.

I wish to pursue the implications this research has for understanding melodramatic meaning by taking it one step further. Characteristically, scholars have discussed how contextual factors within the genre's original circumstances of reception have affected its ideological status. The synchronic, rather than the diachronic, dimensions of meaning have thus commanded scholarly attention. Melodrama's essential historical *variability*—the many faces it has taken on as it has passed through different institutional settings and eras in U.S. culture during the course of its circulation—still remains to be examined.[9] By studying this passage, we can envision and debate the dynamic impact history has on the *meanings* of melodrama, that is, its role in constantly reshaping the genre's ideological function over time.

Such a reconsideration is especially warranted in the case of Sirk. Until very recently, critical analysis of his films has been untouched by the concern in cultural studies with historicizing questions of ideology. Through decades of theory and criticism, Sirk's films assumed a fixed identity as transgressive, based largely on their formal characteristics. What Paul Willemen once referred to as the "Sirkian System"—a visual register characterized by self-reflexive and ironic devices—seemed to indicate so clearly a subversive sensibility that radically different conceptions of ideological identity appeared as either unimaginable or simply wrong.[10] Assumptions about the apparent "self-evidence" of the Sirkian system thus obscured other possible meanings these melodramas may have had, leaving the question of their social and historical reception unresolved.

A brief look at the history of Sirk's melodramas tells us that these films have indeed been subject to a vivid array of meanings through the force of changing cultural circumstances. Besides the academic status that Sirk's films have enjoyed, they have had at least six other significant identities from the 1950s to the 1990s. During the 1950s, Universal-International Pictures presented Sirk's melodramas as slick, sexually explicit "adult" films in accordance with the postwar culture's emphasis on sexual display in representation. At the same time, film reviewers decried his melodramas as "soap operas," typical not only of the crass commercialism of the film industry, but also of the frightening mediocrity of a mass culture with fascist tendencies. Moreover, with Rock Hudson as their star, Sirk's films represented a certain celebration of "normal" masculinity in the face of a social crisis about virility in the postwar era.

In a more contemporary setting, reviewers operating under the influence of the powerful nostalgia of the 1970s transformed Sirk's films and those of many other studio-era directors into "classics," while the revelation of Hudson's gay identity in the 1980s made Sirk melodramas into treatises on the artifice of romance and gender roles in the Hollywood cinema. And, within the highly self-conscious and intertextual climate of today, Sirk's melodramas appear as "camp," as parodic spectacles of excess. Including their academic definition, then, Sirk's films have been historically characterized as subversive, adult, trash, classic, camp, and vehicles of gender definition.

My intention is not to decide which of these versions of the Sirk melodrama is correct. Nor is it simply to combine Sirk's various identities, thereby creating a synthetic picture of a contradictory figure. Instead, I want to examine the institutional, cultural, and historical conditions that enabled these different identities to emerge. In so doing, I hope to contribute to a broader understanding of the relations between the post–World War II melodrama and culture, from the genre's association with postwar attitudes about sexuality, masculinity, and mass culture to its more contemporary rewritings as subversive by film academics, classic by reviewers, and camp by mainstream audiences. Moreover, I hope to contribute to recent research focused on the manner in which institutional contexts most associated with the Hollywood cinema (such as academia, the film industry, review journalism, star publicity, and the contemporary mass media in general) create meaning and ideological identity for films. I am just as concerned with how these habitats of meaning operate—that is, with the principles and developments that guide their strategies of signification—as I am with exactly what visions of melodrama they produce.

As I mentioned, historicizing Sirk and the family melodrama also raises a larger theoretical issue: the relation of historical context to film meaning. The textual focus in past studies of melodrama is part of a tradition in the academy that focuses on narrative cues and visual style to marshal arguments about signification. But, as research in reception theory in literary, media, and cultural studies has recently suggested, intrinsic analysis is generally insufficient for understanding certain dimensions of meaning-production central to a medium's existence. As literary forms, films, and television shows pass through culture and history, they are subject to systems of signification that lie outside textual boundaries, systems largely responsible for negotiating their public identity.

While some theorists, such as David Morley and Janice Radway, have addressed social variations of meaning by focusing on the audience, this book belongs rather to what Janet Staiger has recently termed a "historical materialist approach to reception studies."[11] Like Staiger, I argue that we must consider the contributions that contextual factors, as opposed to textual devices or viewer subjectivities, make to an understanding of how texts mean.[12] The contextual factors that accompany the presentation of a film, including such materials as film reviews and industry promotions as well as specific historical conditions, serve as signs of the vital semiotic and cultural space that superintend the viewing experience. Further, these factors are not just "out there," external to the text and viewer; they actively intersect the text/viewer relation, producing interpretive frames that influence the public consumption of cultural artifacts.

Also central to the present study is a materialist contention, shared by Staiger, Tony Bennett, and other cultural studies scholars, that the text itself has no intrinsic meaning. I will argue that textual meanings are negotiated by external agencies, whether they be academic modes of interpretation, practices of the film industry, or film reviews set within a particular historical landscape. To thus explore the conditions of meaning-production is to forfeit the idea that a film or novel has an essence that can be captured once and for all by the proper critical method. Instead, forms appear as historical chameleons with shifting identities that reveal the impact that culture has on shaping the ideological functions of the media through time. The historical case study is a crucial instrument of this investigation, as it reveals the social conditions and institutions that help constitute contingent meanings for texts as they circulate publicly. As Staiger remarks, the goal of this approach to reception is thus not to posit new textual meanings or values, but to show how meanings and values are produced by social forces. This kind of analysis, then, "does not interpret texts but . . . attempt[s] a historical explanation of the event of interpreting a text."[13]

By historicizing Sirk's films and refusing the notion that they have intrinsic, formally verifiable significance, I hope to demonstrate concretely the importance of analyzing contextual factors in discussions of the social meaning of texts. Although historical case studies may not answer all questions about meaning, they challenge many of our interpretive assumptions. They show how, under different circumstances, films assume different identities and cultural functions, fueling debates about the origins and conditions of textual signification.

However, as we have seen in an earlier discussion of historical approaches to melodrama, case studies tend to concentrate on single practices within the original moments of reception. Thus, much of this research, including Staiger's, has not systematically explored the fuller range of effects that historical context might have on cinematic identity. Films clearly circulate beyond their encounter with any one institutional or social sphere. How can we conceive of the relationship between history and cinema to address this more extensive sense of circulation, to examine the issue of meaning in a *comprehensive*, that is, trans-historical, trans-contextual manner?[14] How is it that films and other media products come to mean *different* things in *different* contexts throughout the course of their life-spans? What do these differences signify about the impact cultural and historical developments have on interpretation?

This broader emphasis seems necessary to address one of the most salient conditions of existence for the Hollywood film: its relationship to diverse regions of commentary over long periods of time that seek to define it. We have not fully come to terms with the habitats of meaning in which the popular Hollywood film dwells at different points in its history, nor with what these habitats could tell us about the shifting terms of a film's ideological identity and reception. What would such a social history of a Hollywood film even look like? What could it reveal about the processes of meaning-production to which a film is subject in disparate circumstances?

To address the questions I have raised about Sirk's authorship, the family melodrama, and film meaning, each chapter is devoted to a specific institutional context or discourse associated with the cultural circulation of films. These are: academia, the studio system, review journalism, star publicity, and what I will be referring to as "mass camp." Each of these contexts, in league with the values of the social formation in which they operate, produces systems of intelligibility and value for Sirk's melodramas that help us understand the role history plays in negotiating and renegotiating meaning. These systems do not, however, exhaust the number of meanings generated in relation to any body of films. Rather, they provide one way to approach the complex web of determinations acting on a film throughout its history and to consider how these determinations work, always differently, to make films meaningful for their various audiences.

In the first chapter, I examine Sirk's relation to developments in film studies from the 1950s through the 1980s. I begin with academia because, on the one hand, without it, Sirk and the family melodrama would not exist as critical categories of interest. On the other hand, academic interpretations have so monopolized considerations of what Sirk's films mean that other possible readings appear naive and incorrect. To approach other contexts as legitimate provinces of meaning, it seems necessary first to contextualize film theory and criticism as a *particular kind* of meaning-production, rather than as the definitive locus of textual "truth." To this end, I explore how concepts of authorship, critical developments, and the process of canon-formation affected how the discipline constructed meanings for Sirk's melodramas through four decades of critical inquiry.

In chapter 2, I turn to film industry practices to address some of the conditions that defined the original circulation of the postwar melodrama. For this inquiry I concentrate on Universal-International's exhibition of Sirk's *Written on the Wind*. Besides being one of Sirk's best-known films, it is almost unanimously revered by critics as his most dazzlingly transgressive work. At the same time, along with *Magnificent Obsession* and *Imitation of Life*, *Written on the Wind* was a big box office success for Universal (ranking the eleventh top-grossing film overall in 1957). The film was subject to one of the studio's most extensive advertising campaigns—a campaign entirely characteristic of the way postwar melodramas were "sold" to appeal to the era's affluent mentality and emphasis on sexuality. The film's strong presence in both academic and industrial arenas pointedly demonstrates the difference that particular institutional and historical settings make to meaning.

Chapter 3 is devoted to film reviewing. By looking at how reviewers evaluated Sirk's melodramas when they first appeared we will be able to see a set of variables involved in reception that differ from those produced by the studio. In addition, the original reviews and those which appeared later in the 1970s by virtue of the first full-scale U.S. retrospectives of Sirk's films allow us to explore the journalistic assumptions governing the production of value for these melodramas within two distinct periods. Analysis of these reviews can cue us to journalism's role in public tastemaking via the creation of popular film canons, against which the success or failure of Sirk's melodramas was measured.

The last two chapters shift the focus from contexts that make direct propositions about film meaning to contexts associated with the consumption of films in a more general and indirect way: star publicity and camp. Chapter 4 discusses the impact of stars on reception by concentrating on Rock Hudson, the actor most identified with Sirk's oeuvre. Hudson starred in eight Sirk films, including *Magnificent Obsession, All That Heaven Allows, Written on the Wind,* and *Tar-*

nished Angels. He was also without question one of the most popular stars of the decade, winning numerous awards as the number one male box office attraction. By analyzing his roles and the bountiful magazine coverage that sought to depict his private life, I examine the function his image served for the postwar era and how that function provided yet another possible significance for Sirk's melodramas during this time.

The question of Hudson's image, however, far exceeds the 1950s in its implications for discussing the relation of star signification and film meaning. Like Judy Garland, Hudson experienced a dramatic reversal in his carefully crafted Hollywood image. As is well known, Hudson was one of the first celebrities to publicly admit he had AIDS. His emergence in the 1980s as a homosexual provoked a media stir that created obvious ironies between his past identity as quintessential heterosexual leading man and his present identity as "afflicted" homosexual. This reversal has undoubtedly helped define contemporary responses to Sirk's films in ways totally unforeseeable by their original creators.

In chapter 5, I address the most widespread kind of contemporary response to Sirk's melodramas—camp. Camp, the recognition of the inherent artifice of media products, is probably the most common social reaction to these films, but it remains the least theorized. Camp may initially seem somewhat incongruous in a book otherwise devoted to institutional contexts, since it is traditionally considered a subcultural phenomenon. But as I hope to show, there is a certain kind of "institutionalized" camp response that is a product of developments within contemporary mass culture. This is not to say that Sirk's melodramas are closed to gay responses; rather, conditions influencing the contemporary reception of these films have reached beyond the subcultural to include the audience at large. Since the 1960s, numerous factors have converged to "democratize" camp to such an extent that we can presently consider it a mass cultural *convention* of viewing past artifacts. This convention deeply affects the manner in which audiences perceive studio era films today. I conclude my discussion of the relation between melodrama and historical context, then, by tracing the particular affinities between melodrama and a mass camp sensibility.

I want to caution that I am not assuming that the audience's perceptions are simply determined by the historical practices I discuss in each chapter. However, we have very little other information pertaining to how people responded to films in the past. Empirical or ethnographic research has strongly defined reception theory in cultural studies. But this research has been confined to contemporary examples or to unusual cases where groups have recorded their responses to past forms. These methods are thus not particularly helpful for addressing the question of reception for films made decades ago. In the case of old films, the

surviving documents from various contexts provide a glimpse into social constructions of meaning that circulated at the time of reception, shedding light on
broader patterns affecting reception than those afforded by the film's formal system itself. Analysis of such contexts, then, does not provide a record of audience
response—in this case, of the many meanings that audiences may have created
for these melodramas. But historical research helps reconstruct the semiotic environment in which the text/viewer interaction took place, showing us discourses
at work in the process of reception.

   It is also important to point out that my study will at no time engage in
conventional textual analysis, rolling back the historical meanings to produce the
"real" meaning of the film in question or delineate what its resistances could be
to the uses such contexts want it to serve.[15] Within these pages, film identity is
always a matter of negotiation between textual features and contextual imperatives. It is therefore contingent upon certain social and historical circumstances.
This contingency does not signify a relativistic free-for-all of meaning—that any
meaning "goes" at any time. To the contrary, it suggests that we attempt to specify the particular ideological functions of a film by examining key moments
within its historical transit.

   Film criticism represents one such moment, a significant stopover point for
a studio era film late in its cultural circulation. More than any other context,
academia mediated the meaning of Sirk's melodramas by according his intentions
the utmost importance in determining his films' significance. It is to this region
that I shall now turn.

Melodrama and Meaning

1

The "Progressive" Auteur, Melodrama, and Canonicity

No critic has been as perceptive as Sirk
himself in articulating some of [his] themes.
Fred Camper[1]

THE HISTORY OF Sirk criticism charts many of the major twists and turns in the field of film studies from the 1950s to the present. In this chapter, I break down this evolution into four general stages: early auteurism associated with *Cahiers du cinéma* and Andrew Sarris in the 1950s and 1960s; the British version of authorship in the 1970s, defined by an interest in "textual politics"; psychoanalysis and its valorization of melodrama in the latter part of the decade; and, more recently, the turn to the woman's film and maternal melodrama by feminism and cultural studies. As we shall see, Sirk's case is richly suggestive for understanding how the family melodrama came to "mean" in an academic context.

As I have already mentioned, my primary goal is *not* simply to rehearse Sirk's critical history, illustrating, as some have done, his importance to the serious study of melodrama in film theory and criticism. Such rehearsals tacitly affirm the authority of past interpretations, rather than question the manner in which meanings were created and perpetuated in the field. Taking a different route, I shall argue that this director's centrality to the discipline gives us the opportunity to reconsider criticism as a specific kind of textual appropriation. Sirk's case provides the occasion to ask how the discipline, during vital periods of its evolution, constructed the significance of the family melodrama.

From this perspective criticism does not reveal the inherent truth of the text; textual readings reveal instead the dynamics and concerns of critical movements. As Jane Tompkins argues in her revisionist work on notions of textual endurance, the persistence of certain texts through time is not a testimony to the universal appeal of their intrinsic merits, but to their capacity to continue to serve as registers of critical trends. What texts mean is continuously transformed by the passage of these trends through time.[2] Sirk's longevity in film studies is interesting, then, for what it can tell us about the transformation of his melodramas via successive developments in the field. Once we grant this historical mutability of meanings in academia, interpretations and values appear as "contingent," radically dependent on the positions and needs of those involved in institutions of evaluative authority, rather than based, as is so often claimed, on the universal givens of the text itself.[3]

To thus contextualize academic evaluations of Sirk's melodramas goes against the common wisdom inspiring critical attention to his films since the 1970s. A dominant mission in relation to Sirk's oeuvre has been to "rescue" his work from the "misreadings" of popular film reviewers and mass audiences, who see only the soap opera and not the refined style and social message. In this and subsequent chapters, I will resist the temptation to valorize academic readings above all others as saving Sirk's films from semantic abuse. I hope rather to question the monopoly that schooled interpretations have had over the "truth" of these films, so that other meanings generated by different locales can emerge as significant to understanding the relation between melodrama and culture.

In examining Sirk criticism, I concentrate on the contribution three significant dynamics in particular have made to motivating, varying, and sustaining meaning for the family melodrama from the 1950s through the 1980s: the interactions between auteurism, other developments in criticism, and canon formation. These dynamics help answer the central questions of this chapter: why specific meanings were ventured at particular times, why some meanings gained and sustained hegemony over others, and why Sirk's films attained lasting value in the field. My study will thus focus on the historical sweep of meaning, rather than provide an exhaustive account of the mechanics of interpretive enterprise.[4] Further, although the intellectual history of film studies figures prominently in my analysis, I must condense this history to suit the boundaries of a chapter, providing summary backgrounds for those moments most germane to understanding Sirk's fate in the academy.[5]

I begin with *Cahiers du cinéma*'s pioneering readings of Sirk in the 1950s. Though a nonacademic journal itself, *Cahiers* was responsible for introducing Sirk to the critical world, as well as for defining how his melodramas would initially be valued by film studies. More than in any other context, melodramatic meaning in academia relied on a concept of authorship, originally championed by *Cahiers*. The family melodrama attained its first recognition through association with the celebrated directors who worked in the genre. Nevertheless, *Ca-*

hiers and the subsequent auteurist work of Andrew Sarris serve only as a prelude to the explosion of discourse on Sirk in England during the 1970s.

Early Auteurism

Like many other Hollywood directors, Douglas Sirk gained initial critical attention from *"la politique des auteurs"* developed by the journal *Cahiers du cinéma* in the 1950s as a reaction to France's sterile, script-dominated, and uncinematic "tradition of quality" filmmaking. *Cahiers* claimed that the film director or auteur was equivalent to any artist as the primary force behind aesthetic creation. Further, its critics argued that films were valuable insofar as the mise-enscène expressed the concerns and visions of the director, thereby discrediting films with a predominance of literary content. Because these contentions often embraced Hollywood filmmakers previously held in critical disrepute as mere minions of a commercial industry, *Cahiers*'s criticism was often self-consciously iconoclastic. These critics produced enthusiastic reviews of genre films by Nicholas Ray, Howard Hawks, Samuel Fuller, and others, flying in the face of established "high art" perspectives on the cinema.[6]

Cahiers had substantial consequences for academic criticism by valorizing Hollywood cinema and making the practice of analyzing films through their auteur's world view the dominant concern for many years. We can understand *Cahiers*'s impact on later U.S. and British criticism as partially a result of the resonance its iconoclastic polemics found in other film cultures. Writing for the avant-garde and alternative magazine *Film Culture* in the 1960s, Andrew Sarris fought against the dominant realist aesthetic of popular review journalism which prized works with obvious social messages (such as Fred Zinnemann's *High Noon* [1952]) over the more vital, subtle, and cinematic films of John Ford and Howard Hawks. At the same time, *Cahiers*'s polemics appealed to younger British critics tired of the traditional, upper-crust values of film critic Penelope Huston and *Sight and Sound*. However, the influence of *Cahiers* was also very much a product of the credibility and public profile its critics, among them Jean-Luc Godard, François Truffaut, and Eric Rohmer, gained as filmmakers of the renowned *nouvelle vague* in the late 1950s.[7] In any case, although the French version of auteurism was later rebuked for its overt Romanticism (fostering interpretations derived from the personal concerns of the creator at the expense of social and political considerations),[8] revisionist work on the concept never managed to banish the authorial study from the ranks of analysis.

While Sirk was not a *Cahiers* fetish-object, like Ray, Hawks, or Alfred Hitchcock, a series of 1955–59 reviews gave him a visibility that would inspire later, more extensive work on the director. These reviews included Philippe Demon-sablon on *Magnificent Obsession* (1954), Louis Marcorelles and François Truffaut on *Written on the Wind* (1957), Luc Moullet on *Tarnished Angels* (1958), and Jean-Luc Godard on *A Time to Love and a Time to Die* (1958).[9]

Although diverse in concerns, these essays tended to acknowledge Sirk's vivid style as key to his status as an auteur. In an otherwise negative review of *Magnificent Obsession* for its trite depiction of the theme of charity, Demon-sablon mentions that Sirk is able to capture the "fugitive passing of a feeling that remains inexpressible" through his mise-en-scène.[10] In "Le film gratuit" Marco-relles notes that *Written on the Wind* represents an "exclusively visual thematic," rather than a "re-creation, from the inside, of beings and the world." But he ultimately criticizes Sirk for never being able to rise above appearances. Because *Written on the Wind* demonstrates an excessive style that remains external to any substantive meaning, Marcorelles judges Sirk as lacking "moral elegance."[11] By contrast, Moullet prizes the gratuitous effects of artifice and excess because they represent the true nature of art. The mise-en-scène may show us "glitter with nothing inside," but that is just the point. Since art is inherently defined by artifice, *Tarnished Angels* becomes valuable, even more sincere, precisely be-cause of a style that refuses to pass beyond surface.[12]

In his review of *Written on the Wind*, Truffaut evaluates style neither as empty formalism nor as self-reflexive aesthetic play; he sees it, rather, as a com-mentary on the modern condition. Sirk's frank use of color represents "the colors of the twentieth century, the colors of America, the colors of luxury civilization, the industrial colors that remind us that we live in the age of plastics."[13] And, finally, Godard appreciates Sirk for his spirited and irreverent contrasts, his "de-lirious mixture of medieval and modern, sentimentality and subtlety, tame com-positions and frenzied Cinemascope."[14]

With the exception of Demonsablon, who associates mise-en-scène with emotion, *Cahiers* critics were attracted to the excessiveness and artifice of Sirk's style. There is no unanimity, however, as to what the vertiginous visual displays mean, attesting to the heterogeneity of *Cahiers* perspectives.[15] Marcorelles judges the mise-en-scène as devoid of substance, Moullet praises it as self-re-flexive, Truffaut considers it an expression of modernity, and Godard revels in its exuberant unconventionality.

At this initial stage of auteurism, then, style is contested in significance. Moreover, critics do not routinely bring their evaluations of style to bear on dis-cussions of the larger narrative themes of Sirk's films. Some tend, rather, to dis-cover the films' meanings in broad aspects of the narrative, unattached to stylistic function. Moullet, for example, mentions Sirk's concern with debauchery in *Tarnished Angels* autonomously from his discussion of self-reflexivity, while Marcorelles addresses Sirk's depiction of a "social giganticism" appropriate to Texas millionaires in *Written on the Wind* in a manner equally unrelated to his assessment of the visuals as empty. In this way, reviewers did not yield a systematic sense of what the personal visions tying style and narrative themes together would be—a major operation of later auteurist work.

Andrew Sarris's subsequent commentary on Sirk in the 1960s made little progress in solving this problem. In 1968 he published *The American Cinema*, a book version of an essay he had written five years earlier for *Film Culture*. Both pieces served to elaborate the French auteurist aesthetic on Hollywood directors.[16] Sarris classified Sirk as a member of the "Far Side of Paradise," along with other directors such as Otto Preminger, Nicholas Ray, and Vincente Minnelli. These directors fell short of the top category, the Pantheon, mainly because of their inability to achieve a consistent, coherent personal vision. Sarris reiterated earlier descriptions of Sirk as a stylist, praising his "formal excellence and visual wit." But Sarris's remarks about the meaning of Sirk's films remain inconclusive. Hinting at a relationship between form and content, he writes, "Even in his most dubious projects, Sirk never shrinks away from the ridiculous, but by a full-bodied formal development, his art transcends the ridiculous, as form comments on content."[17] But Sarris does not illuminate what this content is, even marginally. He insists that Sirk's style is rooted in personal vision, and thus is not simply an exercise in "style for style's sake," but provides little evidence to counter this impression.

Sirk's place in the history of film studies shows that this initial uncertainty in the early stages of auteurism is dramatically resolved by later criticism. This is not to say there is no continuity between *Cahiers* and these later readings; *Cahiers*'s emphasis on mise-en-scène and self-reflexivity continues to serve as a departure point for evaluations of Sirk. But, beginning with *Screen*'s special issue on Sirk in 1971, critics not only resolutely secured meanings for Sirk's peculiar stylistic "signifiers," but escalated him unwaveringly into the ranks of the great auteurs. What we recognize as accurate, more realized readings of Sirk's melodramas depended on a number of interrelated developments in the 1960s and 1970s involving the growth of film criticism in England: among them, the increasingly academic quality of auteur criticism, interviews with directors, and the concerns of British Marxism. These developments help explain why Sirk "burst" onto the critical scene in the early 1970s and why his films suddenly gained such rich significance for the field.

The "Boom" Period

The "boom" period of Sirk criticism in England in 1971–72 comprised *Screen's* special issue on the director; the publication of Jon Halliday's interview with Sirk, *Sirk on Sirk*; retrospectives by The National Film Theatre and Edinburgh Film Festival (the latter followed by publication of *Douglas Sirk*, a collection of essays edited by Jon Halliday and Laura Mulvey); and *Monogram's* melodrama issue. Besides Jon Halliday's contributions, British essays included the work of Fred Camper, Paul Willemen, Thomas Elsaesser, and Mike Prokosh. Non-British sources, such as the French journal *Positif*, the German *Fernsehen und Film*, and the U.S. feminist journal *Women and Film*, as well as Molly Haskell's *From Reverence to Rape*, also demonstrated some interest in Sirk's melodramas in the early 1970s. Much of this writing helped clarify the relationship between Sirk's style and themes, partially through standards of criticism affected by academic traditions.

As William Horrigan has rightly argued, post-Sarris auteurism attempted "to recoup the notion of 'pure style,' and see it not simply as technical flourish, but as profoundly integral, as indeed it is assumed to be in criticism of other arts."[18] Critics had to define the "organic" operation of a director's films, wherein style and theme were clearly related, to verify the director's status as a full-fledged author. In the United States, what David Bordwell has called the "institutionalization" of film studies assisted this mission. Until film became a part of university curricula and an associated publication apparatus in the late 1960s, criticism was often not consistently governed by exegetical imperatives. Once film entered the academy, its study connected with norms of interpretation, particularly those derived from New Criticism, which called for full scale organic explanations of texts. To secure film as a medium worthy of inclusion in the curriculum, these events elevated the film director to a status equivalent to that of the literary author.[19] From this perspective, some early auteur critics did not create what we would now recognize as bona fide interpretations, because they operated in circumstances either predating this process of institutionalization or external to it, that is, within quasi-journalistic systems of writing about film.

We cannot, however, simply superimpose these conditions on England in the early 1970s. Criticism in the "boom" period was not strictly institutionalized, since few university positions in film were available until the mid-1970s. Critics tended to be journalists, intellectuals, and free-lancers, rather than employed academics. As in the case of *Cahiers*, early British film criticism shows how influential sources technically outside academe could be on its critical enterprise. But at the same time, "boom" era Sirk writings display clear affiliations with the exegetical nature of this enterprise, whether because of the background of many of its critics in university-based literary studies or the impact of auteur-centered organic film criticism in journals such as *Movie* and *The New Left Review*. Without doubt, Sirk's more complete authorization rested on the application of organic principles to his films and an already established foundation of auteurist publications, including the *Cinema One* series which featured Jon Halliday's interview.

In addition, the editorial shift that took place with *Screen's* special issue on Sirk signaled rising academic aspirations in British criticism. Under the editorship of Sam Rohdie, *Screen's* commitment to media education for practicing teachers changed to a growing devotion to theory and systematic methods of analysis for intellectuals and cinephiles.[20] As Antony Easthope points out, the journal's connection to regional groups, weekend schools, and other forums[21] helped spread its influence throughout British intellectual culture. In a few years, *Screen* and British theory were mainstreamed into an international academic community. Thus, while not yet technically within academia, "boom" period auteur criticism operated through intellectual traditions of analysis, a supporting network of publications, and aspirations allied with the institutionalization of film studies at this time.

While the standardization of exegesis was clearly at work in resolving the major problem confronting Sirk's authorship—the relation between style and theme—this development cannot fully explain why Sirk gained such prominence in the early 1970s. Terms central to the successful organic construction of the author had to materialize; and these came, as they so often do, straight from the director himself.

The Auteur Machine

Probably the driving force behind Sirk's more complete authorization was Halliday's interview, influenced by *Cahiers's* later work on the director. *Cahiers's* participation in critical recognition for Sirk did not end with Truffaut et al. In 1967, the Studio-Action Théâtre in Paris held a partial retrospective of Sirk's films which prompted *Cahiers* to publish an issue containing an interview with Sirk (actually conducted three years earlier), a bio-filmography, and an essay by Jean-Louis Comolli, titled "L'aveugle et le miroir" or "The Blind Man and the

Mirror."[22] The *Cahiers* interview provided the basic framework for Jon Halliday's *Sirk on Sirk*, a more extensive and tremendously influential interview with the director published in 1972.[23] In addition to *Cahiers*'s direct inspiration, Halliday's interview rose from an increasing emphasis on Hollywood directors in British auteurism, due partly to the influence of the British Film Institute with its *Cinema One* series and the Edinburgh film retrospectives that focused on some of the less touted directors recognized by *Cahiers*, such as Sirk. Without doubt, *Sirk on Sirk*, available to the British intellectual community before its actual publication, strongly motivated the flurry of early 1970s interest in Sirk.

Auteurists, accustomed to interviewing uncooperative or evasive Hollywood directors, discovered that Sirk could and would articulate the intellectual and thematic significance of his films. In Halliday's interview, Sirk provided key information about his background and the philosophical and creative intentions behind his films. He emerged as a European intellectual who had worked in the German theater and had made films for UFA during the Weimar era before coming to Hollywood in the late 1930s. His European sensibilities and conversancy with theories of representation, such as those of Erwin Panofsky and Bertolt Brecht, helped establish him as a serious artist and social critic. As with Fritz Lang, Max Ophuls, Billy Wilder, and Otto Preminger, critics regarded Sirk's transplanted European identity as the basis of a privileged critical perspective on Hollywood genres and the social mores typically conveyed by them.

Sirk's discussion of melodrama through reference to ancient tragedy lent dignity to a maligned genre, and suggested it was capable of significant insights into the human condition (pp. 94–95). In addition, the director consistently compared his aims with those of authors (such as Euripides, Shakespeare, Calderon, and Lope de Vega) who worked ingeniously within genres to present critiques of their own societies. Sirk described his critique as aimed at the bourgeoisie and the family, while Halliday in his introduction places it more specifically against the backdrop of the cultural and political tenor of the Eisenhower era (p. 116). For Halliday, the infirmities presented in many of Sirk's later films are symptoms of the social malaise of the United States in the 1950s, a time of only apparent complacency (p. 11).

Through his reference to tragedy, Sirk was able not only to establish his melodramas as platforms for social criticism, but to bring out their complex structures. These structures include the artificial happy end (that is, the Euripidean *deus ex machina*) and the presence of irony (pp. 95–96, 119). Because of the conventional nature of melodrama and Hollywood narratives in general, Sirk stressed that one must look below the surface to find these complex structures and their materialization of social critique, prompting Halliday to emphasize that "style and content are thus less than ever inseparable in Sirk. Since Sirk's films are . . . many layered . . . they have therefore to be read below their immediate surface" (p. 9).

Sirk's remarks on style make it clear that "things"—objects in the mise-en-scène, including mirrors—are no longer ciphers, vivid stylistic flourishes without certain significance; they embody social critique or a self-reflexive awareness of the conditions of representation (pp. 46, 48). That is, their vividness is associated directly with artifice—an artifice that comments on the world, as it comments on the means of representation. Again, Halliday's introduction acts to cement such interpretive moves; Sirk's films represent a "world of pretense, accentuated by the multiplication of intermediate objects (particularly mirrors and statues) . . . [in which] Sirk's characters can find no way out" (p. 12). Throughout the interview, Sirk elaborates connections between genre, structure, style, and themes such as failure, blindness, impotence, and the impossibility of happiness.

The Halliday text proved to be crucial to the history of Sirk criticism in at least two ways. First, it supplied the "missing link" of coherent meaning that had inhibited the full evolution of Sirk as auteur. The interplay between Halliday's introduction and the interview initiated the necessary work upon the "signifieds" for Sirk's generic and stylistic "signifiers." After Sirk on Sirk, this director's films were saturated with meaning, down to the choice of techniques, such as camera angles and lighting, that reflect his philosophy (p. 40). In this way, as Robert Ray comments, Sirk effectively "remotivated" the meaning of his films for critics.[24] Second, Sirk on Sirk established the primary terms for future treatments of the director. These included melodrama as social commentary, reading below the surface for irony, the false and expedient happy end, the symbolic significance of objects, the idea of self-reflexive style and distanciation, and pertinent themes. Throughout the history of Sirk criticism, Sirk would continue to be a director who manipulated the Hollywood melodrama into performing a social critique of the United States in the 1950s through elaborate structural and stylistic devices. The information in the interviews thus supplied a binding foundation for subsequent interpretations.

Essentially, then, Sirk was redeemed for exegesis through the expression of his own intentions. Or as Fred Camper tellingly wrote in 1971, "No critic has been as perceptive as Sirk himself in articulating some of [his] themes."[25] By the time of Halliday's interview, Sirk had read both Sarris's The American Cinema and Peter Wollen's Signs and Meanings in the Cinema, making it likely that he self-consciously assisted the auteur project (p. 72). As Donald Spoto and Robert Kapsis have shown in the case of Alfred Hitchcock, such incidences of attempted directorial manipulation of criticism were not unusual.[26] But whether or not the director acted consciously in this capacity, the sheer proliferation of published interviews with film authors during the 1960s and 1970s suggests that the interview acted as a tutor-text for the auteurist enterprise.[27] Intention helped provide the necessary terms for a more thoroughgoing account of Sirk and many other directors, thus helping to build a better auteur machine.

Once intentionalized, the process of Sirk's authorization gained its first systematic momentum. But as important as the interview was to the process of meaning construction, it could not account for the variety of interpretations that would emerge in relation to this director's films. In Sirk's case, the interview strongly *oriented* later readings; it established fundamental parameters for approaching these films that virtually no critic questioned. But as we saw in the case of Halliday's introductory commentary, critics acted not only to verify these parameters, but to develop them in relation to existing critical models and perspectives, (as when Halliday converts Sirk's critique of the bourgeoisie into a Marxist exposé of the Eisenhower years). This felicitous intersection between the director's vision and critical developments in the field strongly characterizes the nature of Sirk criticism in and beyond the "boom" period.[28]

Traditionalists and the New Left

Historical retrospect has tended to superimpose a "neo-Marxist" unity on Sirk criticism during this time. While this period did indeed represent the first English language exploration of "textual politics" from a Marxist perspective, many of the essays were untouched by political concerns, reflecting instead a traditional auteurism. Criticism had not yet settled into a single dominant paradigm, as would be the case with psychoanalysis in the mid-1970s. In this regard, the "boom" period occupied a strategic and unique place in the history of Sirk criticism. Benefiting from the semantic labor of the interviews, those writing at this time were able to demonstrate that Sirk was a bona fide author by fully elaborating the relationship between form and content in his films. At the same time, the process of meaning construction was still "young," not institutionalized to the point where a single critical perspective could dominate access to his films. Thus, theorists and critics offered diverse meanings from different perspectives.[29]

This breadth in approach was also reflected in the films covered. In comparison with later treatments, early 1970s critics wrote about a much greater number of Sirk's films, including his European films from the 1930s and the Hollywood comedies, musicals, and dramas he directed for various studios. Due to academic preferences and distribution constraints that narrowed the number of

Sirk's films available to the public, later criticism focused on only a handful of his U.S. melodramas, specifically those he made for Universal in the 1950s. Thus, early critics studied German films such as *Zu Neuen Ufern* (1937) and Hollywood films such as *The First Legion* (1951), both of which since have enjoyed little critical notoriety. The relative openness of the critical terrain reflected the pioneering character of this moment in auteur construction. Film retrospectives and journals such as *Screen* covered both his German and U.S. periods to present Sirk's history and suggest the unity of his oeuvre, while different perspectives laid claim to the relatively uncharted territory of his films left "unsignified" by *Cahiers* and Sarris.

Essays devoted to interpretation of Sirk's films fell into two general categories: traditional auteurist and ideological. My analysis of representative examples of each of these approaches will at times have to go beyond the customary capsule summary of critics' positions to adequately reconsider how these essays demonstrate the interplay between authorial words and critical perspectives.

Traditional auteur articles included Fred Camper's "The Films of Douglas Sirk" and David Grosz's "*The First Legion*," which appeared in *Screen*; as well as several essays from *Douglas Sirk*, particularly Mike Prokosh's "*Imitation of Life*," and Tim Hunter's "*Summer Storm*."[30] These interpretations demonstrated the significance of organic analyses to Sirk's authorization. But, as opposed to the ideological category, they rarely elaborated style and themes through a Marxist perspective. They did not, for example, interpret Sirk's vision as a deconstruction of capitalism nor did they relate his self-reflexivity to a Brechtian theory of distanciation. The "traditionalists," then, did not tend to hitch the Sirk wagon to social critique, despite frequent discussion of pessimistic themes and foregrounded mise-en-scène.

Camper's essay most comprehensively elucidates aspects of Sirk's style and vision that other traditionalists, with some variation, also treated. He opens with three quotes from Sirk's interview concerning the impossibility of happiness, the theme of blindness as it relates to the characters' perception of their world, and aesthetic distance and mirrors.[31] Camper demonstrates how these themes and aesthetic preoccupations are materialized through unrealistic mise-en-scène: "Happiness . . . can never be shown, because the happiness [Sirk] conceives of implies a kind of reality of experience which the very qualities of his images deny" (p. 48). The mise-en-scène's obvious artifice—its unnaturalistic lighting schemes, foregrounded objects, mirror-ridden compositions—denies reconstruction of a real world and the sense of emotional reality such mimesis usually makes possible. Visual artifice conveys a sense of the delusory and ultimately futile nature of the pursuit of happiness as well as the characters' impotence—their inability to see or act effectively. Camper notes that the unconvincing "happy ends" in most of the director's films seal this sense of futility.

Along with the thematic resonances of the "false" mise-en-scène, Camper discusses how Sirk's style produces distancing effects and, ultimately, a self-reflexive aesthetic statement. Sirk's emphasis on artifice creates distance between characters, and in the audience's relation to them. Sirk's films are, in fact, "*about* aesthetic distances, *about* the mirror images and other reflections he uses so well" (p. 47). Camper concludes, "The whole point of Sirk is . . . to show us the beauty of his anti-physical, two-dimensional perspective . . . as an artist, Sirk does not deal in despair but in aesthetic beauty" (p. 51).

Camper's analysis is exemplary of early 1970s Sirk criticism in general, and traditional auteur perspectives in particular. First, his commentary provides systematic and bountiful meanings for prominent stylistic elements: strange objects, unnaturalistic lighting, windows, and mirrors all have thematic and aesthetic purpose. Second, the elaboration of that purpose is directly related to Sirk's interview commentary. Like many other essays, Camper's analysis alternates between quotes from Sirk and critical exposition, each acting as support for the other. Such a dynamic legitimates the director as author, as it substantiates the critic's interpretive enterprise. Third, Camper's article represents a litany of basic elements in Sirk criticism: pessimistic themes, artificial mise-en-scène, distance, self-reflexivity, and false happy ends. Finally, in contrast to a Marxist approach, he links Sirk's style to a purely aesthetic agenda. The surfaces of Sirk's films express beauty, and we are to admire them for that. Thus, Camper's references to lack of realism and distance employ Sirk's testimony to construct the auteur through a more overt focus on aesthetics. While Sirk's expressions of his modernist inclinations were often a part of the vocabulary of traditional auteur critics at this time, the politics of modernism were not.

Given their tendencies toward apoliticism, such interpretations were rarely cited in later Sirk criticism, which focused almost exclusively on the ideological status of his melodramas. They thus fell from critical memory. Early ideological approaches, to the contrary, survived and flourished in later accounts, forming the initial moment of a dominant critical genealogy devoted to "textual politics." Sirk's ascension into the political canon, an aesthetic position reserved for those directors combatting the conventions and ideologies of Hollywood filmmaking, was initiated by the Marxist essays. As we briefly saw in Jon Halliday's commentary, Sirk attracted a following of left-wing writers in the early 1970s. Halliday, a political essayist for *The New Left Review*, translated Sirk's films into critiques of the conservative Eisenhower regime and 1950s bourgeois ideology. He went on to write an article on *All That Heaven Allows* that analyzed the film as an exposé of *"the history of the concealed disintegration of the society,"* representing "Sirk's most sustained dissection of pretense connected with class."[32] Other writers of the time who saw Sirk's melodramas as reactions to the repressiveness of the postwar, middle-class ethos included Paul Willemen and Thomas Elsaesser.[33]

Sirk's avowed goal to criticize the bourgeoisie connected with some British critics' burgeoning interest in examining the relation of film and ideology, particularly after the political upheavals of May 1968.[34] Sam Rohdie's editorial for *Screen's* special issue on Sirk is representative not only of this critical direction, but of several of the larger intellectual wellsprings feeding it. Rohdie explains that Sirk provides the means to carry auteurist studies beyond the purely aesthetic to consider issues related to both a politics of education and a politics of film. He writes: "The 'meaning' and significance of [Sirk's] films are not overt or explicit but must be gathered precisely by means of an analysis of formal procedures. Sirk is anything but a realist. . . . A study of Sirk would 'scandalize' the usual theme-orientated approach to film studies . . . a procedure which regards films as reflections of life." Further, the *Screen* issue does not present "the usual auteur study out of place, out of time, for it seeks to give Sirk's work significance within a context and raises general . . . political [issues] concerned with formal means and ideology while at the same time keeping to the films in their specificity."[35] Rohdie's emphasis on theory, form, antirealism, and ideology signaled the influence of New Left positions of the time.

In the 1960s, *The New Left Review* played a significant role in establishing the goals and character of contemporary British Marxism, as well as shaping *Screen's* editorial directions a decade later. As Paul Willemen has written, *The New Left Review* began publishing in 1960 to "remedy the insularity of the British left by introducing the work of Continental theorists" such as Louis Althusser and Jacques Lacan.[36] In particular, Althusser's conception of the relative autonomy of the superstructure, which questioned Marx's more deterministic model of base/superstructure relations, led to a greater left interest in superstructural phenomena, such as art and theory. The left's commitment to theory was also bolstered by Althusser's privileging of science as a practice that could reveal the operations of ideology, thus producing knowledge about its operations. For radical intellectuals, theory became a new arena of struggle, insofar as it could act like a science to transform ideology into knowledge. The theoretical study of texts, products of ideology at the superstructural level, thus took on great significance.[37]

While Althusser's influence helped sanction *Screen's* move to theory and textual analysis, another Continental source, Bertolt Brecht, helped create a modernist aesthetic that significantly revised prior Marxist aesthetics. The 1964 English translation of some of Brecht's writings in *Brecht on Theater*[38] inspired a shift in the left position toward realism and modernism. As Antony Easthope remarks, prior to the New Left, most "Marxist writing on art had stressed the historical significance of the 'obvious' content of the work, and, with minor exceptions, had seen interest in the formal properties as formalism which deliberately evaded the social significance of art."[39] Brecht insisted on the importance of a formal attack on traditional realist devices to revolutionize perception and consciousness, thereby making realism ideologically suspect. Brecht's modernist vision of a theater devoted to puncturing the illusionistic facade of conventional drama through the deployment of interruptive and distancing techniques had a substantial impact in the 1960s and 1970s, putting formal issues firmly on the Marxist agenda.

In addition, Jean-Louis Comolli and Jean Narboni's "Cinema/ideologie/critique I" published in *Cahiers* in 1969 and translated in *Screen* in 1971, influentially cemented the equation between theory and science, at the same time as the authors emphasized the importance of form in diagnosing the ideological status of texts.[40] Comolli and Narboni offered a series of categories that defined the ideological status of different kinds of films on the basis of their formal adherence to or departure from realist principles, valuing those in the latter category. While prizing modernist films of the avant-garde, the authors proposed that films made within the Hollywood system also had the capacity to subvert dominant ideological values, if they managed to internally disrupt or "make strange" conventions of representation.

Through these and other influences, theory, form, antirealism, and ideology became increasingly important matters for British film intellectuals during the 1970s.[41] For some critics, Sirk's films represented a site to exercise neo-Marxist theory early in this period. Sirk's relevance came about as a result of his Brechtian credentials, evidenced, for example, in his use of mirrors and barrier framings as distancing devices. With his excessive, unrealistic style, Sirk was essentially a modernist in Hollywood, subverting the system and its ideology from within— thus also conforming to Comolli and Narboni's conception of the transgressive commercial filmmaker.

More strongly than any other writer of the time, Paul Willemen relates Sirk's films to a Marxist theory of representation, attentive to Sirk's remarks in the *Cahiers* interview about Brecht's influence on his early theater work. Willemen lists characteristics of the director's melodramas that critique surface reality according to Brechtian premises, prefacing many of them with appropriate authorial comments from *Sirk on Sirk*.[42] One group of devices intensifies generic rules to such an extent that they are "made strange," such as the "use of baroque color schemes" in *Written on the Wind* ("Distanciation," p. 65). Another group represents Sirk's mode of subterranean critique through subtle interference with convention: "Displacements and discontinuities in plot construction . . . contradictions in characterisation. . . . Ironic use of camera-positioning and framing" ("Sirkian System," p. 131). Each of these is an elaboration of Sirk's comments about false happy ends, split characters, and distancing effects, respectively. These generic intensifications and structurally induced contradictions help create distanciation, the prime term for comprehending the function of Sirk's style. Willemen writes, "By altering the rhetoric of bourgeois melodrama, through stylization and parody, Sirk's films distanciate themselves from bourgeois ideology" ("Distanciation," p. 67).

Willemen's discussion goes beyond Brechtian allusions to define Sirk additionally in relation to Comolli and Narboni's argument about subversion in Hollywood. Willemen develops the "beneath the surface" critique offered by the Halliday interview through Comolli and Narboni's political geography of the text. In this geography, the level of content appears to be complicit, but form, the more significant element, attacks the content from within. Sirk's melodramas, via his stylization, are double-leveled phenomena—the typical highly emotional middle-class narrative situations may be there, but cinematic expression undermines them through parody, cliché, irony, and distance. Referring to *Sirk on Sirk*, Willemen connects this stylistic subversion to an unmasking of the disintegration occurring beneath the surface of the complacent society of the 1950s ("Sirkian System," p. 130). Thus, Willemen's construction of meaning for Sirk's melodramas reworks interview commentary to address two of the most significant influences of the New Left—Brecht and Comolli and Narboni.

Thomas Elsaesser joins Willemen in employing a theoretical apparatus to address Sirk and yet stands apart from almost all of the early critics in addressing melodrama as the prime focus of his work.[43] Most critics were especially concerned with how to *resolve* Sirk's relation to what they considered a critically tainted genre. Camper, for example, decried melodrama as "a pornography of feeling," justifying Sirk's films by arguing that they undermined the romanticism at the heart of the genre, endorsing fatalism and despair instead.[44] For many of the early critics, Sirk aesthetically triumphed over the creative constraints of the genre through style. But Elsaesser argued that melodrama had long served as a crucial social barometer during times of ideological crisis, making it as genre a valuable object of study for political analysis. His classification of melodramas by Sirk, Minnelli, and Ray as "sophisticated family melodramas" of the 1940s and 1950s reflected the higher priority of generic considerations in comparison with other critics who were uninterested in generating subcategories of melodrama. It was not until later in the decade, with the onset of feminist and psychoanalytic perspectives, that melodrama more widely enjoyed the status of "good object."

But the centrality of genre in Elsaesser's work is somewhat misleading. His essay is still auteur oriented, particularly in relation to Sirk and *Written on the Wind*. In fact, Elsaesser acknowledges Sirk as the inspiration behind his exploration of the family melodrama. After quoting the director on how he used deep-focus lenses in *Written on the Wind* to bring out the harshness of objects and the violent energy of the characters, Elsaesser writes, "Sirk's remark tempts one to look for some structural and stylistic constants in one medium during one particular period . . . and to speculate on the cultural and psychological context which this form of melodrama so manifestly reflected and helped to articulate" (p. 2). Elsaesser's essay tends to pose elements we have seen defined as *Sirkian* in other criticism as *generic* characteristics of the family melodrama. Despite his generic focus, Elsaesser's definition of the family melodrama is strongly indebted to the terms governing more strictly auteurist studies of Sirk.

According to Elsaesser, the hallmark characteristics of the family melodrama are its heightened visual expressiveness, the psychic and social foundations of its mise-en-scène, and its "double-leveled" meaning. Mise-en-scène and other stylistic issues are keys to unlocking the mysteries of meaning in apparently simplistic forms. To get at this meaning, Elsaesser employs the theoretical apparatus of Freudian psychoanalysis (again, exercising a formative influence on later developments) married to a Marxist perspective. Elsaesser argues that we can best understand the psychological intensity of melodramatic mise-en-scène, the inner world it portrays, through reference to Freud's *The Psychopathology of Everyday Life* and his work on dreams. The peculiarly vivid visuals of films such as Ray's *Rebel without a Cause* (1955), *Written on the Wind*, or Minnelli's *Home from the Hill* (1960) portray the "character's fetishistic fascinations" in sublimated and symbolic fashion (p. 10). In *Written on the Wind*, for example, Kyle's feelings of sexual inadequacy, which surface in his drinking problem, are expressed through shots emphasizing bottles of liquor, oil derricks, and fast cars—all overtly phallic and compensatory reminders of the origin of his malaise.

Further, the symptomatic qualities of mise-en-scène are rooted in the unconscious neuroses and anxieties present beneath the veneer of social stability in the Eisenhower era. Baroque visuals are both an expressive symptom and a critique of the repressive social/sexual regime of the 1950s. Elsaesser uses the term "cinematic counterpoint" to describe how style launches ideological critique. In the sophisticated family melodrama, the stylistic register can create a "counter-current" that goes "against the grain" of the story line typically headed for an optimistic resolution (p. 6). Here, Elsaesser offers another nuance to the Euripidean *deus ex machina*. He finds a conflict between the intense inscription of neuroses at the stylistic level and any ending which would facilely suggest that the problems of the film had been resolved. Cinematic counterpoint describes the double structure of these melodramas in which style plays a central role in the construction of the film's real meaning, and negates melodrama's typical affirmative relation to ideology. It thus reiterates under a new name the "below the surface" nature of Sirk's irony and social criticism.

In each of these early 1970s treatments of Sirk, regardless of approach, we can see that negative themes (blindness, impotence, the decadence of the middle classes), complex narrative elements (false happy ends), and a style that emphasized artifice (garish colors, foregrounded objects, mirrors and reflective surfaces) acted as the basis of the critic's formulation of meaning. Significant commentary or social critique occurred just "below the surface." In this sense the auteur machine was driven by the director, edging closer to the intentional fallacy than many critics—aiming at a more objective analysis of texts—would suspect. In addition, while Sirk was not the subject of the first full-blown exploration of the maverick classic text inspired by Comolli and Narboni's essay—the *Cahiers* editors' work on *Young Mr. Lincoln* preceded it—Sirk criticism at this point seems to have aided the articulation and development of one of the most influential critical categories of the 1970s, the formally subversive "progressive" text. In this sense, the Sirk interviews were among the most important documents of the era of "textual politics" that was dawning in British criticism at this time.[45]

However, not all Sirk critics interpreted these elements in exactly the same way. For Camper, Sirk's films involve tragic themes such as impotence and failure, but attain beauty through their aesthetic of artifice. For Halliday, Willemen, and Elsaesser, formal aesthetics add up to class critique. In the early feminist writings of Molly Haskell and Ellen Keneshea, class critique demonstrates the repressive role and limited options available to the middle-class housewife.[46] Despite some consensus among ideological writers, each uses a different perspective to locate "textual politics." Willemen finds it in structural and stylistic features corresponding to a Brechtian program of representation, while Elsaesser discovers it in the psychic undercurrents (à la Freud) flowing through extreme dramatic situations and heightened mise-en-scène.

Thus, meaning production involved a certain chemistry between authorial intentions and the critic's agenda. While Sirk's remarks created a coterie of definitive elements, the critics' adherence to particular models of interpretation or, in Stanley Fish's parlance, their membership in different interpretive communities (that is, traditional aesthetic, Marxist, Freudian, and feminist) motivated different meanings for these elements.[47] This cooperative enterprise allows us to see what made meaning *possible* (the interviews), as well as the processes that continued to animate and develop it.

In the mid-1970s Sirk's films once again became a central part of academic inquiry. But unlike the potpourri quality of criticism in the "boom" period, critics began to employ a single method—psychoanalysis—to explore the dominant issue in film theory and criticism, the relation between cinema and ideology. For a number of years, no critic in the mainstream of academic practice would employ a method other than psychoanalysis on Sirk's films, nor would they propose readings without a political thrust.

Melodrama and Psychoanalysis

In the latter part of the 1970s, Sirk criticism was published in *Screen, Movie, Framework, Positif, The Velvet Light Trap, Film Comment*, and a variety of other British, French, and U.S. sources. Sirk retrospectives and special screenings began in the United States,[48] and interviews continued.[49] The "boom" period had established Sirk as a director worthy of discourse, an established value that subsequent critics repeatedly affirmed.

During this time, Sirk criticism developed in three general directions. Within the academy proper, it took two routes. The first responded to the theoretical and political work that had been done by Halliday, Elsaesser, and Willemen in British publications, by resolutely endorsing ideological readings of Sirk's melodramas under the influence of a new paradigm—psychoanalysis. The second route rejected the overt theoreticism and leftist leanings of some of this British criticism, responding to Sirk's *oeuvre* more directly through themes (such as fatalism or impotence) from the interviews, creating a second wave of traditional auteurist criticism.[50] In a third movement, Sirk criticism dispersed into more popular and less academic formats such as *Film Comment*. Like the above, these formats tended to replay aspects of Sirk's already constructed authorship, but without theoretical language.[51]

I will focus on the trajectory of the first evolutionary trend, since it is part of the "academic main line," that school of criticism, primarily associated with *Screen*, which was to dominate thought about Sirk and melodrama in the academy. This main line, beginning with the early Marxist approaches to Sirk and gaining one of its most powerful articulations through psychoanalysis, secured the progressive political status of Sirk's melodramas, as well as that of the family melodrama as genre.

Relationships between Marxism and psychoanalysis had been ongoing since the 1960s, with the publication, for example, of Althusser's work on Freud and Lacan, as well as his essay on ideological state apparatuses in which Lacan's theories of subjectivity figured prominently.[52] However, while Marxism and issues of class still formed a part of mid-1970s studies of the cinema, psychoanalysis shifted the emphasis from class to sexuality.

The year 1975 saw the publication of Stephen Heath's piece on *Touch of Evil*, Christian Metz's "Imaginary Signifier," and Laura Mulvey's "Visual Pleasure and Narrative Cinema."[53] Securing the significance of theory to the study of ideology, each essay employed a combination of post-structural semiotics and psychoanalysis, emphasizing cinema as a signifying system focused on sexuality and the positioning of the spectator within dominant culture. A few years before, Juliet Mitchell's influential *Psychoanalysis and Feminism* redeemed Freud specifically for feminist inquiry by defining psychoanalysis as an essential tool for analyzing the unconscious sexual dynamics of patriarchal culture that fostered and maintained the oppression of women. Through these and other sources, Sirk criticism began to pursue more manifestly the sexual implications of the bourgeois order. As Laura Mulvey wrote of *All That Heaven Allows*, the female protagonist's "transgression of class barriers mirrors her more deeply shocking transgression of sexual taboos."[54]

In addition, since the first Sirk issue in 1971, *Screen* had undertaken lengthy studies of realism and the classic text, resulting in a more consensual and sexually-based definition of "aberrant" textual practice. In the early 1970s, discussion of negative themes, distance, and ironic happy ends pitted these Sirkian characteristics against a "normal" practice. For such Brechtians as Willemen the norm consisted of illusionism, conventionality, and audience complicity with spectacle. For Elsaesser the norm existed more as an aesthetic category—a lack of complexity in structure, style, and vision. *Screen* criticism in the latter part of the decade was to resolve such divergences in opinion by coalescing around a concept of classic textual operation, drawn from prevailing psychoanalytic models, which I shall discuss in more detail later.

Another major shift in Sirk criticism, noted by Christine Gledhill, is that the dynamics of earlier criticism which favored auteur over genre began to change. By the late 1970s, critics were classifying film noir, the 1970s horror film, and the woman's film, as subversive, at least partially on the basis of generic characteristics. In studies of melodrama the work of Thomas Elsaesser and Peter Brooks helped establish the dignity, dramatic complexity, and social significance of the genre.[55] In this spirit, critics began to consider the relation of melodramatic form to ideology, without an exclusive emphasis on the director as enabler of critique. However, this shift to generic concentration did not often truly displace the director. The potential for genre films to live up to their transgressive possibilities was frequently realized by the presence of the "right" director, whether it was Larry Cohen, Max Ophuls, Dorothy Arzner, or Douglas Sirk.

We can thus see several modifications in *Screen* perspectives on Sirk and melodrama: (1) traditional aesthetic and Marxist treatments are displaced in favor of a uniform ideological approach—psychoanalysis; (2) gender and sexuality, marginal concerns in earlier treatments, dominate interpretation, though not to the total exclusion of class; (3) the theoretical sense of what constitutes the classic text solidifies; and (4) melodrama begins to attain an overall positive critical status as a genre.

This period was characterized by another change as well, which was not due specifically to theoretical developments but to the nature of critical enterprise as it evolves. Criticism in the aftermath of the pioneering work reacted to its predecessors, attempting to elaborate, revise, or critique prior suppositions; this is part of the inevitable intertextuality of academic enterprise. Laura Mulvey, for example, begins her essay "Notes on Sirk and Melodrama" by criticizing Willemen's progressive readings in "Distanciation and Douglas Sirk" and "Sirkian System." She argues that the ideological contradictions in this director's films are not produced by the exercise of a special authorial agency, but are a congenital feature of melodrama as a genre filled with ideological inconsistencies.

But more than clarifying how critics stage their arguments, such intertextual exchanges begin to reflect a process of selection, delimiting what will survive as valuable from past critical moments. The psychoanalytic phase of Sirk criticism tended to cite and thus ensure the survival of those essays and films from the "boom" period that related to the issue of textual politics. Essays by Willemen, Halliday, and Elsaesser in particular represented the significant critical background, while those by Camper, Prokosh, Hunter, and others in the traditional school quietly receded from view.

Similarly, there was a thinning of the ranks in films considered important for analysis. Critics in the main line of film criticism no longer acted as if they had to prove Sirk's authorship by showing the consistency of his vision over his entire career. Their analyses focused instead on melodrama's transgressive relation to ideology, and Sirk's films insofar as they provided a particularly cogent instance of the transgressive potential of the genre. Thus, films from Sirk's German period, which could not very well act as barometers of U.S. ideology, lost importance, as did many of Sirk's later ventures—particularly his musical comedies (such as *Slightly French* [1949] or *Meet Me at the Fair* [1952]), but even some of his melodramas (such as *Summer Storm* [1944] or *Sleep, My Love* [1948]). While this exclusion can be partially explained through the lack of distribution for some of these films, psychoanalytic and later periods of criticism still selected a very small number of Sirk's available films for study. These were *Magnificent Obsession, All That Heaven Allows, Written on the Wind, Tarnished Angels,* and *Imitation of Life.* The interviews played a role in this selection, since many of these films were favored by Sirk. But, in addition, all of them could be placed against the backdrop of Eisenhower America in the 1950s. This was the locus Halliday established as the most significant for understanding the style and meaning of Sirk's films as social critique, and hence for coming to terms with Sirk's significance for ideological criticism.

Screen-oriented criticism of this period thus witnessed a greater uniformity overall than in the "boom period," both in method and objects of study, as work on Sirk and melodrama coalesced around questions of ideology. However, despite the many transformations heralded by the psychoanalytic phase, the coterie of Sirkian elements remained remarkably stable. Psychoanalytic theory and criticism operated in this case not really to dislodge previous interpretive terms, but to continue to verify them under another name that befitted the change in methodological paradigm. New paradigms gain distinction by making the films in question "their own," activating interpretations not possible under different theoretical conditions. The appearance of psychoanalysis on the critical scene strongly stabilized a core of already established interpretive terms, yet renovated them for a new appropriation born from specific theoretical developments.

Psychoanalytic treatments of Sirk and melodrama arose in conjunction with a Society for Education in Film and Television (SEFT) weekend school held in London in 1977, which was devoted to the study of Hollywood melodrama and its relation to ideology. While not all the work presented at this conference appeared in *Screen*, those writing the key publications of this period were closely associated with the journal's perspectives.[56]

Like Elsaesser, *Screen* critics focused on how the family melodrama exhibited unconscious dynamics that undermined the dominant ideological values the genre might otherwise seem to endorse. Although the extent of subversiveness varied, all critics agreed that the family melodrama raised the contradictions inherent in bourgeois and patriarchal ideologies—particularly repressive in the 1950s—to the surface. Critics regarded the genre's representation of the family as a microcosm of the repressive social and sexual structures of the era. Melo-

drama provided "the locus of contradiction and of potential subversion and dis-
ruption of the dominant ideologies and their operations, most conspicuously in
relation to the family and sexuality."[57]

Major concepts raised at the weekend school to support such assessments
included the "counter-current" produced by mise-en-scène, irony, and the *deus
ex machina* endings. Like previous critics, these writers privileged mise-en-scène
as a site that generates commentary "beneath the surface," undermining the
complicit content of the story line. They also drew attention to the false happy
end as an ironical device that seals the transgressive status of the family melodrama. These valorizing terms persisted even in accounts that questioned the
subversive label. Despite Mulvey's critique of Willemen's progressive reading by
virtue of Sirk's signature, she agrees with Elsaesser that "the strength of melodramatic form [lies] . . . in a cloud of over-determined irreconcilables which put up
a resistance to being neatly settled in the last five minutes." This realization leads
her to praise Sirk over Minnelli for not resolving the tensions and contradictions
raised in the course of the narrative via his ironic *deus ex machina* devices.[58]
The *pull* to evaluate melodrama through the example of Sirk persists, then, as
does the citation of those structural and formal elements established by the interviews and subsequent discourse as key to determining the ideological status
of his texts.

However, in addition to the common terms of stylistic subversion and the
false happy end, we find the specifically psychoanalytic concepts of "excess"
and "containment." These concepts derive from a model of the classic text, defined by such pieces as the *Cahiers* editors' essay on *Young Mr. Lincoln*, Roland
Barthes's *S/Z*, and Stephen Heath's analysis of *Touch of Evil*.[59] These models
redefine the classic text as more than a closed structure reliant on chains of
cause and effect, strict linearity, coherence, and closure. The classic text demonstrates, rather, a process of becoming through a complex interplay between
the forces of containment (understood as both structural and ideological) and
unconscious elements (expressed at subtle formal levels) that threaten to overturn
the coherence of the system. These elements are almost invariably linked to certain expressions of sexuality that challenge the ideological status quo. In *Young
Mr. Lincoln*, Lincoln's symbolic correlation with castration contradicts his folksy
historical image. Barthes's work centers on a confusion of sexual identity related
to castration and impotence, and Heath defines narrative as operating to contain
female sexuality. The classic text is, then, a system struggling to contain prob-
lematic sexual dynamics that can bubble up from "below the surface" to exceed
the conventions of closure and the achievement of containment.

Screen criticism of melodrama, similarly, interprets the genre's subversiveness as a matter of how it does or does not *contain*, or conclusively resolve, the ideological tensions brought up in the course of the narrative. The family melodrama attains a transgressive ideological status by producing *excess* tension that cannot find resolution through the happy end. Two hallmarks of Sirk's style, the false happy end and vivid, critical mise-en-scène, gain new life through these concepts.

For example, Mulvey argues that in *Written on the Wind*, Kyle Hadley's fear of impotence, explicitly rooted in familial and social definitions of masculinity, gives rare insight into "man as victim in patriarchal society, pursued specifically by castration anxiety" (p. 54). Sirk's "minimal attention to a standardized happy end" (Kyle dies) aligns the film with tragedy, while refusing to somehow rationalize his torment. Hence, narrative structure does not serve its usual function of laying to rest difficult ideological conflicts; in this film, closure cannot "manage" the Oedipal problems that have saturated the narrative. Aside from male Oedipal dynamics, Mulvey also discusses the strengths of Sirk's films in relation to the other gender. She defines Sirk's films as women's films, representing a female point of view that articulates the plight of women in patriarchy. In her analysis of the woman's film through a combination of feminism and psychoanalysis, Mulvey represented what was to become a major trend in film theory and criticism.[60]

While Mulvey focuses on the false happy end as a device that figures prominently in the triumph of excess over containment, Geoffrey Nowell-Smith's "Minnelli and Melodrama" is renowned for its psychoanalytic conception of mise-en-scène in relation to these two concepts. Nowell-Smith reiterates that the happy end in melodrama is frequently an implausible device; but its appearance marks "a form of an acceptance of castration . . . achieved only at the cost of repression."[61] That is, charged with restoring the proper social order (marriage, the family), the ending can do so only by repressing challenges to that order. The repressive movement of the narrative in collusion with the dominant social order necessitates the production of excess psychic energy. This energy must be "siphoned off," and it is here that the nature of melodramatic mise-en-scène assumes its significance.

Like Elsaesser, Nowell-Smith argues that the artifice and intensity of melodramatic mise-en-scène can be understood only if one sees them as a manifestation of unconscious processes. But Nowell-Smith cites conversion hysteria, rather than displacement, as more accurately describing the operations of melodramatic form. He writes that in melodrama, "where there is always material which cannot be expressed in discourse or in the actions of the character a . . . conversion can take place. . . . The hysterical moment of the text can be identified as the point at which the realistic representative convention breaks down" (p. 117). Here, the family melodrama's antinaturalism signals something other than self-reflexivity or distanciation. It is read as a symptomatic incoherence that signals a "protest" against the realist convention and the ideology it upholds. Again, like Elsaesser, Nowell-Smith concludes that the family melodrama in the 1950s elicits a stylistic exhibition of neurosis, linked to the sexual malaise of society. In its structural inability to "cope" with these problematics it "opens up a space which most Hollywood films have studiously closed off" (p. 118). In this way, Sirk's remarks about his films' social criticism, mise-en-scène, false happy ends, and ironies were renovated, revitalized, and "updated" as signifiers of excess for psychoanalysis. Indeed, terms central to Sirk criticism obtained increasing influence as they came to define the potential and properties of melodrama itself.

The consensual nature of criticism was due not only to the stabilizing influence of the Sirk interviews, but also, as mentioned, to the Comolli/Narboni-inspired project of the 1970s to define the relation of film and ideology. Whether Marxist or psychoanalytic, critics engaged in progressive readings of Hollywood films often rallied around requisite components of the argument such as closure. In addition, once an author or genre was defined as progressive, the films in question tended to attain a canonical status as such. Few within the main line at this time (and very rarely later) would consistently argue, for instance, that Sirk films supported the class structure or sex roles of the 1950s, or that his excessive style might have different ideological connotations. One early exception to this rule was Steve Neale, who expressed misgivings about formally based ideological assessments of Sirk. He briefly raised the issue of the importance of the original industrial and social context in which these films appeared in considering their social meaning.[62] It is interesting to note that this hesitant aspect of Neale's essay was not picked up by the academic network, under the sway of the progressive paradigm, for further commentary.

Yet it would be a mistake to see the shift to psychoanalysis as nothing more than a seamless consensus. While reiterating fundamental terms of established Sirk criticism, psychoanalysis also generated meanings that differed from earlier approaches. Whereas the pretense and moralism of the petit bourgeois are under attack in Marxist accounts, psychoanalysis centered on the family, Oedipal crises, and sexual identity as representing the repressive bourgeois and patriarchal order. In addition, Marxist critics viewed the density of mise-en-scène as a critique of bourgeois acquisitiveness or as deconstructive artifice, while psychoanalytic critics diagnosed it as a symptomatic reaction against repression. Hence, objects in the mise-en-scène can represent distanciating anti-illusionism or displaced incarnations of a character's deepest anxieties, depending on the methodological orientation of the critic. The point of departure for both approaches is unrealistic mise-en-scène, but psychoanalytic critics interpreted its lack of verisimilitude more as a result of its special relation to both unconscious processes and ideological contradictions than as purely a matter of authorial manipulation of the "right," that is, Brechtian devices.

The example of a single film can help clarify the import of such fluctuations in meaning-making. Marylee's exuberant "Temptation" dance in *Written on the Wind* was initially criticized by Marcorelles as a quintessential example of Sirk's empty style. Since then, critics have attached numerous interpretations to this moment. For Willemen, the dance represents "the use of choreography as a direct expression of character," a Brechtian premise that allowed Sirk to escape the strictures of the industry he was working in and produce self-conscious art ("Distanciation," p. 65). Elsaesser describes the dance as an example of dramatic discontinuity produced from extreme emotional situations, so important to recognizing the complex aesthetic nature of the family melodrama ("Tales of Sound and Fury," p. 12). For Michael Stern, the dance beautifully exemplifies the sexual thematics of the film: frustration and impotence.[63] This moment can signify, then, an example of Brechtian practice, the aesthetic heights of dramatic discontinuity or sexual themes.

This play of difference could easily touch all aspects of Sirk interpretation. What such differences demonstrate is how dependent an element's meaning is on critical perspective. Marylee's dance may clearly exist as a brute filmic fact, but its signification is not so palpable or fixed. Filmic facts are clearly subject to *processes* of meaning construction, in which their meaning is shaped by successive paradigms of theory and criticism. Theory and criticism of the 1970s employed a variety of approaches to articulate the ideological parameters of counterclassic forms, resulting in a continuous re-reading and updating of the progressive features of a given text (via Brecht, Freud, and Barthes, for example). This mobility of meaning suggests that academic readings come to terms with the formal properties of a text through a series of interpretive grids provided by developments in the discipline, rather than through a rapport with the single "truth" of the text.

It is important to point out here that the process of updating does *not* signify the mere imposition of superficial or faddish readings. On the one hand, updating employs certain films to elaborate and secure theoretical developments sweeping the field. During the 1970s, the thus enlivened text often served as a means of politicizing interpretations and viewers, creating new sensitivities to issues of class and gender in publications as well as in the classroom. On the other hand, updating constitutes a vital sustaining activity within the academic institution. By bringing films into relation with new theories, critics make them meaningful for a succession of critical audiences through time. The alternative to such acts of renewal for films and their directors is to be cast into the vault of oblivion.

Once the Marxist and psychoanalytic approaches had further defined how Sirk should be approached, criticism began to demonstrate an increasing uniformity. By the late 1970s, the field of possible interpretations for Sirk and the domestic melodrama had been set, demonstrating a rapid consolidation of interpretive frameworks within the academy. Substantial differences in interpretation almost disappeared as Sirk criticism entered its consolidation phase.

Critical Consolidation

During this period of critical consolidation, which took place in the early 1980s, criticism was in a sense doubly indebted to the past. Not only did it still abide by parameters established in the Sirk interviews, but it also had to acknowledge prior work that had significantly contributed to the definitive goals of ideological criticism—Marxism, psychoanalysis, and feminism. Exacerbating this indebtedness to the past was the fact that there were no new theories that could update approaches to Sirk or the family melodrama. Rather, critics replayed, refined, applied, or countered points of past arguments. While each offered new insights, these substantially relied on established interpretive perspectives.

In keeping with the psychoanalytic phase's general movement toward the analysis of the genre/ideology relation, criticism here focused more exclusively on melodrama than on the redemptive auteur. But Sirk and Minnelli films remained central to discussion as particularly excellent representations of the subversive potential of melodrama. The idea that melodrama laid bare social and psychic conflicts of the 1950s through the microcosm of the family unit no longer had to be argued or proved; it was an assumption upon which critics based their further explorations.

Christopher Orr's "Closure and Containment: Marylee Hadley in *Written on the Wind*," for example, focused on Marylee as an extreme representation of female sexuality, generating an excess that patriarchal structures could not contain through narrative conventions leading to closure.[64] An essay by D. N. Rodowick invoked melodrama's parade of psychological disorders (impotency, hysteria, alcoholism, etc.), its highly expressive mise-en-scène which taps into the inner turmoil of the characters, its formal constitution of ironic distance, and the ambiguity of the happy end to demonstrate the genre's inability to reproduce ideological stability.[65] Thomas Schatz's chapter on melodrama in his textbook *Hollywood Genres* includes a special section on Sirk. His analysis focuses on the significance of mise-en-scène in expressing thematic and ideological conflicts, double levels of meaning, the ironic happy end, and the theme of hopelessness.[66]

Each of these pieces, however, produces interpretations of Sirk and melodrama that nuance familiar critical elements. Orr questions an easy definition of Marylee as exceeding ideological strictures; Rodowick cautions against any simple correlation between history and aesthetic ideology that would understand the text as a direct and spontaneous reaction to social developments; and Schatz designates subcategories of the family melodrama to suit significant differences in plot. But each also shows how overdetermined the discussion of Sirk and melodrama became within a decade of academic pursuit—how scrupulously writing subsequent to Marxist and psychoanalytic developments abided by set analytic perspectives. Criticism here functions to selectively activate established perspectives to further cement interpretive consensus.

What we observe in such periods of criticism is not, as it might appear, a lack of critical initiative. Rather, consolidation is strongly linked to Sirk's canonical status. That is, once Sirk's films became a steadfast part of the political canon through psychoanalysis, possibilities of interpretation became streamlined. Streamlining occurred as institutional practices—pedagogy and publication—transmitted and perpetuated the identity of these films as progressive, creating the conditions for what Barbara Herrnstein Smith has called the "cultural reproduction of value." This phrase refers to an influential pre-classification of significance which institutions pass on to their members, resulting in a binding heritage of value. The academy creates subjects "for whom the objects and texts thus labeled do indeed perform the functions thus privileged, thereby insuring the continuity of mutually defining canonical works, canonical functions, and canonical audiences."[67]

While an author's canonical status over a long period of time can result in a plurality of contrasting interpretations, as it has in the case of Alfred Hitchcock, for example, here canonicity acted quickly to freeze the terms of meaning. Meanings, that is, could not radically change without threatening the political value of Sirk's work, the very reason he had gained and continued to have importance for a field operating under the master paradigm of ideological theory. Certain members of the academy, as subjects of this transmission of value, came to occupy the role of "canonical audience," affirming rather than questioning the politics of the Sirk text. At an extreme, such a tendency found critics operating through a kind of received wisdom; so much so that they could refer in passing to Sirk's "famous ironic subtext," or his "obsessively ironic slant," which forces us "to deconstruct the fiction."[68] The continual affirmation of the transgressive status of the Sirk melodrama in this sense appears as a product of the institutional and intertextual character of academic discourse. The consolidation phase, as particularly representative of this institutional tendency, signified the power that canonicity—that of an auteur, genre, as well as the critical essays themselves—could have over interpretation during a relatively stable period in the discipline.

After the early 1980s, Sirk criticism entered its most recent phase under the auspices of continuing feminist inquiries into melodrama, the impact of cultural studies, and interest in the representation of racial issues in melodrama. This period has both enshrined Sirk melodramas and partially displaced them from the center of melodramatic discussion. It is here that we can examine what happens to an "old" canonical object once the field begins to shift in a different direction.

When Old Canons Die

From the late 1970s onward, the general upsurge in feminist inquiry in film turned discussion of melodrama more strongly toward the woman's film and the maternal melodrama. Mary Ann Doane and Linda Williams, among many others, published essays on such films as *Rebecca* and *Stella Dallas*.[69] The woman's film and maternal melodrama were targeted for special attention due to their concentration on female characters and relationships, as well as their exceptional status within Hollywood production as films designed expressly for a female audience. Studies of family melodrama had not systematically focused on this subcategory of the genre, and had never productively addressed issues of spectatorship. Sirk melodramas began to be displaced from center stage as other subcategories having greater interest to feminist inquiry occupied critical attention. Feminist work in cultural studies only strengthened this displacement. With the growing importance of cultural studies to film studies in the 1980s, criticism often shed the abstract theoretical language of the previous decade to embrace popular culture and make media analysis more responsive to concrete historical and social contexts, as well as the audience.[70] To investigate the reception of popular instances of melodrama by a mass female audience, critics turned to the Harlequin romance, the Gothic novel and film, and television soap operas.

More recent research into melodrama, strongly influenced by feminism and cultural studies, thus witnessed a growing interest in diverse types of melodrama, and often operated without the requirement of the subversive author.

Critics privileged woman-centered narratives with demonstrable ties to the female spectator to gauge the politics of popular representation and response
within patriarchy. Given these series of shifts in 1980s genre criticism, how can
we evaluate the current status of academic discourse on Sirk? Contemporary Sirk
criticism falls generally into three categories: canonical recycling, continued updating, and disciplinary reflection.

Anthologies provide the clearest example of the first category. Christine
Gledhill's collection *Home Is Where the Heart Is* establishes Douglas Sirk as an
important historical antecedent to work on melodrama within film studies, both
in her introductory essay and in the anthology's overall organization. The collection begins with reprints of essays on the family melodrama by Elsaesser, Nowell-
Smith, and Mulvey; it also includes Rodowick's article and one other piece that
employs the critical tropes established by these paradigmatic essays.[71] Key writings on the woman's film and maternal melodrama follow. The anthology, by
preserving what is valuable from past Sirk criticism, acts to enshrine both the
films and the Elsaesser, Nowell-Smith, and Mulvey triumvirate as canonical texts.
At the same time, by placing this criticism in relation to newer material on melodrama, it suggests the director's continuing relevance to the critical scene in the
later 1980s. Still fascinated by melodrama, the academic climate is receptive to
such a revival.[72]

Thus, anthologies represent one mode of survival for Sirk films after the
most recent paradigm shift: Sirk criticism is recycled to act as a foundation for
contemporary explorations into melodrama. Sirk survives by virtue of the anthology's version of academic history assisted by a sympathetic "melodramatic"
critical environment still engaged with questions of genre and ideology. In this
way, the anthology offers a definitive canonical statement—the director's status
as an ideological icon in the field is further cemented by his evolutionary importance. As a result, this kind of forum is not likely to represent struggles over
meaning. Anthologies, as they perform the function of strategic recollection for
a field, affirm and magnify established significance and the interpretive stances
that support it.

All contemporary approaches to Sirk bear the residue of his canonicity; otherwise he would not continue to be the subject of discussion. Other heralded
directors of the 1970s, such as Howard Hawks or Samuel Fuller, for example,
rarely appear at the center of critical dialogue (though this is not to say they
won't be "revived"). What sets the anthology apart from other means of sustaining Sirk's relevance is that its primary function is to canonize. Other recent work
on Sirk has attempted more directly to update analyses of his films—that is, in-

terpret them through the perspectives of cultural studies, feminist, and race oriented criticism. This mode of existence for Sirk criticism basically maintains interest in his films in the way it had always been sustained: by applying new models (such as psychoanalysis instead of Marxism).

Critics who updated Sirk via cultural studies turned to audience considerations by raising the issue of melodrama's most popular reaction: strong emotion. Earlier approaches for the most part eschewed this dimension of the genre. Critics regarded melodrama's "tearjerker" appeal as representing a blind acceptance of the superficialities of the form, which blocked recognition of its more self-reflexive and critical properties. Now with the redemption of mass cultural response, melodrama's peculiar link to the pleasures of catharsis has become pertinent. In "Melodrama and Tears," Steve Neale examines the filmic mechanisms responsible for creating the tears so commonly associated with melodramatic affect, drawing on an assortment of melodramas, including Sirk's. John Fletcher addresses a similar issue when he defends the intense emotionality of *Imitation of Life* (rather than its style) as the point of articulation for the film's cultural critique.[73]

Others updating Sirk from a feminist and/or racial perspective discuss those of his films which can be classified as maternal melodramas or woman's films, often reacting critically to past assessments. Marina Heung, for example, focuses on the representation of motherhood and race in *Imitation of Life*, claiming that this film supports, rather than subverts, dominant ideas about women and race relations. She writes, "Although Sirk's use of deliberate irony may be typical of his other films, *Imitation* stands out . . . in that the conservative thrust of its ending predominates over whatever ironic subtext Sirk might have intended."[74] While many of the established terms of Sirk criticism are present (irony and the question of closure), Heung reverses prior estimations of the ideological function of these elements.

In another essay, Michael Selig similarly raises feminist issues as a means of reconsidering past evaluations of Sirk.[75] Selig's essay reviews 1970s readings of Sirk as Brechtian, to posit the insufficiency of this approach for analyzing the position of women in these melodramas, thus bringing *Imitation of Life* more closely into association with feminist criticism. He also briefly considers the dimension of the audience, through a correlation between the discourse on women in the film and its emotional effect, claiming that the emotional contours of the film are more likely than the Brechtian subtext to raise the viewer's awareness of the difficult position of women within patriarchy.[76] In these discussions, *Imitation of Life* achieves substantial visibility. This is due to its ability to be clas-

sified as both a woman's film and maternal melodrama, and because its treatment of racial issues suits contemporary interests in analyzing the representation
of African Americans in the cinema. As a sign of this film's particular contemporary importance, Lucy Fischer has edited a book devoted to resurrecting the
film's history and critical reception.[77]

Canonical recyling and such updating procedures form the two dominant
types of recent response to Sirk. The last approach, disciplinary reflection, has
been less evident. Though still updating Sirk according to new norms, via the
influence of Michel Foucault, Thomas Kuhn, and other historiographers of institutions, this third approach has different goals from those of the standard updating procedure. Instead of assigning new meanings to Sirk's films, critics here cite
Sirk as an example that helps reveal the operations of academic discourse itself
as it constructs significance. Robert Ray and David Bordwell's remarks on Sirk
fall into this category, as do my own.[78]

For Ray, Sirk's academic treatment provides evidence of how prone texts in
a post-modernist era are to willfully "re-motivated" meanings. For Bordwell, Sirk
is one among many directors whose example can help illustrate the conventions
critics use to build and justify interpretations. My study examines the chemistry
between authorial intention, developments in the field, and canon formation in
motivating meanings for Sirk's films through several stages of critical evolution.
Film criticism is in each of these instances regarded as a practice, a specific
means of appropriating and explicating texts subject to conditions within the
academy. In contrast to canonical recycling, Sirk's example agitates consideration
of the mechanisms that have created value and meaning. But, whether the critic
recycles, updates, or reflects, Sirk is *always* put to a specific use for specific
academic purposes.

While not all current work on Sirk falls neatly into one of these categories,
the grouping helps us map the fate of a once-definitive critical object within a
somewhat changed frame of reference. Sirk's films continue to be discussed because of a general appetite for things melodramatic and political, evidenced in
anthologized recyclings of past criticism and the suitability of some of his melodramas for cultural studies, feminist, or multicultural renovation. His place in disciplinary reflection is facilitated not so much by the melodramatic climate, as by
the retrospective position enabled by over twenty years of institutionalized film
theory and criticism in conjunction with historiographical perspectives on disciplinary practice.

Sirk, then, exemplifies a canon that has not really *died* in terms of publication—not like, say, the once-central Sam Fuller or Howard Hawks. Sirk's com-

mand of the field has changed, but he is still alive and well in academic studies of melodrama as a figure who continues to prove the worth and significance of the genre.

Canonicity and Meaning

In looking at the evolution of Sirk criticism from *Cahiers* to cultural studies, we can observe that interpretations were characterized ultimately by a certain static quality.[79] This quality resulted partially from the tenacity of Sirk's own words over critical enterprise, so that interpretations rarely strayed far from the content of Halliday's interview. But it was also a product of the dominant pursuit of textual politics after the 1970s, and the subsequent constitution of a political canon of directors.

In fact, each step in the history of Sirk criticism signified the increasing hold of his canonical political status over interpretive possibilities. *Cahiers*'s discovery of the director produced a situation of "pre-meaning," wherein style was not fused systematically with significance. The "boom" period developed full-blown organic analyses of the aesthetic and ideological significance of style, but was characterized by a certain pluralism as critics rushed to authorize Sirk. New developments in the field, centered on psychoanalysis and melodrama, began to narrow the field of interpretations and objects for analysis, as critics acted to cement the political value of both Sirk's melodramas and past ideological criticism. Textual politics, supported by Marxism, psychoanalysis, and feminism, precipitated a period of consolidation, wherein critics rehearsed conventions of reading. And finally, as cultural studies, feminism, and racial criticism gained ascendancy, the family melodrama survived relatively unaltered on the basis of a sympatico relation with the new order still interested in melodrama and ideology.

Although there were rapid developments from *Cahiers* to "boom" to psychoanalytic treatments of Sirk's melodramas, the terms critics used to approach these films remained remarkably stable, even repetitive after the early 1970s. Critical memory preserved only those films and essays that confirmed the progressive status of the family melodrama. What came to be seen as Sirk's political value had a direct effect on the possibilities of meaning construction. Through an intertextual network of publication and pedagogy, Sirk's canonical value was transmitted to and reproduced by subpopulations of the critical community, resulting in an essential tranquillity in critical positions. In this way, critical stasis around the family melodrama was strongly supported by the interviews, but truly engineered by a master theoretical paradigm (textual politics) operating in conjunction with a process of canonization.

The impact of political canonicity on the interpretation of the family melodrama raises an issue especially relevant to the concern in the following chapters with investigating alternative historical and institutional settings of meaning production for these melodramas. As Janet Staiger has pointed out, the development of political canons via feminism and other ideological approaches was extremely important in displacing the power base of the more traditional, minority-blind, canon. Political canons not only raised the issue of minority authors, but also practiced an appropriation of works that inspired strategic and instructive ideological rereadings of Hollywood and other kinds of films.[80] However, Sirk's case ultimately represents some of the hazards political canonization represents for ideological criticism. This canonization, resulting in a progressive evaluation of the relation between the family melodrama and ideology, has paradoxically "protected" these films from the ravages of history. This has occurred through both the nature of the textual politics project itself, and the ordinary operations of established canons as they seek to defend valued objects from apparently haphazard or unappreciative interpretations.

The problem with the textual politics project is that progressive readings—that is, specific appropriations of works for specific political reasons—were often imperceptibly transformed into political effects the texts themselves engendered. Film noir, the family melodrama, the woman's film, Max Ophuls, Fritz Lang, and Douglas Sirk remain in our critical consciousness as transgressive because critics, acting out the program established by Comolli and Narboni, judged their formal characteristics as diverging from classic Hollywood practice and the status quo ideology its transparent form carries. What was imputed as formal evidence transformed a particular reading into a state of textual being, thus establishing the film in question as almost unassailably progressive.

The most recent paradigm shift continues to exhibit this convergence between reading and being. There is a strong consistency between the *Screen*-dominated approaches of the 1970s and cultural studies treatments of Sirk's melodramas in several important regards. The mission of the analysis has always been to determine whether the family melodrama is reactionary or progressive; analysis attempts to *settle* the ideological status of Sirk's texts. John Fletcher, for example, defends the ending of *Imitation of Life* as transgressive because it yields an "insoluble impasse," failing to settle conflicts of race, gender, and family relationships, while Marina Heung condemns the film as ideologically complicit in terms of its representation of mother/daughter and racial relations, citing how the emotionality of the ending "lays to rest the subversive energy of Sara Jane."[81]

Despite such a difference in opinions, the stake is the same: the definitive assessment of melodrama's ideology.

In addition, such examinations determine ideological status, as well as spectatorial response (on the infrequent occasions when it is addressed), entirely through formal analysis. Work on Sirk's melodramas continues to make claims about ideology and the spectator solely on the basis of the investigation of filmic structures. Fletcher and Heung both rely on the issue of closure as the determining factor in ideological assessment. And while Steve Neale's work may engage the dimension of the audience through a discussion of melodramatic affect, he approaches the issue by exploring the role of coincidence, knowledge, and point of view within the narrative. Hence, in the case of the family melodrama, ideology and spectatorship have remained largely *formal* issues, approached as things the text itself produces.

The perpetuation of formally based approaches to questions of ideology and spectatorship isolates these texts from their sociohistorical contexts. Attempts to "fix" the ideology of a text remove it even further from the variations in meaning it has been subject to throughout its history and various uses. Among the most important contributions cultural studies has made to the study of media in other areas is exactly that they are not independent, self-determining objects. Determining their meaning is radically dependent on their social location and the predispositions of their receivers, and thus subject to negotiation through time and circumstance. Ideology is not, then, a thing a text *has*; such meanings are *produced* for it. And while a text's formal features may set into motion certain procedures of decipherment for the spectator, these features alone cannot explain the range of meanings a text can have in different contexts of reception. Discussion of a text's ideological significance must, then, come to terms with the *contingent* and *changeable* nature of this identity, to address more adequately questions of history and reception.

Similarly, while creating an important challenge to traditional canons, political canons have often operated in a classical canonical way to lock the text in question away from history and the "untutored" spectator. Like other canons, the progressive version has operated as a defensive mission, tending to "pathologiz[e] . . . all other contingencies," as a means of "warding off barbarism."[82] For many critics, Sirk's value was dependent on removing his films from the terms of their popular reception, since the average spectator tended to miss the social critique and become blindly enamored of the melodramatic content. Sirk had been previously misunderstood, and academic criticism acted to redress the lack of his audience's ironic consciousness by revealing the true political significance of his films.

Thus, Sirk's family melodramas became and remained valuable for film studies through a disavowal of their popularity or possible campiness. The only way to preserve this value was to malign and/or dismiss popular barbarisms which would find "disagreeable" meanings for the Sirk melodrama. By so assiduously protecting his films, critics began to see the possibilities of other ideological identities, tuned into different social, historical, and institutional frequencies, as the enemy, blocking recognition of the role they might play in analyzing the relation of the family melodrama to ideology.

Such silence about errant "barbarisms" indicates that there are still pressing questions to be answered about this relation. It remains now to explore other historical and institutional settings that have figured in the production of meaning for these films.

2

Selling Melodrama

Sex, Affluence, and
Written on the Wind

The past is a foreign country: they do things differently there.

L. P. Hartley[1]

W E HAVE SEEN how academic meaning for Sirk's melodramas depended on an interaction between a central interview, successive critical developments, and procedures of canonicity enshrining the political value of his films. In this chapter I will examine a different world of meaning for Sirk's melodramas, defined by a close alliance between film industry practices and social values of the 1950s. The focus of my analysis will be *Written on the Wind* (1957), extolled by many critics as Sirk's most overtly subversive text, but also a film particularly representative of a certain mode of film production and exhibition in the post– World War II era.

In the course of my investigation of exhibition practices, I will reconsider certain fundamental propositions underpinning the progressive readings of this film and other sophisticated family melodramas of the 1950s. Chief among these are the notion that a historical moment presents a unified ideology, capable of quick summary, and that a film's formal components, if they depart from standards of classical construction, are ipso facto subversive. Critics' characterization of the 1950s as a socially and sexually repressive decade, a necessary backdrop for appreciating the excesses of Sirk, Ray, and Minnelli melodramas as transgressive, does not do justice to the era's complex ideological character. Nor, then, can such a capsule summary address how features of the family melodrama might have been negotiated to different ideological ends through value systems in operation during the original release period.

Specifically, in the 1950s studios related melodrama to dramatic changes in

36

sexual mores and a domestic economy focused on consumption, forging intricate relations between melodrama and dominant cultural ideas. As the case of *Written on the Wind* will demonstrate, Universal-International's exhibition practices made these connections by creating, on the one hand, a generic identity for melodramas as "adult" films in order to capitalize on increasing trends toward sexually explicit representation in the media. On the other hand, exhibition presented melodramatic style as a veritable wonderland of consumer fantasies and goods to appeal to the post–World War II affluent mentality.

In what follows, I will focus on how the industry constructed meaning for melodramas by defining genre and style in accord with postwar discourses on sex and affluence. My argument is that this construction is important to a historical conception of the ideological significance of melodrama. My respective studies of genre and style will first consider pertinent industrial developments that shaped advertising decisions, then the specific aspects of *Written on the Wind's* ad campaign, and finally, the social factors informing industry choices. While stars figured prominently in exhibition strategies, analysis of this factor will have to wait until a later chapter.[2]

Genre: The Adult Film

Advertising campaigns in the postwar era routinely called attention to the sensationalistic content of films. As early as 1945, the poster for *The Lost Weekend*, a film about alcoholism, exclaimed, "How daring can the screen *dare* to be? No adult man or woman can *risk* missing the startling frankness of *The Lost Weekend*."[3] By the 1950s, "daring," "shocking," "frankness," "adult," and other such terms were common in advertisements. Warner Bros. pitched *The Bad Seed* (1956), its film about a murderous teenager, as: "The big shocker is the box-office rocker! Recommended for adults only! . . . We recommend no seating during the last 15 minutes!"[4] MGM employed similar rhetoric for a film called *Slander* (1956):

> Who will be the next victim of Slander? The football coach with a clandestine love nest? A French girl who had an affair with a reformer? A TV headliner who served a 4-year prison term? The Broadway star who was once a drug addict? Slander—a sensational, hard-hitting, no-punches-pulled dramatic exposé done with frankness and fearlessness.[5]

As these examples suggest, the industry typically defined the adult film through a double language that emphasized its social significance to justify titillating indulgence in the spectacles provided by psychological torment, drugs, sex, and murder. This new standard pervasively affected melodramas. But it defined examples from almost every other genre as well, including *The Searchers* (1956), a western with a miscegenation theme; *Love Me or Leave Me* (1955), a musical that focused on violent marital relations; *The Detective Story* (1951), a crime film that mentioned abortion; and *The Moon Is Blue* (1953), a sex comedy.

Selling films through promises of sensationalism was nothing new in film advertising. But in the 1950s a number of industry factors converged to create a specific manifestation of this tradition, resulting in both the production and advertisement of films as adult. The contributing factors included competition with television, the import of foreign films, the status of film censorship, and the Paramount case.

In 1956, *Variety* indicated that besides blockbusters, "unusual, off-beat films with adult themes that TV could not handle" represented an effective route of combat with television.[6] While by this time, studios had created profitable alliances with television by selling their films for television broadcast or by producing television series, industry rhetoric still figured the new medium as a major competitor. The more familiar historical account of this competition focuses on image innovations such as 3-D and Cinemascope which were to fight the new medium by giving the audience spectacles that the small, flat television screen could not. But another strategy clearly lay in the realm of subject matter. By presenting mature narrative situations related to sexual problems, drug abuse, and other sensational subjects, studios attempted to enhance their competitive edge by providing content that the variety shows, family situation comedies, and other television fare could not. Thus, the family melodrama of the 1950s, with its tortured family units and emphasis on psychosexual problematics featured topics far removed from what television could offer in such sit-coms as "The Adventures of Ozzie and Harriet" (1952–66), "Father Knows Best" (1954–63), and "Leave It to Beaver" (1957–63).

However, this trend toward mature subject matter in Hollywood films cannot be explained as simply a reaction to television content. Indeed, the 1950s saw the U.S. exhibition of *La Ronde* (1950), *Summer with Monika* (1952), *Smiles of a Summer Night* (1955), *And God Created Woman* (1956), and other foreign films with sexually explicit content. As Steve Neale has pointed out, the admission of such films into the United States was aided by the reorganization of the film industry after the Paramount case.[7] The separation of exhibition from production and distribution that the Paramount case dictated loosened the control that the Hays Code and the MPAA (Motion Picture Association of America) had previously exerted over imported films, facilitating the creation of alternative distribution and exhibition circuits that could show such foreign fare. The assumption of mature themes by some Hollywood films allowed them to compete, then, with both foreign imports and television. At the same time, the art film, described as realistic (that is, providing revelations about the human condition) while offering daring presentations of sex, may have helped supply the vocabulary that studios used to promote their own melodramas.

Along with the influence of television and foreign films, the status of film censorship during the postwar era helped create a felicitous environment for the production of films with mature subject matter. From the famous MPAA/Howard Hughes dispute over *The Outlaw* in 1946 to United Artists's release of two Otto Preminger films without the MPAA seal of approval—*The Moon Is Blue* (1953), a sex comedy in which the word "virgin" was uttered for the first time, and *The Man with the Golden Arm* (1955), which was about drug addiction—the domain and regulations of the MPAA were almost continually challenged.[8]

The Paramount case, which had played a role in loosening the grip of the MPAA over the distribution and exhibition of imported films, had a similar effect on domestic products. It enabled a somewhat less authoritative relation between censorship and film production. In addition, because of post–World War II attendance problems and competition from television, exhibitors and studios put pressure on the MPAA to soften its moral standards to respond to box office needs.[9] The code was revised in December 1956 to allow references to previously forbidden subject matters such as drug addiction, abortion, prostitution, and miscegenation, while topics like sexual perversion were still banned. By the 1960s, even this last bastion of censorship was finally overcome.

Shifts in the industry were in accord with significant legal decisions against the censorship of certain subjects handed down during this period. In 1952, after a controversy surrounding the banning of Roberto Rossellini's *The Miracle* on the grounds that it was sacrilegious, the Supreme Court granted film First Amendment protection.[10] In the next few years, the Supreme Court disallowed banning a film because of subject matter focused on sexual immorality. Such developments in the film industry and legal structure helped, then, to fuel more permissive screen representations.

Interestingly, ad campaigns often went so far as to call attention to their challenges to censorship as a means of selling a film. *The Rose Tattoo* (1955), for example, was "The Boldest Story of Love You've Ever Been Permitted to See," while *The Sun also Rises* (1957) was a "Love Story Too Daring to Film until Now," and *From Here to Eternity* (1953) was "The Boldest Book of Our Time,

Honestly, Fearlessly on The Screen."[11] Studios thereby made themselves appear as crusaders for the freedom of speech ("honestly, fearlessly") and the right of their audiences to experience mature, realistic content.

Because of major developments affecting content, the film industry produced movies that could compete in a marketplace tuned to the box office possibilities of explicit psychodramas. Indeed, many of the biggest grossing films during this era—*I'll Cry Tomorrow* (1955), *Picnic* (1955), *The Man with the Golden Arm*, *The Bad Seed*, *Trapeze* (1956), *Giant* (1956), *Written on the Wind*, and *Peyton Place* (1957)—were melodramas with social, psychological, and/or sexual problems at their core. For their materials, studios often adapted novels and plays with celebrated adult profiles, enhancing the prestige as well as the notoriety of the films indebted to these prior works. Tennessee Williams's stories, including *A Streetcar Named Desire* (1951), *The Rose Tattoo*, *Baby Doll* (1956), *Cat on a Hot Tin Roof* (1958), and *Suddenly, Last Summer* (1959), were thus converted. So were a host of novels and other plays, including James Jones's *From Here to Eternity*, Lillian Roth's autobiography *I'll Cry Tomorrow*, William Inge's *Picnic*, Robert Anderson's *Tea and Sympathy*, and Grace Metalious's *Peyton Place*. "Racy" topics in these texts included homosexuality, sexual initiation, prostitution, rape, abortion, adultery, sexual frustration and temptation, alcoholism, and murder. It was through this dominant trend in production that melodrama came to be equated with adult subject matter and promises of sensationalism. The film melodrama thus became one of the forms by which the studios could profitably respond to particular industry developments.

Officially released in 1957, *Written on the Wind*, adapted from Robert Wilder's novel by the same title, was not embroiled in any censorship disputes. It obtained the MPAA seal of approval and a rating as "morally unobjectionable for adults" from the Catholic Legion of Decency. However, its production and advertising were deeply influenced by the converging factors during this period, as well as the healthy business adult films were doing at the box office. In the initial stages of planning its ad campaign, Universal described the film as "a searing adult drama that at one time might have been considered too explosive to handle. Today, however, it takes its place among the important Hollywood productions that have dared to treat unconventional themes in a sensitive, realistic fashion."[12]

Trade press reviews, which functioned to present a film's most salable aspects, declared that "this outspoken modern drama probes rather startlingly into the morals and passions of an uppercrust Texas oil family. On shock value alone it would attract B. O. attention," and "fraught with a variety of sensational themes, i.e. adultery, alcoholism, sterility and nymphomania, *Written on the*

Wind will undoubtedly be one of the most talked about pictures in the current crop."[13] Armed with such themes, *WOW,* as Universal often referred to the film, was admirably suited for an ad campaign flying the adult film colors. The various materials involved in this campaign emphasized the spectacle provided by the film's psychological and sexual conflicts as a means of identifying it as a member of the adult genre.

The basic poster for *Written on the Wind* featured a dominant picture of Hudson and Bacall embracing, insert photos of Stack and Malone, and a "mini-scenario" with Malone shrinking back in horror at the prostrate body of Stack under a rather expressionistic-looking tree, along with star and personnel names and the film title. Other, more detailed posters, used as the basis for newspaper ads, emphasized the story and the characters. They described the drama as "the story of a decent love that fought to live against the vice and immorality of an oil baron's wastrel family!" or "the story of a family's ugly secret that thrust their private lives into public view!" Poster copy summarized the characters thus: "Rock Hudson as Mitch, this woman in his arms was now the wife of the man he called his best friend!"; "Lauren Bacall as Lucy, faithful to her husband's name . . . even if she couldn't be to his love!"; "Robert Stack as Kyle, who hid his secret behind a bottle and a hundred million dollars!"; and "Dorothy Malone as Marylee, even a woman will find it hard to understand why she did the things she did!" These advertisements sometimes included lines of dialogue: "Mitch: 'No matter what you think . . . you're the baby's father not me' "; and "Marylee: 'How long can I wait, Mitch, feeling the way I do?' " Images supporting these character descriptions included Mitch and Lucy embracing, Kyle after a fight, and Marylee drinking.[14]

The trailer for *Written on the Wind* amplifies this focus on sensationalistic elements considerably. The first segment announces the film's title, focusing on romantic intrigue. The voice-over narration, "What a woman tells a man—what a man tells a woman—are words too often—*Written on the Wind,*" is divided into phrases that punctuate the three main shot-sequences: a shot of Marylee and Mitch in her sportscar, when she says, "And I'll have you—marriage or no marriage!"; the airport scene between Kyle and Lucy with his admission of love and marriage proposal; and a shot of the Hadley mansion with blowing leaves, followed by the film's title. This segment clarifies the meaning of the film's title by associating it with heterosexual conflict and romance. While the second major segment introduces the stars and the character roles they assume, the third begins to define the film's membership in the adult genre. The narrator describes the film as "a tense, frank drama—woven of the raw realism of life itself." Two shots corresponding to these phrases feature Kyle's drinking (as tense, frank

Advertisement for *The Lost Weekend* (1945). Copyright ©
by Universal City Studios, Inc. Courtesy of MCA Publishing
Rights, a Division of MCA Inc.

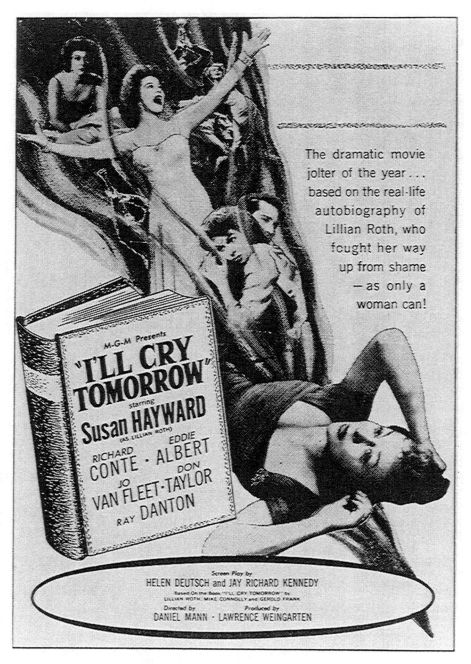

The dramatic movie jolter of the year... based on the real-life autobiography of Lillian Roth, who fought her way up from shame —as only a woman can!

M-G-M Presents

'I'LL CRY TOMORROW"

starring

Susan HAYWARD
(AS LILLIAN ROTH)

RICHARD CONTE · EDDIE ALBERT
JO VAN FLEET · DON TAYLOR
RAY DANTON

Screen Play by
HELEN DEUTSCH and JAY RICHARD KENNEDY
Based On the Book "I'LL CRY TOMORROW" by
LILLIAN ROTH, MIKE CONNOLLY and GEROLD FRANK
Directed by   Produced by
DANIEL MANN · LAWRENCE WEINGARTEN

Advertisement for *I'll Cry Tomorrow* (1955). Copyright © 1955 Turner Entertainment Co. All rights reserved.

Advertisement for *Tea and Sympathy* (1956). Copyright © 1956 Turner Entertainment Co. All rights reserved.

Advertisement for *Written on the Wind* (1957). *Look*, Dec. 1956. Copyright © by Universal City Studios, Inc. Courtesy of MCA Publishing Rights, a Division of MCA Inc.

drama) and Marylee's "pink negligee" dance (as woven of the raw realism of life itself).

The rest of the trailer emphasizes generic type by elaborating character traits and conflicted interrelations. It includes the proclamation of Marylee's promiscuity by one of her "pick-ups," which prompts her father to reach for a gun; a description of Mitch as the family defender, accompanied by the scene of the barroom brawl he wins; Kyle in a drunken rage with a gun, depicted as "too rich" and "tortured by a secret"; Marylee described as "tormented by longings too strong to control," drinking and demanding sexual attention from Mitch; and Lucy's announcement of her pregnancy to Kyle, his ensuing violent attack on her, and Mitch and Kyle's fight, which ends with Mitch's exclamation, "Get out before I kill you!" The narration through this latter scene calls the film "the most revealing study of human emotions ever attempted on the screen."[15]

Generic identification begins to take place in the posters and trailer through a combination of story and character capsules interspersed with dialogue excerpts. The studio selected those aspects of story and character that could best represent the shock value inherent in the film's romantic conflicts and psychosexual problems. The trailer is particularly significant in this regard, as it depicts virtually every scene in the film that could possibly be linked to adult content: sexual insatiability, promiscuity, adultery, pregnancy and questions of paternity, alcoholism, violence, and murderous intrigues. In addition, the narration carefully employs the tactical language of the adult film (that is, revealing/study, raw/realism, and frank/drama), mixing the terms of sensationalism with those of realism.

Story and character capsules were only one means of identifying *Written on the Wind,* however. Advertising often focused on performance as another generic marker. Perhaps because Malone and Stack's characters so strongly embodied the psychosexual problems of the film, their performances received the most attention from advertisements. But Dorothy Malone's performance in particular was key to the adult labeling of *Written on the Wind.* Marylee as resident nymphomaniac dramatically exemplified the film's daring presentation of sex. Trade press reviews singled out her performance on this basis. *Film Daily,* for example, commented that the "most remembered sequence judging by a preview audience's reaction is a short, but dynamic dance by Miss Malone which out-Presley's Elvis." Another spoke of her "lurid machinations" and "wanton characterization" exuding sex in such a "sizzling fashion" that Marilyn Monroe should "look to her laurels."[16] In both cases, Malone is placed squarely in relation to two major sexual icons of the 1950s.

Malone's dance, performed to a jazz rendition of "Temptation," finds a particularly important place in studio discourse as a linchpin of the film's adult identity and appeal. Besides its presence in the trailer and its evocation in trade reviews, this scene also formed the basis for one of the photo layouts, designed for lobby exhibition and for use in media exploitation in magazines. The "Dorothy Malone Dance Layout" featured her in various stages of undress during this moment. Called a "sizzling pictorial group" by the studio, it displayed a number of stills that show Malone changing out of her black underwear into a hot pink nightgown as she dances with reckless abandon. These stills were also used in magazines, in the television trailer, and for a sticker that one could put on a car, window, telephone pole, etc.

Other photo layouts similarly capitalized on scenes that could be associated with adult content. One titled "Men against Women" featured a still in which Kyle slaps Marylee, along with other similar moments of aggression from *Public Enemy* (1931), *The Bad and the Beautiful* (1952), *Pick Up on South Street* (1953), *River of No Return* (1954), and *Backlash* (1956). Here, the studio promoted *Written on the Wind* as part of a stalwart Hollywood tradition, the "battle between the sexes." However, this version of the battle strongly figured male violence against women. Such scenes acted as yet another indication of the mature status of *Written on the Wind*. That is, physical violence against women connoted a heightened and bold expression of heterosexual conflict that translated into the kind of shocking spectacle audiences expected of this type of film.

While the rhetoric of the adult film was undoubtedly essential to the selling of *Written on the Wind*, it was subtended by another major generic concern— that of the romance. In the 1950s, Universal had hired Albert E. Sindlinger, an entertainment market analyst and head of Sindlinger and Company, an audience research firm.[17] One of Sindlinger's most influential findings on attendance patterns concerned the female audience. In the fall of 1956, Sindlinger & Company discovered that for the first time in a year there was a predominantly female audience at first-run showings, though overall male attendance continued to be greater. Females comprised well over 50 percent of the audience for the period's top pictures, including melodramas made in 1956 such as *Giant*, *The Bad Seed*, and *Tea and Sympathy*. These researchers found the increase significant because they believed that the "decline in female patronage was a major factor in causing the attendance decline which started last fall."[18] Thus, their advice to Universal was to develop part of their ad campaign to attract women, a group that had become one of the most visible sectors of the 1950s "lost" audience.

Universal responded to this research by emphasizing *Written on the Wind's* "love angles," its affiliation with romance. As we shall later see, this generic affiliation was not the only means the studio employed to attract a female audi-

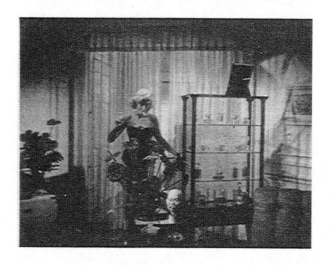

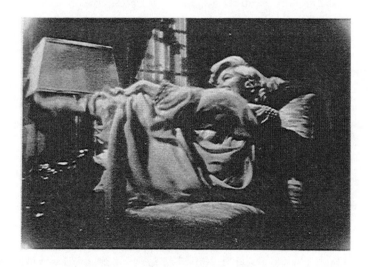

Photo layout for Dorothy Malone's "Temptation" dance sequence.

ence. But here the studio wished to exploit the proven relationship between women and romantic genres by additionally defining the film as a great romance. For example, of the eight radio advertisements written for the film, four were targeted for women's programming, while the others came under the heading of "general audiences." All eight spots were accompanied by the Four Aces's title song, which the studio felt had a direct romantic appeal. General programming spots described the film in terms familiar from other forms of advertising, such as "the drama of a decent love that fought to live against the vice and immorality of an oil baron's wastrel family—and of a shocking secret that thrust their private lives into public view!" The change in copy for women's programming included the lines from the opening of the trailer, "What a man tells a woman, what a woman tells a man, should be Written on the Wind," and a description of the story as that of "an overwhelming love . . . a love threatened by a shocking secret." These spots played during soap opera programming, when the studio was assured of reaching a female audience.

Universal's promotion of the film as both adult and a romance did not, however, actually produce mutually exclusive categories. Descriptions of the film in advertisements that brought out its mature situations made it clear how tied those situations were to romantic conflicts between the four main characters—Mitch, Lucy, Kyle, and Marylee. The adult labeling of *Written on the Wind* was inextricably tied to romantic connotations traditionally associated with melodrama. Through nuances in copy designed for women, Universal associated the film more explicitly with the theme of embattled love, a formula of the Hollywood melodrama. Such an association was probably enhanced by airing the film's ads during radio soaps whose content also showcased romantic conflicts. While pushing the "overwhelming" nature of romance in the film, though, ad copy alluded to the sensationalistic milieu in which relationships would be challenged and realized. Thus, no matter the generic emphasis, the language of love could be detected in the discourse of shock.

The studio created a sense of difference between the two categories more as a matter of strategic rhetoric. To ensure appeal to women who might not be attracted by lurid copy, the studio designed forms of advertisement like the radio ads that specifically associated *Written on the Wind* with romance. Universal used romance to appeal to female audiences not only because women allegedly had a penchant for this subject matter, but as a means of defending against the possibility that some sectors would be alienated by ad proclamations of adult content. In this way, *Written on the Wind* gained a fluid, dual, generic identity with market considerations firmly in mind.

While the melodrama/romance connection was deeply rooted in Hollywood filmmaking and advertising, we have seen how specific industrial deter-minants in the 1950s helped produce a special inflection of melodrama as adult. I would like now to pursue this inflection beyond the institutional horizons of the industry to consider the social context in which adult generic attribution was taking place. That is, the coining of the adult film was not purely a matter of internal industrial determinants. It was both a symptom of and an attempt to capitalize on the rising tide of overt discourses on sexual and other sensational topics during this decade.

The Sexual Display

Film academics studying what Thomas Elsaesser has called the "sophisti-cated family melodramas" of the 1940s and 1950s have typically portrayed the Eisenhower years as socially and sexually repressive. This social order is clearly manifested in television situation comedies such as "Leave It to Beaver," in which family cohesiveness is celebrated, and rigid sex roles portray men as benevolent patriarchs and women as dutiful housewives. From such a monologic perspec-tive, the excesses of *Written on the Wind* seem clearly subversive.

However, as Richard Dyer has argued in his work on Marilyn Monroe, we would do well to reconsider the 1950s beyond its repressive label.[19] This depic-tion of the decade ignores the high visibility and complexity of discourses on sexuality that characterize this era. Along with its sedate images of the nuclear family, the 1950s saw an explosion of discussions and representations of explicit sexuality that made sex an aggressively integral part of public life. By rethinking the 1950s with this cultural development in mind, we can come more fully to terms with the relation between the family melodrama, frequently preoccupied with sexual turmoil, and its original social context.

An examination of the post–World War II era shows that countercultural expressions of sexuality were gaining great currency. Organized gay subcultures, beat generation philosophy, and the routines of the so-called "sick" comedians attacked, respectively, heterosexist presumptions, marriage and monogamy, and propriety regarding what should be publicly said about intimate relations be-tween the sexes.

Gay subcultures became particularly visible in the postwar era, inspired by same-sex experiences abroad and on the home front during the war, as well as by the Kinsey reports in 1948 and 1953 which found that male and (to a lesser extent female) homosexuality was not uncommon.[20] These subcultures began producing magazines such as *Mattachine Review* and *ONE*[21] about gay con-cerns. At the same time, a range of representations focused with candor on the homosexual experience, including Kenneth Anger's *Fireworks* (1947), lesbian pulp fiction by Ann Bannon and others, and particularly Allen Ginsberg's ode to homosexuality, *Howl*, published in 1956 and one of the most influential volumes of poetry published during the decade.[22]

The beatniks' particular form of anticonventionalism espoused the notion of "free love" as opposed to maritally sanctioned intercourse, while "sick" comedians like Lenny Bruce and Mort Sahl not only assaulted the canons of respectable language but openly joked about problems in sexual relationships.[23]

Such marginal expressions of homosexuality, free love, and open, sometimes graphic depictions of sexual encounters and problems begin to demonstrate how punctuated this era was with sexual discourse—not only in the countercultures themselves, but in the massive mainstream cultural response that attempted to understand, condemn, censor, or reform these groups. However, sexually explicit discourse was not simply the product of countercultures; to the contrary, it was in the society at large that sexual representation made its most pronounced and pervasive appearances.

In *Intimate Matters,* John D'Emilio and Estelle Freedman describe the 1950s as part of the rise of "sexual liberalism" in this country that began after World War I, resulting in more permissive attitudes toward sex among white, middle-class Americans. In the 1950s, these attitudes were evident in studies of private expectations, public forums discussing sexual morality, and depictions of sex in the media. For instance, whereas premarital sex was still taboo during the 1950s, other forms of intimacy—dating, going steady, and heavy petting—were more or less socially acceptable means of premarital sexual expression. Middle-class couples headed toward marriage, conversant with Freud and aware of the availability of contraception, placed a great deal of emphasis on sex as a marker of well-being at the same time as they separated its pleasurable from its procreative dimensions.[24] According to Elaine Tyler May, the encouragement of "healthy" heterosexual relations and early marriage by journalists as well as education and psychology experts served as a primary defense against the Cold War demon of homosexuality, interpreted as an insignia of communist activity.[25]

In any case, the term "sexual liberalism" did not connote complete freedom or open-mindedness in this arena of human affairs. Its liberal dimensions, that is, a greater and more open emphasis on heterosexual pleasures of certain kinds, were constrained by a series of boundaries, including the oft-mentioned double standard and the demarcation of other sexualities, particularly homosexuality and African American sexuality, as deviant. However, sexual liberalism did provide a supportive atmosphere for the profusion of sexually frank materials in the media.

As mentioned previously, Supreme Court decisions allowing greater explicitness in sexual representation for public consumption aided the production and exhibition of "adult" films in Hollywood. These same decisions also helped stem the tide of censorship in relation to most of the media; as a result, as D'Emilio and Freedman put it, "sex unconstrained by marriage was put on display."[26] Among other media phenomena contributing to the heightened sexual explicitness in the 1950s were the Kinsey reports, Playboy, the publication of "adult" novels and suggestive paperbacks, and exposé magazines like Confidential.

Both Kinsey reports, Sexual Behavior in the Human Male (1948) and Sexual Behavior in the Human Female (1953), spent several months on the New York Times Best Seller List, each selling almost a quarter of a million copies. Kinsey's unmasking of the actual sexual practices of white Americans caused a public furor, since his findings demonstrated how inadequately traditional moral norms described how people actually lived their sexuality. These reports helped foreground sex and sexual behavior as very much a part of the public cultural landscape.

Many of the other representations within the "sexual display" had the visual objectification of women as their express subject. The 1940s saw this conjunction in such icons as the pinup, featuring scantily clad female movie stars.[27] Playboy, which began publication in 1953, continued to promote the implicit affiliation between sexual explicitness, sexual liberation, and suggestive representations of the female body. Playboy was devoted to an anti-family philosophy of male freedom built on the foundation of a connoisseurship of extramarital pleasures, central among them the image of the sexually available, always "ready" woman.[28] Playboy's first issue sported the now-famous nude calendar photo of Marilyn Monroe, and a later issue that of Jayne Mansfield, two of the most prominent "blonde bombshells" in film. By the mid-1950s, Playboy's success spawned a number of imitators interested in capitalizing on the "girlie" aspects of its format; these included Rogue, Nugget, and Dude.

The paperback book industry, which was booming by the 1950s, also sported sensationalistic covers featuring women in a state of undress or other compromising positions, with titles such as Three Gorgeous Hussies, Women's Barracks, I, Libertine, and Junkie. In addition, these and other successful paperbacks at the time, including From Here to Eternity, The Man with the Golden Arm, Mickey Spillane novels, Lady Chatterley's Lover, From Russia with Love, and Peyton Place, drew obscenity charges from the House of Representatives's Gathings probe into paperback publication for portrayal of explicit sexual encounters.[29]

While forums such as Playboy and paperbacks seem to posit a direct relation between sexual display, the sexual objectification of women, and a predominantly *male* spectator, there were types of explicitness that were strongly aimed at female readers. Paramount among these were exposé magazines such as *Confidential*, appearing in 1952. *Confidential* enjoyed tremendous popularity by indulging in what its publisher called "sin and sex." This magazine, like the spin-offs it inspired in the 1950s, including *Dare, Exposed,* and *Uncensored,* depicted social ills and the private lives of celebrities through lurid innuendo to create maximal sensationalized effects. Incriminating headlines such as "Why Robert Wagner Is a Flat Tire in the Boudoir," were common. Exposé magazines borrowed from the already proven successful story formula of the confession magazine (such as *True Confessions*) that grew in popularity after World War I, a time which also saw a revolution in morals and manners creating a more permissive attitude toward sex. The point of the confession story ("I had to prove my love/the night before the wedding") was to give the reader "a glimpse into someone else's most intimate affairs," with sex as a perennial subtext.[30] Publishers found that women, initially the undereducated working class but increasingly the middle class as this formula found its way into fan magazines and even some general circulation magazines like *Look* and *Life,* particularly enjoyed this combination of "authentic revelation" tinged with highly emotional problem oriented scenarios, often sexual in nature.

The growing frankness of sexual discourse during the 1950s, including the demarginalization of pornography, should not cause us to view the decade as a heretofore unrecognized Sodom and Gomorrah. Despite changing rules of censorship, such media events renewed the fervor of reformists and groups bent on challenging the morality of the sexual display. Similarly, while homosexual subcultures and their representations grew, so did their persecution at the hands of Cold War ideologues; while images of Monroe and Mansfield pervaded the media, so did discussions of the sanctity of the family and traditional sex roles; while *Confidential* flourished, so did *Better Homes and Gardens.* In other words, an emphasis on the sexual display does not redefine the 1950s in some new monologic way; instead, it alleviates a simplistic depiction of the decade by revealing how central discursive adventures into explicit sexual territories were. Subsequently, this era appears as one driven by contradictory and sometimes combative representations of sex, manifested in a wide range of popular forms from Monroe and *Playboy* to "Father Knows Best" and Walt Disney films.

However, to return to *Written on the Wind,* it is clear that Universal prepared part of its advertising campaign to dovetail with the decade's interest in sexual display and the sensational. What the example of *Written on the Wind* suggests is that both industrial and cultural factors influenced the production and exhibition of films with adult content. Exhibition strategies, far from representing some hyperbolic and mendacious Barnum-esque ploy, assumed the task of presenting melodrama in accord with social developments around more permissive representations of sexuality and other potentially volatile topics. Film advertisements, then, attempted to align films with the prevailing winds of discourse, here through generic attribution.

In addition, the manner in which the postwar culture of heterosexual display targeted both genders helps clarify the intent behind Universal's ad copy for the film. As we have seen, certain media forms courted men through the explicit representation of the female body placed in the exhilarating space of pre- or extramarital pleasure. Others, particularly scandal magazines, attempted to appeal to women through the rhetoric of the exposé, which depicted "private" problems through the lens of sensationalism. On the one hand, then, the centrality of Marylee/Malone to Universal's advertising acted as a bid for the male audience. With her newly peroxided hair and performance as a nymphomaniac, Malone can be seen as one of the many Monroe surrogates during the 1950s and very much a part of the decade's correlation of explicit sexuality with female sexuality. On the other hand, the dual pitch (realism and sensationalism) that characterized the majority of the advertising linked with media industry notions of women patrons attracted by inflamed confessional narratives ("Marylee: Even a woman will find it hard to understand why she did the things she did"). This underscores the point that the studio's "pure" romance angle was not their only means of attracting women; they also inflected romantic conflict with sensational overtones as a means of pursuit.[31]

The importance of this social background for *Written on the Wind* is that it strongly suggests that the labeling of this and other films as "sophisticated family melodramas," implicitly understood as transgressive ideologically, should not be taken as the last word in generic classification or ideological assessment. For such a background represents what Tony Bennett and Janet Woollacott have called a "culturally specific" instance of generic construction, that is, a process of definition arising from a particular institutional and social location.[32] This proposition counters the tendency of most genre theory and criticism to permanently define a given text's generic identity by describing its adherence to certain conventions. Bennett and Woollacott's perspective allows us to examine how texts are drawn into different generic relations depending on specific social and historical situations—how, that is, a text can be associated with various genres over time, which may draw it into "different social and ideological relations of reading."[33]

Thus, we must retreat from the standard pursuit of the definitive "master" characterizations to investigate how media forms assume diverse generic identities that may change their ideological meaning.

What I am arguing here is that during the 1950s such a "culturally specific" construction of generic identity for *Written on the Wind* and other melodramas occurred. It occurred through affiliation with a transitory "local genre"—the adult film—forged by a mixture of institutional and social factors. This generic frame selectively activated filmic elements, such as psychosexual and romantic conflicts, tormented characters, and erotic performances, to foster an ideological identity for the film which was commensurate with the era's strong emphasis on sexual display. This climate, underwritten by a renewed heterosexual fervor in the anticommunist, post–World War II years, created a voyeuristic audience ethos focused on the objectification of women and a lurid sensationalizing of social problems and human relationships.

As a result, studios produced scores of melodramas featuring psychological and sexual excess, from film adaptations of "racy" novels and plays to films by "sophisticated" directors—Sirk, Minnelli, and Ray. With themes of psychological dysfunction, sexual identity crises, illicit sexual relations, frigidity, illegitimate birth, family strife, violence, and drug abuse, it is not difficult to see how Minnelli's *The Cobweb* (1955), *Tea and Sympathy* (1956), *Some Came Running* (1959), and *Home from the Hill* (1960), as well as Ray's *Rebel without a Cause* (1955), and *Bigger than Life* (1956) would join Sirk's films in their adult appeal.

As the strong presence of reformers indicates, increasingly explicit representations of sex were not without subversive implications. If the "sophisticated family melodrama" attained a transgressive status during this time, it was not because its representations of sexuality proved an exception to the repressive rule of the Eisenhower years; it was because such representations were so much a part of a dominant, and for some objectionable, trend in filmmaking. However, the issue of ideological status is not so easily resolved. At the same time that these films may have represented a liberation from the forces of censorship, the climate of sexual display tended to associate sex with traditional patriarchal pleasures and a domestic ideology that saw women as avid consumers of conflicted romantic narratives in the style of *True Confessions*. The film studios, *Playboy*, *Confidential*, and other mainstream media forums thus articulated sex for consumption within value systems that ultimately affirmed cultural continuity.

While there are obvious differences between the industry's atomizing of the film into story, character, and performance extracts and the academy's exegetical analysis, both institutions foregrounded filmic features that would support appropriate generic identities and ideological values. Both have focused on psychosexual problems, but have constructed the ideological value of these problems in very different ways. The industry, influenced by developments around sexual spectacle in the 1950s, associated these problems with various voyeuristic plea- sures. The academy interpreted nymphomania, sterility, etc. in *Written on the Wind* as symptomatic Oedipal protests against the oppressiveness of the family structure in the 1950s, its reading conditioned by the development of ideological theory after May 1968. For the former, Marylee emerges as a specific figure of sexual display. For the latter, she represents a critique of familial repression under patriarchy. From a historical perspective, each institution represents a "culturally specific" instance of generic construction which acts to illuminate filmic mo- ments for given audiences according to the demands of context.

Amidst this discussion of generic classification, I have focused mainly on how industry and social factors activated meaning through story and character references, leaving out one of the most significant features of these melodramas: style. Film theory has strongly based arguments about the family melodrama's transgressive status on mise-en-scène. As I discussed in the previous chapter, critics consider Sirk's visuals as the major source of expression for the distanciat- ing and symptomatic critique of the Eisenhower era's complacent social order. By exploring the studio's effort to use exhibition strategies as a means of affiliat- ing aspects of *Written on the Wind*'s vivid mise-en-scène with social values of the 1950s, a different ideological universe of meaning for the family melodrama emerges.

Shifting attention away from the market possibilities of sex and romance, Universal sold the style of the film as an arena in which domestic fantasies con- cerning class and feminine identity could be realized—thus attempting to appeal to another dimension of 1950s ideology: the upwardly mobile desires of the middle-class family, particularly women. Without missing a beat, Universal shifted ad strategies away from a predominant concern with the erotica of un- censored permissiveness to the acquisitive desires of the nuclear family.

Mise-en-Scène: Consuming Visuals

While generic designations for *Written on the Wind* sprang from a number of industrial developments specific to the post–World War II era, decisions on how to sell the style of the film were less affected by the upheavals of this pe- riod, maintaining instead an unruffled continuum with longstanding, industry- wide traditions of exhibition. As the work of Jeanne Allen, Diane Waldman, and Jane Gaines has demonstrated, from 1900 through the 1940s the industry pre- sented aspects of mise-en-scène, such as sets and costumes, as spectacles for consumption. This it did literally by selling film fashions in stores, and figuratively by presenting glamorous visuals to appeal to the acquisitive fantasies of its spectators, particularly women who were considered the primary purchasers of commodities.[34] This decision to sell style as a commodity was influenced at different historical moments by the presence of a strong consumer culture.[35] By promoting film visuals as "goods," the industry hoped to make profitable financial and psychological alliances with a social ethos focused on buying. As we shall see, Universal acted totally in accord with tradition when it considered style a resource that could be used to appeal to two distinct kinds of acquisitive impulses: the desire for upward class mobility and female dreams of self-improvement.

In the context of the 1950s, Sirk's films were part of one of Universal's attempts to produce "prestige" pictures, a contrast to their usual schedule of low-budget horror films and series.[36] The concern with better production values naturally gave his films a certain lush visual patina, touted by trade reviewers as "lavish," and "14 karat."[37] This circumstance of production underwrote Universal's promotion of *Written on the Wind*'s style as extravagant. But the studio's strategies were also conditioned by traditional industry attempts to depict film visuals as sites for consumer desires, and by the specific social context provided by the affluent ideology of the post–World War II era. Although about the destruction of a rich family, the film showcased aspects of its upper-class lifestyle that Universal could exploit to appeal to the anticipated desires of its audiences.

Universal defined the style of *Written on the Wind* through press books and press releases.[38] Studios typically used press books to sell the film to the exhibitor, as well as to provide copy for use in local or "point-of-sale" advertising in newspapers and magazines. Among other things, press books contained what we can call background stories on a film's mise-en-scène, which elaborated production decisions involved in creating its most notable aspects (that is, those aspects regarded as having the greatest potential for appeal to a consumer consciousness). Advertising focused on style digressed from the film itself, making a series of associative connections between film and external concerns. Through background stories, the studio associated visuals with authentic or everyday places, as well as with conceptions of "better worlds" defined by spectacle. As in the case of genre, we have the terms realism and spectacle as integral parts of advertising rhetoric.

Press copy offered the "21" Club as a set-piece in the authentic category. The "21" Club served as a setting for a sequence occurring early in the film, when Mitch (Rock Hudson) brings Lucy (Lauren Bacall) to meet Kyle (Robert Stack) for the first time to conduct some business. Art director Robert Clatworthy assembled this set-piece using materials from the real club, including menus, napkins, and glasses, flown from New York to Los Angeles. Here as elsewhere in studio promotion (including trade press reviews), matters of style were not subsumed under the director's name; rather, they were presented as accomplishments of numerous personnel.[39]

Other realistic descriptions of style operated through a more marked correlation of decor with everyday space. For example, Universal circulated an article titled "Hollywood Set-Decorator Gives Tips on Home Beautifying," by Julia Heron, the set co-designer. This type of article graced the pages of women's magazines in the 1950s, promoting a connection between film decor/star fashion and the average home decor/female self-image. The copy ran:

> No .matter how much you spend on your home, if it is not decorated correctly to match your personality, size, shape and coloring, then you can look like nothing in a $100,000 mansion. . . . Just as you could look out of place in your own home if the interiors are all wrong, so can stars. . . . Because Dorothy Malone is a statuesque blonde with blue-green eyes, I backgrounded her with pastel tones. I avoided angular shapes in furnishings, because Miss Malone is tall, and also chose drapes and furniture that would set off the beauty of the actress, but at the same time pinpoint the dramatic moments of the story. . . . This particular home also had to look ostentatious because of the wealth of the family, and here I had to deliberately use some bad taste.

This article continues to advise the average woman about the coordination of her figure type and coloring with interior decoration, thus making the decor of the film into a visual classroom offering home and personal appearance lessons.

In addition to Heron's piece, publicity included fashion layouts for each one of the female stars to further emphasize the film's visual elements as sites of emulation for the female spectator. Both layouts feature "working women" outfits; Malone's consists exclusively of the blue business suit she wears at the end of the film. This suit, though hardly representative of her general attire during the film, is clearly intended as a slightly different type of appeal to women through professional imagery. Besides being used to attract the homemaker, Universal also employed female stars and fashions as a means of enticing the interest of women in the work force in the 1950s. Ad executives saw a chance to appeal to this population by foregrounding its female stars in their roles as working women in the film. As another part of this plan, Universal held advance screenings in local sites focused on select women's groups. These groups included secretaries, beauty-salon operators, women's clubs, professional women's organizations, and dress-shop personnel among others—working or "active" women, some of them involved in the appearance industries themselves.

Those advertising strategies concentrating directly on spectacle raised mise-en-scène to the level of an extravagant visual "feast," a series of images crafted from Hollywood's keen sense of showmanship which would gratify the senses of the audience. Two such set-pieces were the Hadley Building and the "stairway of the stars." The studio touts the Hadley Building, office of the Hadley oil empire, as "the largest ever built for a motion picture office building . . . so massive and out of place, it will probably be as long remembered by audiences as the performances of Hudson, Stack, Miss Bacall, and Miss Malone. Such giant sets have long played an important role in big film hits." This monument is then placed in a lineage of large "star" set-pieces, such as the pyramid in *The Egyptian* (1954), the airliner in *The High and the Mighty* (1954), and the whale in *Moby Dick* (1956).

The studio treats the "stairway of the stars," deployed centrally within the Hadley mansion and seen frequently in the film, as a monumental spectacle with a Hollywood history of precedents. Press copy refers to this forty-eight-step winding staircase as the "most often used stairway in film colony history," having a thirty-year history beginning with *Phantom of the Opera* (1925). This combination of spectacle and internal history, however, ultimately emphasizes the theme of "women and staircases." The publicity claims that "it takes a circular staircase to bring out a girl's sex appeal. . . . That stairs and sex appeal go together, that curves seem curvier as the owner ascends with well-modulated swing and sway has been proven many times over." This association of staircase and sex appeal is credited to Flo Ziegfeld, who discovered "the entertainment value in a set of circular stairs . . . for the sole purpose of exhibiting breathtaking showgirls to their best advantage." Dorothy Malone is singled out as a "staircase actress" par excellence: "She and the stairs, if not Hudson, were made for each other." This piece cites other actress/stairs combinations, among them Scarlet O'Hara in *Gone with the Wind,* Shirley Temple in her number with Bojangles, and even Lady Macbeth in her "out damned spot" soliloquy, as they prove that staircases provide an opportunity for an actress to combine "good acting ability with magnetic attraction."

These appeals to varieties of realism and spectacle fall into categories of film advertising almost as old as the invention of movies itself. Publicity on films stressing authentic recreations and monumental set-pieces were in evidence in the earliest days of narrative filmmaking.[40] And certainly, production companies still fashion public perceptions of a film's visuals by promoting discussion of mise-en-scène as authentic (for example, with the recreation of *The Washington Post* newsroom in *All the President's Men* [1976]) or spectacular (for example, with set design in *Alien* [1979] or *Dick Tracy* [1990]). But while such a distinction between the advertising rhetoric used for the "21" Club and for the "stairway of the stars" clearly exists, the discourse on realism is in this case strongly permeated by considerations of spectacle.

The "21" Club's reproduction does set up an obvious relation to a realistic referent. Art personnel definitely wished to lend the mise-en-scène an air of credibility. However, such publicity also promises audiences vicarious access to a sophisticated urban location. Universal attempted to offer audiences the thrill of temporary class displacement by bringing them into relation with an elite locale.

Heron's account of decor, as it attempts to construct a direct and intimate relation between what one sees and one's private universe, deals more complexly with the interplay between the real and the spectacular. It "domesticates" the mansion's decor and the female star's aura by associating them with the realm of the housewife. In the process, Heron projects an image of woman that is inseparable from an aesthetics of interior decoration and vice versa. "Home beautifying" is implicitly understood as the beautification of self. However, though press copy parallels the mansion and character with the family home as the everyday habitat and site of self-expression of the housewife, it is the glamorous appeal of a mansion and star that makes these aspects of mise-en-scène an attractive site for emulation. Hence, once again, the radiant spectacle of wealth provides an essential basis of publicity for *Written on the Wind,* even in sales pitches seemingly otherwise oriented. This does not eradicate the domestic project of Heron's description, but acts as part of its foundation.

The signification of privilege (the "21" Club, a mansion, a star) existing throughout the references to the authentic and everyday suggests, then, that the visual is never free from articulation as spectacle of a certain class-based type. This sense of the visual was echoed in one review, titled "WOW Is Lavish." This review called the film a "plushy little item," describing it as a story about "human failure in the midst of great wealth with the result that the audience is dazzled purposely with everything that money can buy. . . . There's plenty to look at in this show."[41] Style thus attains a class dimension as a display of capital, invoking the acquisitive predispositions of the audience.

Those set-pieces touted as spectacle further amplify aspects of the mise-en-scène as literally sights worth seeing. The Hadley Building and the "stairway of the stars" are evoked as they evidence riches and glamor, including that of Hollywood itself. But, most significantly, the discussion of spectacle poses a strong alliance between the "look" of the film and the female body. Once again, Dorothy Malone's character provides a key image in this regard. Malone's character is associated with the staircase and the immediate forum for looking it provides, mixing class with sexual spectacle.

The class and sexual dimensions of mise-en-scène were most likely enhanced by another dominant visual feature of the film: Technicolor. *Variety* reported that in 1955–56, less than 50 percent of all films produced were shot in color.[42] Color, still not universally used, maintained some of the novel and specialized status it had had since the 1930s. As Steve Neale notes, color was "overwhelmingly associated, aesthetically, with spectacle and fantasy," and hence with suitable genres such as the musical, the adventure film, animated features, and westerns into the 1950s.[43] The effects of color in each of these genres was to escalate mise-en-scène into primary content and into the register of dazzling spectacle. With its high-key effects, sparkling lighting, and crisp definition, Technicolor connoted the spectacular possibilities of the visual and concomitantly, its pleasurable consumption.

Given the somewhat still novel identity of Technicolor in the 1950s, we can speculate that its use assisted the studio's elaboration of *Written on the Wind*'s mise-en-scène as lavish, enhancing the correlation of decor with the exoticism of upper-class spectacle. Less speculative is the relation of color to female imagery. That the use of color has been strongly associated with the appeal of the represented female body has been thoroughly documented.[44] The industry perceived the visual pleasure inherent in Technicolor as being inextricably tied to the female image and its ability to sell films. Color, then, advanced the visual objectification of women, here through mise-en-scène and cinematography which served to augment other industry strategies in this direction.

Each of these studio strategies—association of the film with a display of capital, and a double use of the female body as sexual object and as model for the everyday woman—is also evident in one of Universal's major media tie-ins. Universal joined with the Colgate Palmolive Company to develop a promotional campaign for *Written on the Wind* on "Strike It Rich," a CBS quiz show sponsored by Colgate. The campaign began on October 1 and ran for five weeks.[45]

"Strike It Rich" was itself an interesting phenomenon in broadcast history. It debuted as a radio show in 1947, and began airing on CBS-TV in May 1951 during the day with Warren Hull as the emcee. By June of 1951, the show was also running on Wednesday evenings. At the time of the tie-in with Universal, the show was being aired six times a week on radio and television, an obvious mark of its popularity.[46] The contestants on "Strike It Rich" referred to by CBS publicity as the "quiz show with a heart," were real people (or in some cases actors or stand-ins) who had serious problems and needs; they were completely destitute or physically handicapped, for example. These contestants would appear on the show and tell their stories. The person with the most impressive hard-luck story would win an amount up to $500, depending on audience response. The show's quiz format was based strongly on audience participation.[47]

Written on the Wind was merchandised through spot-promos during the show and through a contest titled "Miss Strike It Lovely," itself promoted on television and through Colgate Palmolive dealers. The winner of this beauty contest would receive a complete wardrobe and a trip to Las Vegas, and would act as a public relations envoy for the film, traveling coast-to-coast for a month. Five final contestants made appearances on "Strike It Rich," the winner a UCLA co-ed named Phyllis McKeen.

The concept for this tie-in replicates other publicity strategies we have seen in several ways. The quiz show appeals to the audience through one of the basic dreams of capitalism: good fortune and sudden wealth for the common folk. Supervising this premise is the notion that capitalism is basically a benevolent system that looks after the downtrodden. The choice of this show for *Written on the Wind*'s media exploitation underscores the studio's attempt to affiliate the film with fantasies of class displacement. Through the tie-in, we have an interplay between the sudden wealth and good fortune formula of the show, and the depiction of riches within the film itself. At the same time, the contest, like every beauty contest, offers the female body as spectacle and model, that is, as an opportunity for objectification on the part of male audiences, and emulation on the part of female audiences—the strategized "double whammy" of publicized female representations. Thus, the tie-in with "Strike It Rich" replays and emphasizes components of promotion that orient the film ideologically in terms of class and gender.

As we can see, Universal's promotion of mise-en-scène for *Written on the Wind* relied heavily on traditional industry strategies for selling the visual dimensions of a film. The promotion of the "21" Club, the "stairway of the stars," and the Hadley Building and mansion presented the film as upper-class spectacle, full of elegant locations to attract the material vision of film patrons. "Strike It Rich" helped associate the film with dreams of capital through a quiz show format that promised the downtrodden a chance for a windfall. At the same time, the female star and the beauty contest acted as vehicles for male pleasure as well as female self-assessment. Mise-en-scène was thus invoked as a landscape full of visions of class mobility, sex appeal, and feminine identity. As in the case of genre, this aspect of Universal's pre-selling attempted to represent satisfaction for both male and female spectators, the former with presumed interest in the female body, the latter with domestic scenarios and self-image, and both potentially fascinated by the lifestyles of the rich and famous.

The Ideology of Affluence

Although decades old, the industry's strategies for selling style were grounded in specific 1950s social ideologies. Like the earlier postwar period, the 1950s saw an immense consumer boom. The period after World War II saw the first dramatic increase in domestic affluence since the Great Depression. This period of abundance was enabled by many factors. There were substantial consumer savings accrued during the period of wartime rationing when goods of all kinds were scarce; after the war, a public craving for goods coupled with these savings and an increase in income among the middle and working classes created a sensibility geared toward spending. Suburbanization greatly enhanced the demand for durable goods such as cars and home appliances. And, perhaps most important, while government and military spending helped stimulate domestic prosperity, those in power also foresaw that inflated consumer spending was necessary to maintain domestic prosperity. Government and big business encouraged the public to buy more than they might need to help secure the future of burgeoning production.

Particularly helpful in this process was the tremendous growth of installment credit and advertising in exhorting people to buy. The growing availability of credit cards caused consumer indebtedness during the 1950s to grow from $73 billion to $196 billion, while by the end of the decade advertisers were spending $12 billion on their campaigns.[48] As Paul Baran and Paul Sweezy have noted, advertising during this time had a greater effect on the economy than the military.[49] That is, advertising played a key role in developing the consumerism deemed so important to a healthy economy. Part of its pervasiveness was due to television, which through its corporation sponsored shows and commercials made advertisement an intimate household experience. In addition, advertisers saw themselves as having a role in changing the traditional consumer aesthetic, based on thrift and necessity, to one based on hedonistic pleasures in buying. To this end, they often employed sociologists and psychologists to conceive selling tactics that would thus stimulate consumption.

Domestic affluence, then, occurred through such developments as a deprived postwar mentality about spending, suburbanization, and the initiatives of government and big business, including the role of advertising. In the 1950s, the years 1955–57 represented the peak of this affluence.[50] In addition, the availability of goods functioned as an important signifier of the superiority of democracy to communism.[51] Upward mobility gained a patriotic edge, appearing as a social desire strongly aligned with the virtues of the American way. Economic imperatives and social developments were thus joined to this ideological mission, bolstering the desirability of consumption even further.

What importance did the ideology of domestic prosperity have in creating socially prevalent ideas of class and feminine identity? The call to consumerism helped foster the idea of a uniform classlessness—the hallucination of a middle-class lifestyle shared by all. This image thrived in the face of a still ethnically diverse population, as well as an active, striking working class feared capable of communist inspired insurgence. Just as it had at the turn of the century, the spectacle of consumption communicated through the media encouraged the working class to aspire to middle-class values (by becoming good consumers) in the hopes of stilling any class unrest.

George Lipsitz has discussed television's role in creating the homogenizing effects of this consumerist ethos, calling the new medium "an instrument of legitimation for transformations in values initiated by the new economic imperatives of postwar America."[52] Lipsitz examines how developments in television programming participated in the "death" of 1940s class consciousness against the already inhospitable climate of suburbanization, rampantly growing consumption, and McCarthyism. Working-class, immigrant centered television situation comedies, such as "The Goldbergs," "I Remember Mama," and "The Life of Riley," were gradually phased out at the end of the decade in favor of white, middle-class family sitcoms, such as "Father Knows Best" and "Leave It to Beaver." But even before this displacement, their plot lines often staged a conflict between traditional ethnic family values and new values associated with suburban lifestyles and consumerism, emphasizing the legitimacy of the latter to ultimately ease the social transition to a mentality based on material satisfaction.[53] Thus, television served as a particularly cogent example of a social force that helped create the consumer consciousness business that advertisers required for an expanding domestic economy, at the same time as it promoted the desirability of ethnic and class conformity.

As the major consumers in society, women historically had been the key to economic expansion on the domestic front. Historians of the turn of the century and the 1920s, two prior instances of such expansion, have found that marketplace strategies aimed at women often fostered a strong connection between the act of consumption and (once again) female self-identity.[54] That is, strategies promoted a psychology of identity for women in which the acquisition of things was intimately tied to self-realization.

In the 1950s, several social and economic ideologies enhanced this connection. Among them were "togetherness" and what Betty Friedan has called the "sexual sell." Both of these ideologies promoted a sense of female well-being by emphasizing a link between the role of housewife and material satisfaction.[55] *McCall's* coined what would become a catch phrase of the time, "togetherness," in May 1954. The concept of togetherness emphasized new possibilities open to the housewife, who with her husband and children could achieve a lifestyle of comfort unknown to previous generations. Family "togetherness" meant a unified effort, spearheaded by the housewife, to gain security through the purchase of material goods. Such a concept made home life seem vital, while giving the housewife an important role in constructing the secure universe that would flourish through her expert, upwardly mobile purchasing sense.

While "togetherness" promoted the significance of the female role as house-wife and focused family life on consumption, the "sexual sell" used by advertis-ers in their pitches to women acted as a similar kind of identity-machine. As Betty Friedan has argued, the advertiser in the 1950s sold women an image of female liberation that was understood strictly as it pertained to buying new prod-ucts that would promote either a woman's efficiency and creativity in the home or her beauty and youthfulness.[56] The "sexual sell" of household appliances and cosmetics equated the purchase of things with a housewife's "identity, purpose, creativity, self-realization, even . . . sexual joy."[57] In both "togetherness" and the "sexual sell," the position of women as consumers was secured by tying their sense of self and the well-being of their families to marketplace offerings.

Although the 1950s ideal was of the housewife, the postwar era also saw a higher employment of wives than ever before. Within this all-encompassing ethic of consumption, however, work was seen as a means of saving the family from the embarrassment of not being able to purchase what it needed for the home.[58] Work for wives was thus justified as it allowed the family to attain a middle-class standard of living based on consumption.

Universal's advertising strategies for *Written on the Wind*, focused on the spectacle of wealth and female appearance, were motivated, then, not only by hoary traditions of the industry, but by capitalistic social ideologies. These ide-ologies attempted to create a sense of classless identity and female self, both housewife and working woman, that would assist the expansion of the domestic economy by instilling upwardly mobile acquisitiveness as key to the persistence of democracy and to the achievement of family and personal happiness.

The importance of this social context for Universal's promotion of style is twofold. First, it allows us once again, as in the case of genre, to consider how strongly interrelated film production, publicity mandates, and historical condi-tions are. *Written on the Wind* and other films with adult themes were produced within a climate of growing sexual permissiveness in representation of the time, with advertising serving the purpose of foregrounding those elements that would support such a framework of reference. Similarly, the production of films with lush visuals was strongly influenced by publicity considerations in the 1950s which sought to exploit the contemporary decor and fashions showcased in certain films as a means of advancing Hollywood's relation to consumer society. The rich mise-en-scène of family melodramas (as well as perhaps other popular genres of the time like the musical) did not result simply from directorial decision, but from socially influenced industry demands to render style *consumable*. The particular intensity of melodramatic mise-en-scène, understood later by film academics as the signature element of subversive cinematic counterpoint, appears here in a new light: as part of the pageantry of plenitude for a bourgeois society awash in the ideology of domestic affluence.

Secondly, this confluence of film, advertising, and consumer culture raises the possibility of a particular mode of viewing a film that is not necessarily based on a coherent reconstruction of the filmic system, but on attentiveness to its surfaces as they provide a spectacle of consumption. Calling this kind of viewing "the consumer glance," Mary Ann Doane writes that such a glance

> hovers over the surface of the image, isolating details which may be entirely peripheral in relation to the narrative. It is a fixating, obsessive gaze which wanders in and out of the narrative and has a more intimate relation with space—the space of rooms and bodies—than with the temporal dimension. It is as though there were another text laid over the first—a text with an altogether different mode of address. . . . In this other text, the desire to possess displaces comprehension as the dominant mechanism of reading.[59]

Although we are accustomed to thinking that a true reading of a film emerges from an organic analysis of narrative and style as intrinsic systems, Doane's remark raises the possibility of considering the role social factors play in creating other modes of textual apprehension. In the case of *Written on the Wind*, advertising, underwritten by social developments, solicited two kinds of apprehension. In conjunction with the sexual display and a booming consumer society, advertising attempted to cultivate, respectively, voyeuristic and acquisitive responses. Generic associations with the adult film depicted the downfall of the wealthy Hadley family as a forum for a continuous showcasing of psychological and sexual problems, in which the objectification of women and the sensationalism of the exposé figured prominently. Similarly, the association of mise-en-scène with upwardly mobile displays of class and female appearance portrayed style as a stage upon which acquisitive fantasies could be enacted. In this way, advertisements presented the film to appeal to a "roving" spectator, someone whose attention would be drawn by what the surfaces of the film had to offer of such spectacles. With its concentration on sensational topics and middle- to upper-class decor, the postwar family melodrama was not likely to disappoint an alinear, spectacle-driven sensibility.

Examples of social readings like those geared toward voyeurism and consumption are particularly important to consider in relation to assessments of the film/ideology relationship. They do not necessarily produce a unified text with a coherent ideology, but suggest that institutional and social forces can act to produce a heterogeneous text offering a variety of viewing pleasures—grounded in various kinds of social ideologies—to its audience.

From such a perspective, we cannot consider the family melodrama of the 1950s as necessarily subversive to the repressive regimes of the decade. Rather, as I hope to have demonstrated, such films often helped realize the heightened sexual depictions and affluent ideologies that marked the culture. By contextualizing the family melodrama in this way, we can begin to understand why audiences of the 1950s did not "get" the subversive critique of the family and of the era's repressive sexual politics: they may have been subject to a cultural order that rhapsodized on the pleasures of excess offered by representations within an increasingly sexual and consumerist climate. Although the industry's advertised identities for the film directly challenge the academic sense of what the film really means, they offer us a way of grasping some of the historical conditions at work in a significant moment of a film's reception.

The film industry represents, however, only part of a complex field of significations entering into the social meaning of the postwar melodrama. To approach other practices associated with meaning production, I turn in subsequent chapters to reviews, star discourse, and camp.

3

Tastemaking

Reviews, Popular Canons, and Soap Operas

The denial of lower, coarse, vulgar, venal, servile—in a word,
natural—enjoyment, which constitutes the sacred sphere of culture, implies
an affirmation of the superiority of those who can be satisfied with the
sublimated, refined, disinterested, gratuitous, distinguished pleasures forever
closed to the profane. That is why art and cultural consumption are
predisposed, consciously and deliberately or not, to fulfill a social function of
legitimating social differences.

Pierre Bourdieu[1]

UNTIL RECENTLY, film academics had disdained reviews as antithetical to the serious study of films. To many, mass media reviews seemed unconversant with the complexities of film language, devoted instead to accounts of plot and character aimed at the quick fix of evaluation. In the early 1970s, Marxist criticism labeled such popular commentary as "culinary," complicit with bourgeois standards insofar as it addressed films from the point of view of entertainment and consumption, failing utterly to reflect on questions of ideology. The critical program introduced by Comolli and Narboni's "Cinema/Ideology/Criticism" essay accordingly relegated the review to the status of "specious raving" that must be surmounted to achieve committed scientific and political analyses of films.[2]

Contemporary historians have begun to redeem reviews as important sources of information about reception. From this perspective, reviews are not just pieces of failed criticism, but types of social discourse which, like film advertisements, can aid the researcher in ascertaining the material conditions informing the relation between film and spectator at given moments.

While there is some evidence that reviews influence attendance decisions, we cannot blithely assume that they dictate public response.³ Their value for reception studies lies rather in their mobilization of terms that attempt to define how a film will be perceived in the culture at large. Robert Allen and Douglas Gomery have referred to this activity as the "agenda-setting" function of popular criticism. By establishing a critical vocabulary and appropriate frames of reference, reviews do not tell "audiences what to think so much as . . . what to think *about*."⁴ Popular critics thus offer a program of perception to the public, comprising a set of coordinates that map out and judge the significant features of a film. These coordinates, whether moviegoers agree or disagree, help to establish the terms of discussion and debate.

In addition to this mobilizing function, reviews also represent materials that signify the cultural hierarchies of aesthetic value reigning at particular times. As a primary public tastemaker, the critic operates to make, in Pierre Bourdieu's parlance, "distinctions." Among other things, the critic distinguishes legitimate from illegitimate art and proper from improper modes of aesthetic appropriation. As the epigraph suggests, it also often secures a class position far from the vulgar crowd in the process. As examples of such arbitrations of taste, film reviews do more than provide information about how a particular film was received. They also offer some insight into broader cultural attitudes toward art and the public during given historical periods.

With these perspectives in mind, I will analyze the relation of Sirk's melodramas to the significant moments of their popular critical reception: the films' original exhibition in the 1950s and the Sirk retrospectives two decades later. In reviews that were not influenced by the studios, Sirk's films generally fared badly in the press when they were first shown. However, a much different situation arose in the 1970s, when popular critics, after having assimilated auteurism, extolled these films as the work of a bona fide artist.

The differing aesthetic fates of Sirk's melodramas were intimately linked to the nature of the canons established by the presses of both times. These judgments, in turn, were strongly informed by more general intellectual attitudes toward mass culture respective to each period. I have, accordingly, a double aim in the analysis that follows: first, to ascertain the effects of popular canons on specific evaluations; and second, to explore the relation between popular film criticism of Hollywood melodramas and pervasive aesthetic attitudes toward mass culture.

Reviewing in the 1950s

By the 1950s, popular film criticism appeared in newspapers of every type, as well as a broad range of magazines.⁵ Liberal sources such as *The Nation, The*

New Republic, Commentary, and *Partisan Review;* the middlebrow literary periodical *The Saturday Review;* and *The New Yorker,* an upscale magazine for the sophisticated urbanite, consistently reviewed films. The Catholic press similarly featured a standard "screen" section in a lay publication, *Commonweal,* and two clerical sources, *America* and *Catholic World. Library Journal,* the official organ of the Library Association of America, reviewed films based on books. Besides these specialized presses, *Time* and *Newsweek,* mass-circulation magazines aimed at the middle classes, ran movie columns. And last, there were a number of periodicals devoted entirely to film, among them *Film Culture, Films in Review,* and the British *Monthly Film Bulletin* and *Films and Filming.*

In addition, several books of reprinted film reviews, media criticism, and history were published by renowned critics writing in the post–World War II era. These included James Agee's *Agee on Film;* Arthur Knight's *The Liveliest Art;* a number of books by Gilbert Seldes, including the reissued *The Seven Lively Arts, The Great Audience,* and *The Public Arts;* and Robert Warshow's *The Immediate Experience.*[6] Through newspapers, periodicals, magazines, and books, criticism of the cinema thus joined the cultural rituals devoted to tastemaking.

While the liberal sources ignored Sirk's melodramas, reviews of his films appeared in virtually every other type of publication. Some of these reviews, particularly those appearing in newspapers, lauded the adult nature and extravagant "look" of these melodramas along the lines encouraged by Universal's sales campaign, discussed in the preceding chapter. Given the redundancy of these positive reviews with industry discourse, I turn rather to a group of reviews operating according to more autonomous journalistic criteria. Appearing mainly in East Coast and otherwise urban periodicals and newspapers, these reviews offered negative evaluations of Sirk's melodramas, in part influenced by a dominant canon of the time that endorsed realism in dramas. This general critical context supervised value judgments for drama, including the adult melodrama, that genre to which Sirk's films belonged at this time.

The Realist Canon

Annually, *The New York Times* published its list of the ten best films of the year, along with the results of the New York Film Critics awards. In the post–World War II era, several types of pictures fared especially well with these critics. These included sophisticated comedies like *Love in the Afternoon* (1957), big budget, Technicolor musicals like *The King and I* (1956), and foreign films like *Rashomon* (1951) and *Mr. Hulot's Holiday* (1954), as well as a great number of domestic dramas. The ten-best list of the *The New York Times* from 1949 to 1959 named serious dramas such as *Pinky, The Heiress, Sunset Boulevard, All about Eve, A Streetcar Named Desire, Death of a Salesman, Stalag 17, From Here to Eternity, High Noon, On the Waterfront, Marty, The Bridge on the River Kwai, The Defiant Ones,* and *The Diary of Anne Frank.*

In terms of the New York Film Critics awards, drama had the clear edge over the other favored genres. Films and directors committed to exploring overtly serious themes carried away the honors. The critics designated Fred Zinneman as best director three times during this period, for *High Noon* in 1952, *From Here to Eternity* in 1953, and *The Nun's Story* in 1959. The former two films also won best picture awards. Elia Kazan and his films were similarly saluted. Kazan and *A Streetcar Named Desire* won in 1951; in 1954 both director and film were again honored with *On the Waterfront.* Other directors earning both awards were Delbert Mann with *Marty* in 1955, David Lean with *The Bridge on the River Kwai* in 1957, and Stanley Kramer with *The Defiant Ones* a year later.[7]

Adulation of many of these and other dramas was strongly influenced by new standards of filmmaking in the postwar era. Hollywood found a new "realism," which was indebted to a number of aesthetic influences, among them U.S. war documentaries, Italian neo-realism, and developments in the theater. In each case, war documentaries such as *The Battle of San Pietro* (1944), neo-realist films such as *Open City* (1946), and plays such as *Come Back, Little Sheba* (1950) or Tennessee Williams's *A Streetcar Named Desire* (1947) presented the plights of ordinary people through a desolate, often socially critical world view and sparse style.[8] In doing so, they appeared to eschew the glamour and optimism of more conventional dramas, attaining a different look that seemed to signify reality, particularly in comparison with what reviewers regarded as Hollywood's typical illusionistic fare. These forms thus helped establish an apparently unvarnished narrative and visual style as a new standard for dramatists with realist ambitions. From the semidocumentary espionage film, *The House on 92nd Street* (1945), to the more darkly flamboyant film noirs such as *They Live by Night* (1948), to the spate of social problem films, including *Crossfire* (1947) and *The Men* (1950), to such theatrical adaptations as *Death of a Salesman* (1951), U.S. dramas of different types strove to meet the criteria of postwar verisimilitude.

In 1952, Bosley Crowther, motion picture critic for *The New York Times,* chairman of the New York Film Critics, and one of the era's most influential reviewers, coined a term for the new realistic films which further identified their attributes. These "downbeat" films "substitute grim realism for romance and prove that all is well that ends bad." In the process, they not only monopolized Academy Award nominations, but had tremendous success with the public, who, against producers' expectations, had begun "swarming" to films that ended unhappily. Films that sidetracked romance and refused happy endings included *A Streetcar Named Desire*, in which the heroine is carted off to an insane asylum in the film's closing moments; *Decision before Dawn* (1951), whose ending signals doom for the spy hero; and *Death of a Salesman*, which ends with the father committing suicide. While, as Crowther admits, upbeat films were still as popular as ever, and Hollywood had had success with tragic films before, downbeat films created an identifiable movement that simultaneously attained critical and popular success. For Crowther, postwar filmmakers seemed more motivated to come to terms with the problems of the world, while audiences similarly had matured in their screen desires.[9]

Thus, the postwar era saw the emergence of a kind of realism whose aesthetic codes were based on a defiance of Hollywood conventions: dramas provided overt social themes instead of "escapist" illusionist fare; ordinary middle- or lower-class characters instead of glamorous sophisticates; a black and white style instead of luxuriant spectacle; violence, overt sexuality, and death instead of romance and happy endings; and a pessimistic rather than optimistic tone. It was not that these films actually attained verisimilitude through this defiance, acting as transparent mirrors of some objective reality; they were as artificial as any representation. Rather, this particular historical moment created and legitimated this particular definition of aesthetic realism.

The sheer omnipresence of such anticonventional films does not, however, tell us exactly *why* they became the dominant critical canon of the time. The reasons for their canonicity are related to traditions of film reviewing that had been in place long before the postwar era. The proliferation of realist films did not shape new attitudes in popular film criticism; rather, it gave the critic a rich opportunity to exercise conventions of evaluation that had been in force for at least two decades. I am referring to a timeworn antagonism to Hollywood glitz on the part of urban periodicals and the general primacy of film content in review aesthetics.

Reviewers often opposed the Hollywood film industry to motion picture art. This comparison was typically rooted in the industry's perceived proclivity for effect (the giddy spectacle of artifice) over substance (mature content with social relevance). From this perspective, industry businessmen were no more than "shark-suckers," who would "continue to demand that the commercial screen be reserved exclusively for the presentation of elegant untruths, gilded dreams, and badly refracted memories," at the expense of religious, social, and economic realities.[10] Dramas would inevitably come to be praised or damned on the basis of their relationship to this binary opposition. Hence, for some, *Gone with the Wind* (1939) personified the labor and expense of one of Hollywood's "super-pictures" in Technicolor, resulting in a film "which is a major event in the history of the industry but is only a minor achievement in motion picture art."[11] By contrast, films such as *The Grapes of Wrath* (1940) and *Citizen Kane* (1940) earned reviewers' respect, either by treating social and economic hardships with integrity or by exhibiting a degree of intelligence and character found to be lacking in the slick products of the movie business.[12]

Critics of the 1950s, then, sustained certain traditions of assessing dramas when they nominated Hollywood realist films for top awards. While musicals, by contrast, were often praised for their display of the industry's illusionistic pyrotechnics and zest for entertainment, critics insisted that the worthy drama demonstrate signs of alienation from the industry. By thus apparently canceling out commercial origins, the drama could attain a significance and seriousness of purpose that aligned it with high art. The anticonventionality and concerns of the postwar realist film fit perfectly into this scheme.

The specific criteria typically used by critics to judge films, derived from Anglo-American traditions of moral criticism, created a focus on film content that similarly encouraged the canonization of postwar dramas. In his collection of reviews, *The Great Films*, Crowther defines the reviewer's aesthetic as concerned with "those films in which the content has been of . . . originality and significance . . . aptly combined with cinematic technique." While he acknowledges the importance of style and its "fit" with content, Crowther's emphasis is on the latter. It is strong content that provides "a fresh, stimulating, expanding and meaningful experience . . . a new awareness of the human condition in exciting and absorbing ways." The great majority of films that have met this test have been "ones that are strong on observation and criticism of society."[13]

Thus, the realist canon emerged from an intersection of downbeat productions in postwar Hollywood with preexisting negative attitudes toward the film industry, and content-oriented moral criticism that found inventive films with strong social themes attractive. While it might seem that the flamboyance of the adult melodrama would exclude it from serious attention within this aesthetic, reviewers found a way to extend their canonical notions of art to the genre.

The Adult Melodrama Revisited

As I discussed in the previous chapter, the 1950s saw the production of a great many "adult" films, films with sensationalized social, psychological, and sexual themes. Postwar melodramas were frequently characterized this way, not only by the studio but by reviewers as well. The studio tended to identify the adult film as both socially relevant and sensational, focusing its advertising campaign on the latter. Reviewers were sensitive to each of these dimensions of the adult film. But, in favorable reviews, no matter how "wanton" the spectacle might be, they typically envisaged the social themes in these films as fertile territory for the application of the realist canon. That is, critics could easily offset the adult film's clear sensationalism by emphasizing its social verisimilitude. The explicitness of these films acted as a signifier of an "authenticity" reviewers perceived as insightful of the human condition. The often topical dimensions of these films—such as alcoholism in *I'll Cry Tomorrow* (1955), juvenile delinquency in *Rebel without a Cause* (1955), the case study on cortisone misuse reported by *The New Yorker* that inspired *Bigger than Life* (1956)—helped confirm their status as culturally significant documents.

Arthur Knight, one of the main reviewers for *The Saturday Review*, thus defined *Baby Doll* (1956), perhaps the most controversial film of the time because of its blatant sexual content. Knight wrote that it was certainly "one of the most unhealthy and amoral pictures ever made in this country." However, its documentary style and Kazan's approach to characters "strongly resembles the techniques of Balzac and Flaubert." Through reference to two preeminent French realists, Knight justifies the film's excesses as presenting "another chapter in the human comedy."[14] *Newsweek* echoed these sentiments when it described the film as "controversial realism . . . a horrified visual report on a sordid environment full of appalling people, which should stand as an authentic model for some time to come."[15]

Bosley Crowther similarly praised the film version of Grace Metalious's *Peyton Place* (1957), a crystalline representative of the adult melodrama figuring rape, abortion, adultery, and other such subjects, as "a drama of personal tensions and incongruities that has something of the irony and terror of the film version of 'An American Tragedy.'"[16] Even the Catholic press often found merit in the "racy" adult film on the basis of its realist offerings, despite the influence of the Legion of Decency. *America*, for example, commented that *Cat on a Hot Tin Roof* (1958), a film with a homosexual subtext, was a "powerful drama in which the characters are vivid and believable human beings . . . and in which there is enough groping toward reconciliation and love to justify the nerve-jangling sound and fury that preceded it."[17] *Commonweal* pronounced the film's theme as "lovelessness and its baleful consequences," which the reviewer found had "tragic pertinence for many contemporary audiences."[18]

Through perceived relevance and authenticity in message, situation, or character, bolstered occasionally by reference to authors (such as Flaubert) with established prestige, the adult melodrama was thus redeemed and made valuable within the horizons of the era's dominant realist paradigm. In this way, the positive review recast adult films from the studio's promotion of their romantic/sexual content and consumable style, to foreground the relevance of their social problems and stylistic verisimilitude as the ultimate test of their quality.

However, these films were just as subject to mixed or negative reviews when critics found fault with their reproductions of "human realities." These failures usually fell into three categories: lack of plausibility, immorality, and inappropriate style. In 1955 reviewers found, for example, that *Rebel without a Cause*, *I'll Cry Tomorrow*, and *Man with the Golden Arm* suffered from insufficient explanation of why their characters became, respectively, juvenile delinquents, alcoholics, and drug addicts.[19] Critics worried that these films sacrificed coherent psychological motivation to exploit the audience-grabbing emotionalism inherent in their spectacles of human degradation. As for immorality, *Commonweal* presented a typical complaint when its reviewer wrote that *Picnic*'s (1955) vivid reality would be "more effective if its tone weren't so amoral. . . . It assumes that virtues such as honor, honesty, and chastity are pretty old-fashioned stuff."[20] Last, reviewers detected a conflict between realist aspirations in the story and the stylistic choices made. Crowther wrote that in *Rebel without a Cause* there was "a pictorial slickness about the whole thing in color and Cinemascope that battles at times with the realism in the direction of Nicholas Ray."[21] Visual variables could undermine the codes of dramatic authenticity so prized by the canon.

Thus, histrionic performances without sound character motivation, outright sordidness, or a lush visual style could endanger the codes of dramatic naturalism needed to convey the message of the 1950s realist drama. Moreover, critics generally associated these shortcomings with the interference of Hollywood. They regarded the industry's market-based penchant for designing films with sensationalistic content and style as a potential contaminant to the transmission of social message and dramatic integrity.

Reviewers evaluated Sirk's melodramas almost exclusively through this sense of failed realism. However, none of the more or less politely qualified criticisms encountered thus far prepares us for the vehemence of the Sirk reviews. While critics recognized the adult content of these films, discussion rarely ascended to the level of debates over their social significance or morality as it did with other adult films. Instead, reviewers saw Sirk's melodramas as the ugly quintessence of Hollywood commercialism, torpedoing his films on grounds of implausibility and style.

These condemnations were additionally underwritten by a delicate distinction between melodrama and soap opera. Although it was sometimes still a suspicious genre critically, reviewers recognized melodrama as a major forum for the expression of social problems in the postwar era. The term soap opera could be appreciated for similar concerns. But more often than not, it conjured up associations with the worst exploitative impulses of Hollywood, and, in a broader sense, a Pandora's box of fears about mass culture itself.

Sirk Reviews

Arthur Knight and Lee Rogow of *The Saturday Review* were two of the few critics of the time who had anything charitable to say about Sirk's melodramas. Of *Magnificent Obsession*, Rogow wrote, "The remarkable thing about the film is the proof that these great cheap formulas can touch the fringes of real emotion." Similarly, Knight conceded that Zuckerman's screenplay for *Tarnished Angels* "retained a surprising amount of the raw emotion of the book," while *Imitation of Life* presented audiences with "life as they would like to believe it, and it makes good movie material—at least for a matinee."[22]

Albeit with somewhat grudging praise, each critic redeemed these films based on the reigning aesthetic for drama by emphasizing their apparent adherence to an *emotional* realism. Most other critics found a destructive tension between any realism offered by these films and the fakeries of the culture industry, personified by a combination of soap opera formulas and Hollywood commercialism.

Reviewers consistently traced a lineage between Sirk's narratives and mass-circulated soap operas in magazines and on the radio as a means of illuminating their eclipse of realism. As early as 1944 James Agee commented that Sirk's adaptation of Chekhov's *The Shooting Party* for *Summer Storm*, "looks as if Mr. Sirk had wanted to be faithful to something plotty, melodramatic, and second-grade, with psychological possibilities in it which he, or his actors, failed to make much of . . . most of it had for me, the sporty speciousness of an illustrated drugstore classic." Parodying a line from one of these "classics," Agee writes, " 'Speaking of women,' " murmured the Baron, toying with his aperient."[23] Although meant in a playful sense, in bringing together women and aperients (that is, laxatives), Agee's imaginary quotation foregrounds an association between women and the debasing effects of mass culture that continued to underwrite assessments of Sirk's work.

For example, Crowther later evaluated *All That Heaven Allows* (1955) as "one of those doleful situations so dear to the radio daytime serials." In this "frankly feminine fiction," Crowther wrote, "solid and sensible drama plainly had to give way to outright emotional bulldozing and a paving of easy clichés." *Time* referred disparagingly to the film as a woman's picture, lamenting the fact that the "the characters talk *Ladies' Home Journal*ese and the screen glows like a page of *House Beautiful.* The moviegoer often has the sensation that he is drowning in a sea of melted butter, with nothing to hang on to but the clichés that float past."[24]

Commonweal put these sentiments in somewhat stronger terms in its review of *Magnificent Obsession* (1954). Its reviewer suggested that

> Perhaps there is some defense for soap opera on radio: at least a woman can go about her work as she half-listens and day-dreams over their preposterous stories. But soap operas in the movies are something else again. Even a handsome Technicolor opus like [this] . . . gets tiresome as its characters . . . go through one empty situation after the other—situations that have almost no relation to real life.[25]

Although later champions of Sirk, the British in the BFI's *Monthly Film Bulletin* criticized all of his melodramas on the basis of their relation to the artifice of soaps and Hollywood. A critic called *All That Heaven Allows* "a complacent reconstruction of a thirties magazine serial world which is as laboriously predictable as it is fatuously unreal. . . . Rock Hudson manfully imposes sense where possible on the sentimental proceedings." *Written on the Wind* was "Hollywood moonshine of the slickest vintage. A streamlined piece of magazine fiction, mounted with superb physical gloss."

The *Monthly Film Bulletin* saved its harshest criticism for *Imitation of Life,* of all Sirk's films perhaps the one with the most obvious relation to social problems. Noting Hollywood's penchant for "high-class pulp fiction" which has "led to many a confession tale and glossy family saga," the reviewer argued that "when their novelletish emotional entanglements are coupled with a fashionably 'liberal' theme, the result can be eminently dislikeable. . . . Its onslaught on the emotions is almost entirely synthetic . . . its attitude toward its racial problem is debased and compromised."[26]

The question of style added to the problems Sirk's films had in reproducing a realist aesthetic to the satisfaction of reviewers. *Written on the Wind*'s decor was "luxurious and the color is conspicuously strong, even though it gets no closer to Texas—either geographically or in spirit—than a few locations near Hollywood."[27] Reviewers continually registered this kind of negative association between Sirk's mise-en-scène and Hollywood artifice. *Newsweek* called *Imitation of Life* "a picture rich in decor but lacking in imagination and restraint"; while *Catholic World* resented the combination of a "theatrical atmosphere and success story . . . full of phony glamour" without relation to "anything that ever happened in real life" with a story about racial prejudice. What aroused the reviewer's particular indignation was the fact that the studio hoped to attract an audience for the film based on "its lavish color production, its tearjerking qualities, and the irresistible circumstance that Lana Turner wears more than one million dollars worth of jewelry and a wardrobe of equal opulence and bad taste."[28]

The polar opposition between soap plotting and Hollywood commercialism, on the one hand, and social and dramatic integrity on the other, licensed reviewers to conduct unapologetic parodies of the dramatic structure and situations of the films in question. As just one example, John McCarten of *The New Yorker* wrote of *Magnificent Obsession*,

> Although he doesn't seem to be the brightest fellow in the world, there are really no flies on our hero mentally, and at length he becomes a brain surgeon as sure with a scalpel as a shad boner in Fulton Fish Market. Sawing away on his sweetheart's head—I believe he is trying to clear up a slight case of astigmatism—the man knows real peace of mind. But it's movies such as this that prevent me from feeling likewise.[29]

Thus, although Sirk's films shared many characteristics with adult melodramas, including serious social content, melodramatic story lines, and an often elaborate style, they were more often subject to wholesale condemnation by periodical reviewers. For reviewers, Sirk's films so embodied the antirealism and aesthetic liabilities of soaps and Hollywood greed that they generally refused to admit them to the realist canon. At every point, critics opposed the Sirk film to relevant subject matter, plausible dramatic situations, psychological realism in character, and a style that would function as expressive support. Instead, his films supported the mass cultural dream machines by offering their audiences tacky, sensationalistic formulas and cheap emotionalism. Further, the Sirk soap was clearly linked to a leisured domestic female audience whose taste, in reviewers' minds, signified the debasement of art into sentimentality and cliché. Reviewers castigated the "fatuous" unreality of the soap opera through a visible antipathy to the feminine. The best one could hope for in these formulas is that someone would "manfully impose sense where possible."

While the realist canon played an important role in determining the meaning and value of these films in the postwar era, it is unlikely that realist preoccupations alone could explain the intensity of Sirk's aesthetic ostracism, particularly its peculiar gender dimensions. In fact, reviews reflected prevalent, often vituperative, attitudes toward mass culture that characterized intellectual discussion in the 1940s and 1950s. Sirk's critical status during this time was determined additionally by more general cultural prejudices that perceived affiliations between his melodramas and the negative capabilities of mass culture.

As we have seen, Sirk reviews chronicled the generic relation of his films to a number of soap opera predecessors: magazine fiction, radio soaps, and "high-class" pulp fiction (that is, best-sellers). Although not mentioned by name, these reviewers were referring generally to such popular 1940s radio soap operas as "The Goldbergs," "Stella Dallas," "Woman in White," and "Guiding Light," as well as to the omnipresence of romantic fiction in women's magazines like *McCall's*, *Ladies' Home Journal*, and *True Story*. More specifically, Sirk's films were sometimes based on the work of best-selling authors like Lloyd C. Douglas (for *Magnificent Obsession*) and Fanny Hurst (for *Imitation of Life*), authors whose popularity sometimes stood in the way of serious critical attention.

Given these affiliations, one could say that Sirk's melodramas lacked the appropriate patrimony. Except for *Tarnished Angels*, which was based on William Faulkner's "Pylon," Sirk's melodramas lacked the prestigious ancestry of a Tennessee Williams or a Pulitzer Prize-winning play by William Inge. For critics, Sirk's melodramas had *matrilinear* roots in forms explicitly regarded as feminine in substance and appeal. As some recent theorists have pointed out, the feminine did not fare well in past debates about the nature and effects of mass culture. Critics writing from the 1930s through the 1950s defined mass culture's aesthetic bankruptcy and even endangerment of *real* art through the feminine metaphor of passivity; they invoked this trait to describe the susceptibility, mindlessness, and sheer capacity for manipulation that the culture industry relied on to dominate cultural production and reception.[30] The judgments against Sirk's films were heavily freighted by this kind of implicit equation of things female with the threatening and debilitating potentials of mass culture.

Soaps, Totalitarianism, and Taste

During the Cold War era, as intellectuals began to shun Marxism and radical politics because of their public association with communism, the realm of mass culture assumed a special importance. As Richard Pells argues, intellectuals "no longer assailed their traditional enemies—the capitalists, the political bosses . . . — with the old ideological fervor. But if they wished to preserve a little of the radical heritage, they could concentrate on popular tastes and values as the new opiates of their countrymen." By assailing the media, "writers might demonstrate their dislike for the quality of American life without having to challenge the nation's political or economic institutions as well." In this way, the critique of the media often strategically displaced more direct assaults on the government, while preserving the image of the socially committed liberal intellectual.[31]

The exponential growth of mass culture during the postwar years provided a provocative terrain for this alternative cultural mission. Intellectuals saw the expansion of mass culture which had begun in the pre–World War II era as heralding a new cultural "democracy." This democracy was characterized, on the one hand, by the mounting popularity of forms associated with the average individual, such as television shows, best-sellers, magazine fiction, paperbacks, comic books, radio soaps, "B" movies, and hit music. On the other hand, more pervasive networks of dissemination for cultural products had arisen, resulting in the wide availability of a variety of fictional types. Television, for example, had the ability to deliver programming to a large number of households, while changes in print distribution found material from the great novels to comic books to pinup magazines, ready for purchase in drug or candy stores. Many felt the dominance of popular forms in combination with mass diffusion would result in a forever changed relationship between mass and literate cultures, wherein the former would subsume the latter, determining what was valuable through the sheer act of consumption.

As Andrew Ross has pointed out, two general positions toward this new, apparently more democratic state developed among Cold War liberals. The first stemmed from Theodor Adorno and Max Horkheimer's antifascist critique of mass culture as exercising a form of social control. Dwight MacDonald, for example, compared mass culture's enforcement of the same standards for everyone with fascism, totalitarianism, and communism. From this perspective, capitalist culture, represented by the endless, profit motivated production of formulaic products, was the enemy of true democracy, obliterating social differences and empowering a protofascist mob of common people. The second position rejected a blanket condemnation of mass culture. Popularity was no longer a sign of fascism, but a mark of how well a fictional type responded to deep social needs (for example, in Robert Warshow's discussion of the western, the genre provided a serious cultural orientation toward violence). Ross argues that this therapeutic argument was an important moment in Cold War liberalism because of its attempt to disassociate capitalism from the specter of totalitarianism. By stressing the potentially benevolent effects of mass culture on diverse populations, U.S. society appeared as an order that assisted, rather than obstructed, the development of human potential.[32]

Among intellectuals on both sides of this debate, postwar developments in mass culture also aroused particular concern about the standards of public taste. In 1953, for example, *The Saturday Review* ran a series on the "Common Man" and the "temper of taste in America today," in the face of changes brought about by mass communications. On one side of the discussion stood the negativists. Increasingly dissatisfied with the intellectual quality of what was being purveyed, they asked, "Can we have the Age of the Common Man without an Age of the Common Denominator?"[33] These writers equated democracy with a "tyranny of mediocrity" that would "seriously displace or possibly annihilate literate culture." The standardization and proliferation of texts within the culture industry led to "a 'democracy' of taste," which meant a "practically unanimous demand for Grade-B movies."[34] Modern culture was thus characterized by a "new democratic snobbery" that preferred the popular arts to the classics and, in its confusion of the best with the most generally acceptable, revealed "a spiritual confusion which is subtle and insidious."[35] For these writers, the strong links between popular objects of mass culture and their audiences threatened a permanent displacement of good taste by a powerful self-congratulatory mediocrity.

However, in the same series, there were those who defended mass culture as a potential democratic culture. While admitting that mass culture could cause a vulgarization of taste, they argued that mass communications also exposed more people to the very best of world literature and substantive films, and that such exposure could actually help raise the level of public taste.[36] Critics such as Gilbert Seldes held out hope that the producers of mass culture would assume their social responsibility and develop better programming to elevate the audience's sensibilities. While both negativists and hopefuls were committed to concepts of a literate culture, the latter openly advocated the potential virtues of modern cultural production.

The growing defenses of mass culture in both political and aesthetic discussions led to analyses that claimed the worth of certain of its artifacts, including western pulp fiction, science fiction, comic books, and genre films. However, even within this more generous climate, critics continued to invoke soap operas as embodying the worst kinds of corruption of spirit and taste that the culture industry could produce.

Adorno and Horkheimer's passing references to soap operas in their "Culture Industry" essay established the genre as exemplary of the totalitarian operations of mass culture on art and subjectivity. The dramatic formula of most mass cultural artifacts, built on the housewife's "getting into trouble and out again . . . embraces the whole of mass culture from the idiotic women's serial to the top production." The endless repetition of such clichés not only threatens to engulf the authentic work, but stunts the "mass-media consumer's powers of imagination and spontaneity." Further, women's serials co-opt subjectivity and emotion through their explicit relation to states of inwardness: emotion appears as "mere twaddle . . . an embarrassingly agreeable garnish, so that genuine personal emotion in real life can be all the more reliably controlled."[37] Bernard Rosenberg, a writer very much in this camp, wrote similarly in 1957 that "sleazy fiction, trashy films, and bathetic soap operas," are among forms that threaten "not merely to cretinize our taste, but to brutalize our senses while paving the way to totalitarianism."[38] In their popular formulaic structure and artificial relation to emotions, soaps signified the mark of the beast of fascism in its desire to control aesthetics, subjectivities, and political mentalities.

Soaps also played a role in discussions of taste among the hopefuls. In 1948, Paul Lazarsfeld and Robert Merton questioned assumptions of the blanket social control exercised by media, while being concerned about the conformism and "narcotizing dysfunction" the media could produce. However, within a framework designed to temper fears about the depraved effects of the media on public taste, they nonetheless asserted that "the women who are daily entranced for three or four hours by some twelve consecutive 'soap operas,' all cut to the same dismal pattern, exhibit an appalling lack of aesthetic judgment." Calling for an analysis of this state of affairs, they ask, "What is the historical status of this notoriously low level of popular taste?"[39] Gilbert Seldes agreed with this position when he singled out "neurotic daytime serials" as that which the broadcast industry had to move away from to assume the role of raising public taste.[40] Even researchers and critics who had some faith in the promises of a mass democratic culture believed that soaps and their female audiences hampered mass culture's more utopian possibilities by representing its potential for aesthetic depravity and automated reception.

As we can see, then, reviewers' reception of Sirk's melodramas in the 1950s was influenced by a host of interrelated factors, both critical and cultural. In terms of specific review standards, Sirk's films affronted the realist canon by their perceived relation to the artifice characteristic of Hollywood commercial imperatives and soap opera formulas. These evaluations in turn took place within broader circumstances, in which the mass culture debates of the Cold War period fingered soaps as the incarnation of mass media evil. But while we can see what climates of opinion helped shape and justify critical opinion toward Sirk, it remains to ask what was at *stake* in these judgments, what was ultimately at issue in their particular equations of Sirk and soap operas with bad taste.

Recalling the epigraph for this chapter taken from Bourdieu, the case of Sirk and soap operas stands as a classic instance of critics' tendencies to reject "lower, coarse, vulgar, venal, servile—in a word, natural—enjoyment" as a means of insulating themselves from the "commoners" who allegedly identify with the spectacles offered by popular representations. In their "disgust at the facile," nowhere better represented than in the parodic recounting of soap plots or moralistic condemnations of their formulaic pleasures, critics claimed a superior status for themselves as cultural watchdogs of taste. At the same time, they created a debased image of the masses as aesthetic incompetents and threats to a civilized world. Critical canons of good taste could be ventured and sustained, in fact, only by constituting a heathen underclass of tasteless consumers to serve as a radical, aesthetic Other. Since these consumers were primarily perceived as women in the case of soaps, the fallout of such social and aesthetic hierarchization may have subtly aggravated deeply held convictions about sexual difference, which figured a certain disdain for women at the same time as it assisted their social and moral marginality.

The 1950s did not provide, however, the last word on popular Sirk criticism. Completely transfigured in many ways by the 1970s, the critical establishment had another significant opportunity to judge the work of this director.

The 1970s: Retrospectives

After their original release, Sirk's melodramas, like the work of so many other directors, reappeared publicly via retrospectives from the 1970s through the 1980s. In New York City, a prime location for such activities, screenings invariably took place in museums, theaters wholly or partially devoted to revivals, and other institutions associated with public intellectual life. Specific revival enterprises for Hollywood films in New York included the Museum of Modern Art, Theater 80, St. Marks, Carnegie Hall, the Bleecker Street Theater, the Regency, the Thalia, and the New York Film Festival.

Such forums differed from mainstream commercial theaters in presenting old films as part of enlightened culture, edifying for an urban cognoscente, rather than as simply entertainment for the average moviegoer. Assisting this enterprise were a cadre of film reviewers often similarly situated within an alternative framework, whether *The Village Voice* or *The Soho Weekly News*. Within this context of exhibition forums and presses, Sirk's films earned sustained, appreciative reviews for the first time in a mass cultural environment. Reviewers praised and defended his films, making their past degraded status appear as the product of a sorely misguided critical mentality.

The growth of exhibition site as archive clearly aided the critical rewriting of past products of the film industry. But the radical shift in perspectives on Sirk and other directors owed to at least two other factors that likewise encouraged a valorization of "Old Hollywood" during this time. The first of these concerned the nature of the critical canon of the 1970s, shaped by heated discussions of the "New American Cinema." Within these discussions, the "Old" in many cases appeared as better and more authentic than the "New." This preferential treatment was not simply a product of journalistic whim; it was part of the overall thrust toward nostalgia that marked public discourse and popular culture during the 1970s. The second, and perhaps more patently obvious, of these factors was the penetration of academic auteurism into journalistic writing on film. The combination of nostalgic revisionism and auteurism helped the Sirks of the film world to emerge as revered talents in review journalism during this time.

The New versus the Old

And seeing *Psycho* again is rather like visiting a historical monument or a national shrine; when one approaches the legendary staircase where Martin Balsam was stabbed . . . you're awed to think that this is where it happened, as though you were surveying one of the battlefields of the Civil War.[41]

In the 1960s, the term New American Cinema reflected, on the one hand, the economic and organizational differences in filmmaking after the demise of the studio system, with a rise in corporate takeovers and independent film production. On the other hand, it was a catchall phrase used to describe various types of films being made through the 1970s. Most now familiarly associate the label with the bold generic and stylistic experimentation carried out by filmmakers such as Robert Altman in *McCabe and Mrs. Miller* (1971), Terrence Malick in *Badlands* (1973), and Woody Allen in *Annie Hall* (1977), whose films broke with past traditions of style and construction. But reviewers of the time also applied the label to commercial blockbusters such as *Star Wars* (1977) and *The Deep* (1977), which crystallized the economic conservativeness of corporate Hollywood, as well as to more humble offerings like *Rocky* (1976) and, farther on the fringe, *Jackson County Jail* (1976), which seemed to purvey a low-budget honesty in the face of flashy or commercial projects. The New American Cinema could be by turns innovative, crass, or refreshingly simple.

But no matter what the nuance, as Robert Ray has pointed out, the New American Cinema was heavily indebted to the Old. Besides a flurry of nostalgia films such as *The Way We Were* (1973), *American Graffiti* (1973), and *That's Entertainment* (1974), Hollywood incessantly replayed generic formulas of the past, often with parodic overtones.[42] Thus, *The Pink Panther* (1964), *Bonnie and Clyde* (1967), *Little Big Man* (1970), *Star Wars*, and *Jackson County Jail* were among a great number of contemporary films that reworked, respectively, the conventions of the comedies, gangster, westerns, science fiction serials, and "B" movies of the preceding decades.

What is of interest here is not so much the details of this ultra-reflexive development, but rather how reviewers' responses to this aspect of the New

American Cinema shaped an aesthetic—an aesthetic that had ramifications for determining the merits of classic Hollywood. Inevitable comparisons between the two eras arose which were laden with "value judgments."

"The system" provided one of the arenas in which the New was constantly brought into association with the Old. Articles in *The New York Times* and elsewhere discussed how the business contrasts between the studio system and the contemporary corporate megalith affected filmmaking aesthetics. In one such article, Garson Kanin praised the old studio heads with whom he had worked as both director and screenwriter, saying that they might have been "pirates and barracudas, but however crass, cruel and ruthless they were, they were simply crazy about making movies. I don't find that true about the present generation of tycoons." He continued, "I can't believe that the head of Trans America is any more interested in movies when he buys out United Artists than he is in, say, automobiles, when he buys out Budget Rent a Car." Kanin bemoans the loss of both the old studio heads' personal touch and the "individual imaginations of a Lubitsch or a Ford or a Preston Sturges." Imagination is sacrificed within the "strictly commercial" and businesslike aspects of contemporary filmmaking, where producers "seem intent on calculating what will appeal to the widest possible audience. Instead of trusting their own instincts, they tend to opt for the proven, the tried, the familiar . . . blockbusters, sequels, repeat formulas." Kanin then concludes, "Goldwyn would hate it. He'd say you can't hold the public with sensationalism, you can only hold them with good stories."[43]

Reviewers for *Film Comment*'s issue on the 1970s seemed to sum up such sentiments when they complained about the conservatism of the film industry: "The generation that grew up on *The Graduate* took over Hollywood and went into plastics," and "Instead of making *Star Trek II*, why don't they give $10 million each to David Lean, Sergio Leone, Joseph L. Mankiewicz, and Orson Welles?"[44]

Such pieces participated in relandscaping the past, depicting bygone eras as simpler and less corrupt. Here, what was at one time perceived as the seat of capitulations to mammon—the studio system—is nostalgically redefined as an artisanal culture that provided a safe haven for individuality, personal craftsmanship, and ingenious creativity; this in contrast to the perceived eviscerating effects of large-scale, postindustrial corporatism on artistic enterprise.

Specific aesthetic arguments echoed this perspective when reviewers contrasted the films of both eras. Some criticism remained relatively content to trace the total indebtedness of New to Old, that is, how *The Electric Horseman* (1979) presents us with "an exact, perfectly restored specimen of the 1930s Frank Capra populist-political comedy—a *Mr. Smith Goes to Washington* with Frye boots and videotape."[45] David Ehrenstein of *Film Comment* argued similarly that *Coming Home* (1978) was "more than reminiscent of *Written on the Wind*." Citing correlations between the characters played by Bruce Dern and Robert Stack—the gun under the pillow, the self-destructive neurosis—as well as the romantic triangle and a dance to compare with Dorothy Malone's "Temptation" number, Ehrenstein insists that despite its political trappings, *Coming Home* "practically *is Written on the Wind*, refurbished and updated—a melodrama."[46]

The implicit contention that the contemporary was often nothing more than an imitation of the past typically, however, had a more critical partisan edge. One reviewer complained that the 1970s was "a modish antique store of a decade that pilfered issues and styles from more vital times."[47] Chief among offenders in this regard was Brian de Palma. In "The Man Who Would Be Hitchcock," a review of de Palma's latest venture, *Obsession* (1976), Walter Goodman wrote that "to compare Alfred Hitchcock, even at his second or third best, with Brian de Palma is not fair sport; it's like putting Muhammad Ali in the ring with Andy Warhol."[48]

Alternative sources agreed. Andrew Sarris's reviews in *The Village Voice* frequently condemned contemporary films for so unsuccessfully attempting to "repackage the past." Sarris noted as early as 1964 a strong "deficiency of newer films in comparison to older," criticizing *The Pink Panther* for borrowing from *Duck Soup*, *The Awful Truth*, and Hitchcock's *Foreign Correspondent* and *To Catch a Thief*. In treating the same issue in later years, he cited the imitativeness of *Smokey and the Bandit* (1977), *Star Wars*, and *Sorcerer* (1977), excoriating the last of these as a rip-off of H. G. Clouzot, John Huston, and David Lean. None of the contemporary manifestations of old traditions could "come close to matching their craftsmanship."[49]

Hence, critics faulted some of the generically recycled films of the newer era as lackluster imitations of more glorious examples of artistic integrity and originality. As in the case of business comparisons, reviewers engaged in historical revisionism to create their canonical objects, obscuring how commercially oriented and formulaic classic Hollywood cinema had been as well. As the quotation at the beginning of this section suggests, films from the past could even attain the kind of sacred, enduring monumentality usually reserved for epic historical events.

This penchant for rewriting the past at the expense of the present was no doubt supported by the intense romanticizing of earlier periods of history that marked the 1970s. If, as historians tell us, widespread nostalgia tends to appear at times of social discontent with the present, then this decade was a prime candidate for the nostalgic sensibility.[50] Those writing about the 1970s experienced it as a time of profound social dislocation, a founding sentiment for what many referred to as the period's nostalgia wave or "boom."

This sense of dislocation was partially instigated by the legacy of the 1960s. Vietnam, the King and Kennedy assassinations, Kent State, racial violence, Civil Rights, hippies, gay liberation, and feminism challenged notions of "natural" and rightful orders that had operated for decades.[51] Besides inheriting troubling features from the recent past, specific events occurred during the 1970s that caused a painful "rediscovery of limits" within the exercise of U.S. global and domestic power. These included the failure of the Vietnam War, the rise of the OPEC cartel and ensuing energy shortage, and our decreasing hold on outer space with the collapse of Skylab, as well as Watergate, Three Mile Island, and a host of other internal social problems such as rising unemployment, high interest rates, divorce, and inflation.[52] In each of these instances, the decade seemed to have no positive character of its own. Rather, its events aggravated a public sense of sheer social instability, a disintegration of "simple" national values, as well as decisive U.S. power, under the influence of advanced capitalism and increasingly complex world affairs.

Public dissatisfaction with the decade was often expressed through a drama of historical comparisons, wherein the present was judged as a "departure from superior past realities."[53] To play this role, the past had to be sanitized of serious social strife, a sleight of hand engineered by the nostalgic imagination. The querulous social sensibilities of the 1970s willfully and wishfully reconstructed bygone eras as pre-industrial and pre-corporate utopias, where traditional values of individuality, creativity, home, and family reigned. Prior historical moments were thus neatly packaged by the therapeutic urge for stability that underpinned such revisionism. The past, then, served primarily as a reactive, escapist alternative to the pressures and chaos of an incipient postmodernity. While conservatives celebrated the nostalgic sentiment, radicals criticized its whitewashing tendencies and neglect of contemporary social conditions.[54]

The 1970s commitment to the past was evidenced in such diverse phenomena as the reincarnation craze, postmodern architecture's "pastiching" from preceding styles, and the huge historical preservation movement, which attempted to save historic sites and communities from the bulldozers of urban renewal. But it was more properly in popular culture that relations to the past attained a strongly nostalgic component. Cultural manifestations of this phenomenon included renewed interest in the 1950s, pre-television Hollywood musicals, romantic comedies of the 1930s, the radio serials of the 1930s (which had been so thoroughly trashed a few decades earlier), fashions of the World War I era, swing bands, F. Scott Fitzgerald, and even a revived Beatlemania toward the end of the decade. In addition, tributes to bygone eras constituted a substantial percentage of media productions. While the New American Cinema was replaying key classic genres, big Broadway musicals featured *Hello, Dolly* and *Grease*, while television sported "Happy Days" (1974–1984) and "Laverne and Shirley" (1976–1983), which, like *Grease*, revisited the 1950s.

The social malaise of the 1970s thus gave birth to a nostalgia that helped create a reverence for the past in compensation for a disjointed and dysfunctional present. In this context, film reviewing appears as one more cultural voice calling out in the 1970s wilderness. The critical regard for the old masters of Hollywood cinema, as well as the pessimism about current trends, serves as another indicator of the dynamics of the 1970s nostalgic imagination. Reviewers created an aesthetic hierarchy that confirmed alienation from the present through a vision of classic filmmaking free of corporate taint and full of the individuality, originality, and vitality found lacking in contemporary industry products.

By itself, however, the nostalgic tone of the 1970s cannot explain why classic films attained such canonical heights; the forces of auteurism had a more visible hand in this process. However, the substantial yearning for yesterday during the period created an agreeable cultural environment for the revisionist work of the auteur critics, which relied so heavily on the celebratory rewriting of historical persons and artifacts into the contemporary script.

Public Auteurism

During the 1960s and 1970s, newspaper and magazine articles devoted to classic directors abounded, a fact assisted by the continuing productivity of many of these directors. Essays titled "John Huston: I Want to Keep Right on Going," "Nicholas Ray: Still a Rebel with a Cause," and "It's a Wonderful Life, but . . . : New Light on the Darker Side of Frank Capra" provided the means of attesting to the creative genius of these directors. These articles documented their past glories working in the Hollywood system and their often negative appraisals of contemporary commercial Hollywood.[55] Thus, interviews with directors served as a prime site for the articulation of the split between New and Old and the kind of nostalgic sentimentality about the studio system and individual creativity characterizing aesthetic hierarchies of the time.

Sirk's public authorization owed in part to this drama of comparison. Along with Fritz Lang, Max Ophuls, and others, critics invoked Sirk as an exemplar of the foreign director working within the Hollywood system as a means of discussing the relative successes of contemporary transplanted foreign directors such as

Roman Polanski and Miloš Forman. Naturally, the reviewer concluded that it was easier to make the "transfer" when Hollywood was an organized system, rather than the big commercial venture it was in the 1970s.[56]

But in terms of judgments established through an interplay of Old and New, Sirk's stature as a director was enhanced by his links to the New German Cinema—a foreign cinema widely canonized during this time. Jean-Luc Godard and Rainer Werner Fassbinder had both written essays on Sirk in the early 1970s that journalists later used to validate Sirk's authorship for the public via the aura of foreign artistry. But it was more properly Fassbinder's review of Sirk's work in a reprint of his "Six Films by Douglas Sirk" in *Film Comment* and his frequent proclamations of indebtedness to Sirk in his own work that helped the latter to gain validity.[57]

Fassbinder's discussion of six of Sirk's melodramas, among them *All That Heaven Allows* and *Written on the Wind*, ends with the lines: "I have seen six films by Douglas Sirk. Among them were the most beautiful in the world."[58] Fassbinder's euphoric admiration demonstrated, as did most auteur criticism of the time, that the apparently hokey exteriors of Sirk's melodramas housed a social criticism of the United States, articulated visually through a self-reflexive mise-en-scène that pointed to the flawed materialism of the bourgeoisie. The fact that such statements were made by a foreign director closely identified with political filmmaking, and in particular with the overt political transformations of melodramatic material in films such as *The Merchant of Four Seasons* (1971), lent an authority to this kind of appraisal.

Fassbinder's remake of *All That Heaven Allows* in *Ali, Fear Eats the Soul* (1974) paid further homage, as did the particular character of his melodramas. His films seemed to simulate Sirk by using melodrama as a platform for social criticism. Stylistically, Fassbinder employed a baroque mise-en-scène complete with the Sirk trademarks of mirrors and doorways as distancing devices. While the content of the New German director's work was played out in a more overtly incendiary fashion, the parallels nonetheless reinforced the sense that Sirk's films had been a significant influence on a significant cinema.

The Fassbinder connection, then, served a double purpose: it resuscitated Sirk for a contemporary audience through association with a prestigious foreign cinema, at the same time that it placed Fassbinder's films within more accessible Hollywood generic traditions. In addition, the European roots of both Sirk and Fassbinder dovetailed nicely with the "anti-Americanism" of 1970s criticism in relation to the corporately produced works of the New American Cinema.

While this particular discourse on the Old and the New contributed to Sirk's authorization at the time, journalism's auteur critics provided detailed interpretations of his films that went further in giving Sirk a public profile as an artist. Creating value for objects of mass culture in the public sector relied as much as academia did on establishing the aesthetic worth of their authors. As mentioned, most public critical commentary on Sirk was initiated by retrospectives beginning in the latter half of the 1970s. This commentary was marked by a blend of Andrew Sarris's conservative auteurism and the more politicized perspectives of the left-thinking *Screen* and other academic journals, which often found an ideologically agreeable climate in newspapers affected by 1960s alternative culture. More directly, those affiliated with academic auteurism sometimes wrote these reviews.

In introducing Sirk to the cultured masses for the first time, revivals often replicated the "discovery" phase in academics in the early 1970s, discussed in chapter 1. At the Carnegie Hall Cinema in 1976; the Museum of Modern Art in 1977; and the largest retrospective, sponsored in 1979 by Columbia University's School of Art, the Museum of Modern Art, the Goethe Society, and the Thalia Theatre to celebrate Sirk's return to the United States after a twenty-year absence, retrospectives presented films outside the pantheon of his 1950s melodramas. These included Nazi era films such as *Final Chord* (1936) and *La Habanera* (1937), as well as later U.S. films such as *Hitler's Madman* (1943), *Sleep, My Love* (1948), *Thunder on the Hill* (1951), *Has Anybody Seen My Gal?* (1952), and *Sign of the Pagan* (1954). In addition, in keeping with the rhetoric of discovery, reviews rehearsed Sirk's autobiography as a means of substantiating his artistic credentials, and defended him rigorously against prior criticism that had derided him on the basis of his association with "tearjerkers." However, programs consistently included Sirk's renowned melodramas, as well as the perspectives that had created their special status, revealing that revival institutions were well aware of Sirk's canonization in academia.

George Morris's review of the 1979 retrospective for *The Soho Weekly News* demonstrates how important academic interpretations were to popular reviewing at this time. Morris credited the early auteurists with recognizing that "Sirk's work was unified by one of the most dazzling personal visual styles in the American cinema." He then established the director as someone who, like fellow émigré directors Preminger and Lang, was "fascinated by the contradictions within American society and culture." Sirk used the "hoary clichés and exhausted conventions of the so-called 'woman's picture' " to explore these contradictions "with irony and detachment." On a deeper level, "he was questioning the basic assumptions and ideals that were supposedly sustaining this country during the Eisenhower era. Sirk actually subverts and ruthlessly criticizes the middle-class values that his films superficially endorse." For elements of

Sirk's visual signature that support their subversive intents, Morris mentioned mirrors that "splinter reality," and "oppressive objects and decor" that "externalize the inner tensions of the story."[59]

Morris's interpretation provides a particularly detailed example of the penetration of the early *Screen* and *Monogram* projects into review discourse, especially the work of Paul Willemen, Jon Halliday, and Thomas Elsaesser. The reviewer depicted Sirk as a director who redeemed a questionable genre, launched a social critique of middle-class conceits of the Eisenhower era "beneath the surface," and employed self-reflexive and symptomatic imagery.[60]

This penetration was clear even in writers who had previously interpreted Sirk's films apolitically. Fred Camper, who had written about Sirk for *Screen* in the early 1970s without *Screen*'s characteristic left perspective on the director, now defended him as someone who revealed "an understanding of America far more subtle and profound than that of almost any other filmmaker." Among other things, Camper described how *Written on the Wind*'s mise-en-scène—"an exploration of a labyrinthine set of possible relations between people and costumes, people and objects, people and decor"—critiqued the materialism of U.S. life.[61] Similarly, for Andrew Sarris, Sirk's perverseness "consisted of gilding fables for the masses until they meant the opposite of what they seem."[62] In referring to Sirk's style as "artfully artificial," "relentlessly reflective," and ironical, Sarris's reviews were tinged with a sense of textual politics absent in his earlier comments on Sirk in *The American Cinema*.[63]

While few reviewers actually cited academic sources, academic interpretations were absorbed into the system of certain magazines and newspapers, acting as a ready-made stash of meanings upon which the reviewer could draw. Review discourse differed from academic in shunning theoretical "jargon"; but these critics nonetheless rendered academic readings more accessible to the public.

This is not to say, however, that all critics responded reverently to prior schooled interpretations. These interpretations often appeared as so immersed in their own lofty logic that they lost purchase on reality. For example, MOMA's retrospective of four of Sirk's German films in 1980 prompted Jonathan Rosenbaum to applaud Sirk's "consummate craftsmanship" but question the presence of a Brechtian subtext or social criticism in his films. He noted that there is a "curious unresolved split between Leftist and campy readings," made even greater by the fact that audiences rarely see the former and seem to revel in the latter.[64] Academia still serves as a point of departure here. But Rosenbaum questions its position on the director in the face of reception, sensing that academics ignore mass audience response because such response contradicts aesthetic propositions required to make Sirk a political auteur.

More recently, we can see a rare example of a marriage (rather than "an unresolved split") between left-oriented academic and camp readings in Sirk criticism. J. Hoberman's review in *The Village Voice* of *Written on the Wind*, shown at the Public Theater in 1987, focuses on the artifice of the film in such a way as to fuse academic insights with camp. Quoting Halliday and Fassbinder, Hoberman shows himself to be a critic conversant with academic readings. Citing Sirk's background as a European intellectual, Hoberman recognizes how the artifice—the excess of the film with its exaggerated colors, decor, and use of mirrors—renders a "distanced antinaturalism," that self-reflexively critiques the brash consumption of the petit bourgeois in this "quintessential American movie of the 1950s."

At the same time, his review treats the film's excesses in an appreciative yet parodic manner aligned with a camp aesthetic. Here, exaggeration is revered for its own sake by those savvy enough to recognize the alternative pleasures embedded in its departure from the conventional aesthetics of good taste. *Written on the Wind* is "trash on an epic scale, it's a vision as luridly color-coordinated, relentlessly high-octane, and flamboyantly petit-bourgeois as a two-toned T-Bird with ultrachrome trim." The film is "meta-trash" focusing on "the vanity of trash" itself.

Hoberman's understanding of the film rests, then, on its transcendence of schlock through its strange combination of lurid style and self-reflexive social critique. This combination is especially clear in his response to Malone's "Temptation" dance. He remarks, "One cares for the grotesque Malone because her continually thwarted sexuality poses the greatest threat to the patriarchal order . . . in the film's most hilarious excess, her inflamed strip-mambo literally knocks the father dead."[65]

This review provides a fitting finale to review discourse on Sirk's films for several reasons. *Written on the Wind* maintains its academic identity as a self-reflexive critique of the petit bourgeois and patriarchy through its exaggerated mise-en-scène and use of color. At the same time, by so thoroughly embracing the campy, overdrawn aspects of the film, Hoberman addresses the "repressed other" of interpretation. That is, he poses a reading of Sirk's melodramas based on their implausibility and "bad taste" that auteurists had all but stifled, and 1950s New York critics had used to condemn his work. But instead of taking this latter tack, Hoberman gives the film a rave review through a camp reading that celebrates its unconventional artifice. Thus, we see a blending of past comprehensions of Sirk's melodramatic excess that includes academia's self-reflexive and symptomatic readings, as well as accusations of bad taste by past critical establishments, now repossessed as a sign of quality by a "hip" camp aesthetic.

In sum, whereas Sirk had almost no status as an artist in the 1950s, 1970s nostalgia helped create the conditions for his public embrace as an old master, while journalistic auteurism enthusiastically granted him an aesthetic status by offering a relatively stable set of interpretations, domesticated from their academic sources and offered to an urban cognoscente. In each case, review journalism assigned meaning and value to Sirk's films in relation to a series of existing canonical ideals, that is, realism in the 1950s and nostalgic auteurism in the 1970s. These ideals were themselves fueled by social developments, ranging from postwar film production to post-1960s alienation.

If I stopped my analysis here, we might well be left with the impression that this "revolution" in Sirk's public profile signified the vast differences between 1970s and 1950s critical establishments. In fact, there are fundamental consistencies between the two that would belie such an impression.

During both periods, reviewers based their evaluations on a conception of Hollywood as a crass, commercial, formulaic, hence aesthetically and even morally bankrupt institution. I argued that in the 1950s, through their affiliation with industry commercialism and its association with corrupted mass cultural formulas, Sirk's soap operas helped represent a kind of zero-degree cinema, against which other films could be judged as successful. Critics constructed the "realist" film, with its perceived platform of social content supported by dramatic plausibility and a suitably expressive style, as an antibody to the common Hollywood virus represented by Sirk.

Similarly, 1970s critics, particularly of the alternative presses, treated certain films of the New American Cinema as negative aesthetic benchmarks on the same grounds. *Star Wars*, a *Voice* cinematic whipping boy of the time, was no more than a "sensationalistic factory product." It stood as an example of pure commercialism, which created escapist fantasies tinged with reactionary politics and manipulated the audience into passive consumption. For Sarris, the "lowest common denominator has become the magic number for success stories in the industry."[66]

From this nucleus, a constellation of films with less overt commercial ambitions and perceived greater complexity emerged as aesthetically superior. There were "Heroes and Villains in the Arts," with filmmakers like Andrej Wajda occupying the former role, George Lucas the latter.[67] Foreign films, particularly those by Wajda, Godard, and filmmakers of the New German Cinema, merited attention on almost everyone's ten-best lists, as well as numerous awards from the New York Critics circle. Such U.S. box-office failures as *New York, New York* (1977) and *Pennies from Heaven* (1981) became critical successes in the *Voice* based on their departure from "the melancholy trend of infantilism" characterizing the mainstream in films such as *The Deep* and *The Other Side of Midnight* (1977).[68] Small-scale ventures like *Heartbeeps* (1981) or *Handle with Care* (1977) were championed because of the affiliations their directors (Allan Arkush and Jonathan Demme) had with independent filmmaking, and their knowing use of film conventions coupled with a lack of inflated ambition.

Critics valued all of these different kinds of films for their opposition to the evils of the film industry: its official optimism and lack of complexity, ambiguity, and realism, as well as its catering to what Molly Haskell (borrowing from Siegfried Kracauer) referred to as an updated "shop girl" mentality—a naive, emotional, and ultimately passive subscription to the desires of the culture industry.[69]

Despite positive changes in critical attitudes toward the mass media given the adversarial and alternative function many served in the 1960s, Adorno and Horkheimer's position toward mass culture still occupied a central role in the more recent reviewers' manner of constituting aesthetic hierarchies. Whereas in the 1950s Sirk's films had been generally reviled as the seat of a "mindless," totalitarian mass culture represented by Hollywood, now some films of the New American Cinema occupied that place. What changed between the two eras of film criticism was not the fundamental manner of creating critical canons; it was rather the *identity of the specific films* that would play the necessary *bête noire* role of Hollywood aesthetic bankruptcy and defilement of audience mentalities. Instead of Sirk, Lucas.

In this way, review journalism in alternative presses maintained the basic structure of aesthetic hierarchies from the past, spun from a notion of a corrupt mass culture. Sirk's appreciation at the time was a product not only of a shift in cultural and critical winds via nostalgia and auteurism; he was also the indirect legatee of a fundamental feature of review aesthetics, which simply required more recent films to represent the zero degree.

There is, finally, one other parallel between the two critical establishments that works against a sense of their absolute differences. While the more contemporary attitudes toward Sirk underwent radical change from the past, this change did not include appreciation of any cathartic pleasures Sirk's melodramas might offer as soap operas. I have suggested that 1950s critics segregated themselves from the masses by repudiating the "natural" enjoyment afforded by products of mass culture through judgments based on a refined sense of realism. What Bourdieu would call such a Kantian "taste of reflection" is as applicable to those in charge of Sirk's later aesthetic salvation. In most critics championing his films' social critique, self-reflexivity, and, in particular, distanciating effects, there is still a refusal of the "vulgar" enjoyments suspected of soap operas. This refusal again functions to divorce the critic from an image of a mindless, hedonistic crowd he or she has actually manufactured in order to definitively secure the righteous logic of "good" taste. It also, as Haskell's remark about shop girls suggests, perpetuates negative notions of female taste and subjectivity. Critiques of mass culture seem always to invoke a disdainful image of the feminine to represent the depths of the corruption of the people.

The process of tastemaking in both historical periods operated, then, to create hierarchical differences between the aesthete and the masses through the construction of canons and aesthetic positions antithetical to the perceived unrestrained and tasteless pleasures of the crowd.

4

Star Gossip

Rock Hudson and the Burdens
of Masculinity

STARS OCCUPY A privileged place in the social apprehension of films in mass culture. Films often attract audiences and remain in the public memory on the basis of celebrity performers (a "Humphrey Bogart" or "Mel Gibson" movie). The prominence of stars in mass media interviews and feature stories strongly enhances their status as significant cultural icons. Indeed, celebrity coverage ranks as one of the most visible, pervasive staples of the mass media, and one of the key forms mediating the relation of people to their culture.

Edgar Morin's work in *Les Stars* introduced the notion that the star phenomenon was best analyzed as a combination of both movie roles and offscreen personality (constructed by studio press releases, magazine stories, etc.).[1] While movie roles could create a certain definition of star persona (such as Lauren Bacall's friendly femme fatale in *To Have and Have Not* [1944]), personal details were at least equally important in adding an aura to stardom (the fact that Bacall and Humphrey Bogart fell in love during the filming of *To Have and Have Not*). Biographical revelations were a constituent part of the celebrity image, creating dimensions of fascination and meaning for stars beyond any specific role they might play. This perspective suggests that to capture a star's meaning, the analyst must attend to an inherent intertextuality spanning from film roles to "extra-filmic" sources depicting the actor's offscreen self. The star thus emerges as a "structured polysemy," a signifying entity composed of multiple but finite meanings, generated by diverse texts and subject to change over time.[2]

By examining the various sources that constitute star identity within specific historical contexts, the theorist can explore the relation between a star's popular meaning and the social function this meaning serves. The star is never a mere celebrity, but a bundle of media constructed traits that reflect cultural preoccupations, whether we consider Shirley Temple and the Great Depression or Marilyn Monroe and 1950s conceptions of female sexuality.[3]

But, aside from the star's significance as a cultural barometer, there is another, equally important dimension of star study. As Richard de Cordova suggests, analyses should ask the question of how the presence of a star affects the reception of a film.[4] The exact relationship between a celebrity's intertextual persona and its impact on viewing a particular film may be difficult to determine with certainty. But the star's strong social presence and ability to attract audiences suggest that it has a particular power over the consumption of artifacts that requires serious consideration.

Rock Hudson: Creating the Image

Of all the stars who have passed through the Sirk universe, including Jane Wyman, Robert Stack, Dorothy Malone, and Lana Turner, Rock Hudson is the actor most identified with this director and his work at Universal Pictures. Hudson gained his first major success in a starring role in *Magnificent Obsession* (1954), and appeared in seven other Sirk/Universal films during the decade: *Has Anybody Seen My Gal?* (1952), *Taza, Son of Cochise* (1954), *Captain Lightfoot* (1955), *All That Heaven Allows* (1955), *Battle Hymn* (1956), *Written on the Wind* (1957), and *Tarnished Angels* (1958).

During this time and into the 1960s, Hudson enjoyed tremendous popularity as a beefcake idol and romantic lead. However, extra-filmic information about him late in his career dramatically transformed this image. In the 1980s, Hudson was the first major celebrity to publicly announce he had been diagnosed with AIDS, revealing his long-hidden homosexuality and virtually dismantling his previous ultraheterosexual identity. Given Hudson's close association with Sirk films, his role in each decade as a central cultural symbol, and the drastic revision of his persona, he represents a particularly compelling case with which to explore the impact star discourse has on the meaning of Sirk's melodramas. I will thus analyze the media's construction of Hudson's persona in the 1950s and 1980s— the two moments in his career when he attained his greatest social importance—to examine how his star image affected the perception of Sirk's films within such different historical contexts.

While it is very tempting to look on the 1950s ironically, equipped with 1980s revelations about Hudson's gay identity, an ironical approach to the decade could easily disregard Hudson's actual importance to postwar culture. During the 1950s, Hudson had the kind of iconographical sexual significance critics usually associate with the more flamboyant types represented by Marilyn Monroe, Elvis Presley, and Marlon Brando. In contrast to these figures, Hudson embodied a certain brand of sexual normalcy, a normalcy every bit as important in defining the tenor of the times as the more excessive. As I will later argue, Hudson's image functioned defensively against changing conceptions of masculine power and sexuality in the post–World War II era. In a society obsessively concerned with the problem of male "weakness," posed as a result of such social specters as the "modern woman" and the "homosexual menace," the media developed Hudson's image as proof of the widespread appeal and endurance of uncomplicated virility. They helped sustain, that is, a certain brand of traditional masculinity in the face of great public turmoil over appropriate social and sexual behavior for men.

Between 1948 and 1959, when he began his career with a bit part in Raoul Walsh's *Fighter Squadron* and enjoyed the heights of his popularity with *Pillow Talk*, Hudson appeared in nearly forty films. Most of his early appearances were bit parts until he caused a sensation among female fans with his small role as a gambler in Anthony Mann's *Bend of the River* (1952). After this, he secured the lead in a number of films from 1952 to 1954, including *Scarlet Angel* and *The Lawless Breed*. But it was not until *Magnificent Obsession* that his leading man status intertwined successfully with that of romantic heartthrob. *Magnificent Obsession* grossed eight million dollars, and Hudson reportedly started receiving three thousand fan letters a week from teens and older women. While critics frequently related Hudson's appeal to his "good looks," his acting ability received short shrift until *Giant* (1956), for which he received an Academy Award nomination for best actor.

Hudson's box-office stature after 1953 was manifested in the numerous magazine and industry honors he received, as well as by his prominence in magazine coverage. He was voted the most popular male movie star by *Modern Screen* in 1954, *Look* in 1955, *Photoplay* in 1957, and by theater owners the same year. From 1957 to 1964, the Film Buyers of the Motion Picture Industry consistently named him the number one box-office attraction, which meant that audiences bought more tickets for his movies than anyone else's. Magazine features helped declare his unequivocal popular status: among almost countless others, *People*, *Look*, and *Life* each ran cover stories on Hudson, respectively titled "Rock Hudson: No. 1 Lover," "Rock Hudson: Why He's No. 1," and "Hollywood's Most Handsome Bachelor."[5] Hudson was unquestionably the strongest box-office attraction Universal had from the mid-1950s through the early 1960s, and arguably the most popular male star of the time overall (albeit with stiff competition from Cary Grant).

During this period, Hudson appeared in westerns, war films, adventures, costume dramas, romantic comedies, and melodramas. Within these genres, Hudson's roles included American Indians, army officers, swashbucklers, gamblers, bachelors, doctors, journalists, and gardeners. But despite such diversity, Hudson's starring roles emphasized a consistent persona: a strapping, physically appealing, clean-cut, often sensitive, and ultimately morally upright character. The largest role of his early career, that of boxer Speed O'Keefe in *Iron Man* (1951), demonstrated how he would be typecast in his later films. In this film he plays a young, wholesome boxer whose honesty contrasts with a "dirty" fighter played by lead Jeff Chandler. Similarly, in *Bend of the River*, while his character begins as ambiguous in terms of good and evil, by the end of the film he has joined with protagonist Jimmy Stewart and even gets the girl.

Hudson's parts in Sirk films helped cement this persona. In *Taza*, he is the good Indian who allies himself with the white man against other warring Indians to secure peace in the West. In *Magnificent Obsession*, his character (Bob Merrick) begins as a careless playboy who indirectly causes the death of Jane Wyman's husband, and then directly causes her blindness. Stricken with a sense of painful responsibility, inspired selflessness, and love for Helen Phillips (Wyman), he returns to medical school to learn procedures that could restore her vision, eventually saving her sight and her life. *All That Heaven Allows* accentuates the essential simplicity and uncluttered rightness that lay at the center of Hudson's particular kind of masculinity. His character, Ron Kirby, is overtly linked with nature both by his gardening vocation and his lifestyle. Kirby is presented as the "natural man"—earthy, generous, soft-spoken, and unassuming. As someone who rejects social artifice, preferring the woods and down-to-earth friends, he stands in contrast to the cronies of his beloved, Cary Scott (Jane Wyman). Similarly, in *Written on the Wind* and *Tarnished Angels* (despite his drinking problem in the latter), he appears as the personification of stability in contrast to other players tormented by psychological and sexual problems.

Even in films that toyed with his wholesome persona, such as *Magnificent Obsession* and George Steven's *Giant*, in which he plays a bigoted patriarch, the narratives were preoccupied with restoring his "good guy" status. Hence, we see a fairly quick transformation of Merrick from an irresponsible ladies' man to a committed lover and doctor, while *Giant* ultimately finds Hudson's character battling over the rights of Mexican patrons to be served in a white Texas cafe. Like Bette Davis's awaited transformation from dowdy spinster to radiant, independent woman in *Now, Voyager* (1942), Hudson's roles in films like these served to magnify his typage through a kind of dramatic striptease that would eventually reveal the "real" image of the star behind the disguise of the character in question.

Until the release of *Pillow Talk* in 1959, the first in a series of sex comedies with Doris Day that included *Lover Come Back* (1961) and *Send Me No Flowers* (1964), the majority of Hudson's film roles depicted a romantic hero whose relative lack of emotional complexity was matched by generally unerring moral instincts supporting basic social ideas of right and wrong. Although coded visually as beefcake, Hudson's sexual allure remained on the path to monogamous devotion in his early films. The Day/Hudson trilogy and Hudson's other sex comedies of the 1960s founded his second wave of popularity and a new persona—the bachelor playboy—apparently at odds with his earlier, more pristine image, the ramifications of which I shall discuss later.

While film roles were undoubtedly important in providing the contours and appeals of Hudson's star image, extra-filmic coverage added prolific and significant dimensions to this image that clarified how it was to function within the culture at large. As mentioned, Hudson received prodigious press coverage during the 1950s in fan, women's, and general circulation magazines. The kinds of stories appearing in these magazines—behind-the-scenes accounts of the star's personal and romantic life—originated in the story formulas of confession magazines in the 1920s, which focused on intimate revelations about ordinary people's lifestyles and love problems. From confession magazines, fanzines, and scandal rags to respectable middle-class sources, publishers found that such "inside" stories sold. Mass media "gossip" featuring apparently private information about notable people had a sizable market value resting largely on a female public.

Star gossip typically relied on biography as a foundation for its revelations about star lifestyles and romantic status. These biographies were inevitably derived from studio press books which provided the "official" life story of the star. The basic life story tended to chronicle the star's childhood, adolescence and adulthood, building to the moment he or she was discovered by Hollywood. Each step of the chronology was punctuated by facts about his or her romantic relationships. No matter what the variations in the writer's perspective or in particular details included in the account, the same major biographical facts tended to form the basis for most star commentary.[6]

The backbone of the official Hudson biography was comprised by the following information. Hudson was born Roy Scherer on November 17, 1925 in Winnetka, Illinois, in a poor section of a well-to-do neighborhood. His parents divorced when he was four, and he was later adopted by his mother's second husband, Wallace Fitzgerald. His mother subsequently divorced Fitzgerald, a Marine Corps officer whom Roy never liked. From an early age, Roy worked odd jobs to help support the family, including soda jerk and window washer. He was a bad student in high school, but liked by his classmates who remember him as quiet, shy, good-looking, and a "one-woman" man. He was drafted by the Navy, where by almost wrecking a plane, he was transferred to permanent laundry duty. After the Navy, he worked at a post office and as a truck driver. His truck driver friends urged him to try to become a movie star, and through a mutual acquaintance, he was introduced to Henry Willson in 1947, who was in charge of talent for David O. Selznick.

Biographies reported that "When Willson asked him if he could act, Rock told the truth, 'No.' 'Good,' answered Willson." Thus began Hudson's famed transformation at the hands of Willson, who hoped that Hudson's good looks would appeal to female fans. However, as Roy Fitzgerald, he had a crooked eye tooth, a slouch, a bad haircut, a Midwestern twang, and an uninteresting name that had to be changed for this appeal to be truly realized. Willson fixed all of that. As the man who created the names of Tab Hunter and Rory Calhoun, he coined Rock (from the Rock of Gibraltar) and Hudson (from the river), and took charge of necessary cosmetic and locutionary alterations to add finesse to Roy's new identity.

Hudson's career began slowly with a one-liner in *Fighter Squadron*, which allegedly took him thirty-four attempts to get right. After a few more films, he landed the part that made him a screen idol in *Magnificent Obsession*. Since coming to Hollywood, Hudson dated script girl Betty Abbott, starlets Vera Ellen, Terry Moore and Julia Adams, and Henry Willson's secretary, Phyllis Gates (whom Hudson married in 1955 and divorced in 1958).

Fanzines recounted these details with adulatory rhetoric and often with assurances that theirs was an especially exclusive look into the actor's life. For example, Joe Hyams's "The Rock Hudson Story," published in *Photoplay*, the most successful fan magazine of the decade, offered itself as an unprecedented study of the "real" person behind the star hype. Hyams's purpose was to counter Hudson's simple "beefcake" image by giving an account of his complexity as "a solid, stable, intelligent young man who has built up an almost uncanny ability to take life as it comes and make not only the best but the most of it."[7] Like other star stories, Hyams's biography was intended as a backdrop for an elaborate work of characterization, defining traits, hobbies, and romantic dispositions that would help define the person behind the celebrity. In Hyams's account, Hudson emerged as a handsome, shy, easygoing fellow who "laughs about misfortune." As Hyams wrote, "Rock is and always has been a stranger to worry and anxiety" (91). We learn that Hudson loves music, collects records, dances the jitterbug expertly, and adores food. Hyams established Hudson's tremendous appeal to women with quotes from fans (women who proposed to him or were saving up money to buy him cuff links without their husband's knowledge, etc.), but qualified this hysteria by describing his dating life as selective and seriously focused on one woman at a time.[8]

Despite Hyams's proclaimed desire to counter the beefcake image, his essay joined every other biography in promoting and capitalizing on Hudson's obvious sex appeal to fans by featuring numerous photos of Hudson's naked upper torso, as well as his embraces with co-stars and real-life dates.[9]

Hudson's romantic status in "reel" and "real" life was so important that there were types of essays devoted exclusively to this subject matter: lifestyle and marital status reports. Lifestyle and marital status were often inextricably linked in magazine articles. In the early 1950s, essays on Hudson's bachelor status abounded, as they did for other unmarried male stars. In "How a Hollywood Bachelor Lives," the writer described Hudson's house (a mountaintop glass and redwood structure) and lifestyle (the fact that he is a casual host, barbeques steaks, has parties centered around his player piano, and sleeps in the raw in the summer) to characterize his particular embodiment of a single male's home existence.[10] Supporting photos show him with a dog, in his convertible, and answering the phone outside the shower wrapped in a towel and baring his chest.

After his marriage to Phyllis Gates, the home continued to be the site most revealing about the star.[11] *Photoplay*'s "Planning a Heavenly Love Nest" described Hudson's dream home as a direct extension of his personality. This nest, for example, would be built on high ground, for "a fellow who has . . . wanted an uninterrupted view of whatever world he found himself in." In addition, it would be close to nature (relating to his past as a golf caddy and his summer trips), have an unplanned decor (jokingly referred to as Early Ad Lib), be filled with the kind of chairs he likes ("big, deep and comfortable with a hassock in front so a guy could stretch out and take it easy"), and be free from draperies with fringe and doilies ("Rock's dislike for these decorations was developed at an early age" when he visited an older woman's house decorated in this manner and tipped over a Christmas tree).[12] Despite his marriage, this essay was at pains to sustain an image of "free" masculinity for his fans by so strategically minimizing any sense of domesticating feminine influence in decor.

Press coverage of Hudson, then, generally depicted his humble Midwestern origins, uncomplicated personality, love of nature and the simple pleasures of life, and his appealing manliness. Throughout, Hudson emerges as a rather unexceptional fellow except for his torso. This depiction owed partially to the studio's desire to conform to contemporary public tastes about stardom in the post–World War II era. During this time, the public resented the aristocratic profile of the star that traditionally had been generated by Hollywood publicity. The film industry responded by portraying the "real" lives of its stars through ordinary, domestic, middle-class imagery.[13] But Hudson's media identity owed more strongly to other factors that better explain his tremendous popularity and particular significance to 1950s culture. The media used Hudson to popularize a certain "alternative" conception of masculinity.

An "Alternative" Masculine Ideal

Magazine stories explicitly presented discourse on the home as discourse on the "natural" man. We see Hudson the bachelor living on top of a mountain in a redwood house with a dog, eating steaks. Through such associations with rugged individualism and nature, Hudson emerges as a historical throwback, a quasi—Paul Bunyan figure who has maintained innate masculine characteristics unpolluted by fame or civilization. The description of the "heavenly love nest" in relation to his marriage sustains this impression. Although describing interior decor, a province typically affiliated with domestication and women, the mise-en-scène of the nest is carefully described in terms that evacuate the feminine. The unplanned, disorganized decor, chairs structured for men, and an absolute rejection of anything feminine like doilies and fringe, attest to the domination of a pure masculine ethos opposed to cultivation. Such elaborations corresponded nicely to the wholesome roles Hudson played in 1950s films, particularly his gardener in *All That Heaven Allows*. In addition, while promoting his sex appeal through beefcake photos, the press balanced their flagrant display by consistently downplaying Don Juanism, emphasizing that "Rock is the farthest thing from a 'ladies' man."[14] In this way, Hudson emerged as a wholesome, conventional, ultra-American, and pristine masculine type.

Given such conventional definitions of Hudson's image, why, then, refer to him as an "alternative" masculine ideal? His extra-filmic and filmic identities were so associated with normalcy that there appeared to be absolutely nothing different about him. However, when we place his image in the context of the 1950s, the reasons for his "alternative" label become clearer.

As Richard Dyer has pointed out, the popularization of psychoanalysis in the 1940s and 1950s inflected prior brooding, introspective portraits of masculinity in stars affiliated with the Romantic tradition (such as Valentino) with an overtly neurotic twist.[15] The best known "psycho-stars" of the 1950s—Montgomery Clift, Marlon Brando, and James Dean—presented a tormented version of masculinity, characterized by emotion, violence, and a brutal interrogation of self-identity and social convention. Even actors who previously had been defined as all-American heroes, such as James Stewart and John Wayne, appeared in semi-psychotic roles that challenged their prior wholesome characterizations (such as, respectively, *The Naked Spur* [1953] and *The Searchers* [1956]).

There were those biographers of Hudson who attempted to attach him to this trend of the new romantic hero. One writer, for example, uncovered Hudson's fear of performing, bouts with anxiety, and suppressed anger.[16] Such accounts probably related Hudson to the more obviously troubled and increasingly appealing personas of young actors like Dean and Brando, modifying his persona to compete in a world of attractive neurotics. But such presentations never overtook the simplicity incarnate Hudson profile, Hyams's description of Hudson as a "stranger to worry and anxiety." To most fans, Hudson was "the boy next door, the captain of the football team, and favorite Hollywood hero."[17] In addition, Hudson's press coverage could not have been at more complete odds with the equally prolific star gossip on Brando and Dean.

Although both Brando and Dean came from the Midwest as well, reporters found nothing prosaic or admirable about their off-camera behavior. Brando's antics alone were prodigious. They included the constant presence of his pet raccoon, Russell, feeding raw eggs to a kitten on a hotel dining room table, yoga exercises on hotel lawns, setting off firecrackers in hotel lobbies and strolling through them with his head encased in a rubber monster mask, running broad jumps into pools, rude silences, messy clothes, and wild stories about eating grasshoppers and gazelle eyes.[18] These activities perhaps overshadowed Dean's penchant for beating tom-toms on table tops, setting fire to napkins or pouring bowls of sugar in his pocket if he felt he was not getting enough attention at restaurants.[19]

Hence, Brando acquired a "screwball" reputation that reporters linked to a "completely uninhibited animal nature, born of a Bohemian upbringing,"[20] while Dean could be labeled, even amidst the adulation he enjoyed after his death, "sadistic, uncouth, arrogant, cruel, and a filthy slob."[21]

Brando's unconventionality, like Dean's, even caused reporters to psychoanalyze them. A scandal magazine, *Rave*, declared Brando the "world's worst lover." This report claimed that Brando's love life was a "mess" because he happened to be "one of the most neurotic and unfortunate men, a dyed-in-the-bedsheets Don Juan." Calling his "inadequacies" as a lover more psychic than physical, the writer cited psychiatric opinion of Don Juanism, which finds that it is rooted in "doubt of one's own virility, and a loveless childhood." The future of his love life depended "on what luck he has on the psychoanalyst's couches he's been resting his curly head on lately."[22] Such speculations were probably only enhanced by mass coverage of Brando's nervous breakdown and his treatment by a psychiatrist in 1954 before the filming of *The Egyptian*, in which he was scheduled to star. Dean's sociopathic behavior was attributed to the "confusion of adolescence," which turned him into "a sullen, bad-mannered rebel."[23] However, for some, "there was nothing in (his) boyhood to account for the eccentricities, exhibitionism, and downright bad manners" that Dean later acquired in Hollywood.[24]

While the psychoanalytic examination of these actors by the popular press no doubt generated excitement in fans over their "bad boy" appeal, it also served as a means of explaining and defusing the Brando/Dean assaults on civilized behavior and social norms as the conduct of "sick," maladjusted people. Magazine information on Hudson often acted exactly in the spirit of this sort of defensive gesture. That is, constructions of his image presented him as an alternative to the psychoanalytic romantic hero, a testimony to the continuing appeal of the normal in the face of disturbing new trends in male stardom. Above all, the Hudson persona communicated a masculinity that was always nonthreatening and that supported the tradition of a "clean-cut," masculine ethic. He was seen as providing relief from many actors of the time who "have been sensitive and spooky like Jimmy Dean; the public got tired of decay. So now here's Rock Hudson. He's wholesome. He doesn't perspire. . . . He smells of milk. His whole appeal is cleanliness and respectability—this boy is pure."[25]

The role of Hudson as foil to the psychoanalytic tenor of post–World War II Hollywood was nowhere more apparent than in an essay in the fan magazine *Filmland*, which I quote at some length because of its particular relevance here. Ironically titled "Hollywood Exposé," this article featured Rock Hudson, George Nader (another young, aspiring Universal star), and their dates on a picnic. The article began, "Hollywood a crazy, mixed-up town? Peopled by oddballs and weirdies? Let's take a look at four typical citizens. . . . Sorry to disappoint you."

> In a madhouse town, where battiness is practically a vogue, these two guys are terrifically, sensationally, super-colossally normal. This makes them the odd ones. After all, when everybody else is talking about his psychiatrist, his divorce, or his love affairs, these two haven't a thing to say. . . . Rock and George resent being thought strange simply because they act like normal citizens and avoid the pill-taking, psychiatrist-seeing gang like the plague. With a lot of other normal outcasts, they live in Hollywood just as they would in Anytown, U.S.A."[26]

Some captions to photos of the picnic read, "Hey, we nearly forgot the lemonade"; "Rock, George, and their dates devour a lunch of sandwiches, chicken, fruit, and milk": and "Nader's good boy scout training," as he cleans up.

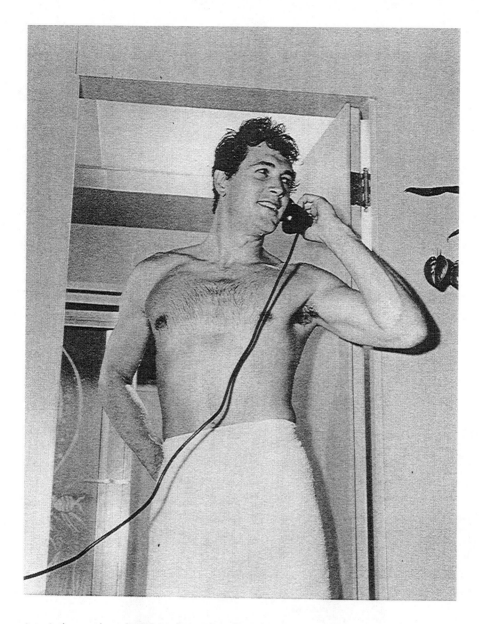

A typical torso shot of Rock Hudson. Photo by Sid Avery, © 1952. Motion Picture and Television Photo Archive.

The middle-class pleasures of a Hollywood bachelor. Photos by Sid Avery, © 1952. Motion Picture and Television Photo Archive.

Here, the term exposé is reversed in its usual association with shocking facts to refer to the continued presence of normality in a sea of disintegrating personalities. The picnic is a bit of Americana that invokes "a happy, normal, good time," a boy-scoutish banquet with lemonade and milk, pre-sexual, uncomplicated in its pleasures, and apparently nature's answer to psychiatric therapy. Such a perspective also served as the basis of a *Saturday Evening Post* spread featuring a game of charades and a backyard barbeque with Hudson and his friends.[27] Through this kind of iconography, wholesome Hudson appeared as a kind of antidote to an overdose of unstable oddballs—drugged, divorced, and uncertain of their identities.

Another look at Hudson's film roles confirms how extra-filmic and cinematic images joined together in endorsing this function. Hudson's film persona was almost absolutely foreign to the neuroses and violence characterizing the screen male during this period. Even in films like *Magnificent Obsession* and *All That Heaven Allows*, in which he falls in love with an older woman, the Oedipal alarm bells that could easily go off with a Paul Newman or James Dean are muffled by Hudson's image of stalwart normalcy. Further, in many roles, Hudson specifically represented a moral and psychological counterpoint to the deep chaos and social rebellion represented by the psychoanalytic male. This is evident in his pairings with neurotic characters—for example, the alcoholic, symbolically castrated, and Thanatos driven Stack in *Written on the Wind* and *Tarnished Angels*; the power hungry and potentially sexually subversive Dean in *Giant*; and the incestuous Kirk Douglas in *The Last Sunset* (1961).

In each of these films, Hudson not only provides the voice of reason, but acts as an ideological anchor of sanity. Even in his later sex comedies, his zestful bachelor contrasts with other male characters who have therapists. In *Lover Come Back*, for example, Tony Randall plays a businessman who cannot exercise his power effectively and says things like, "My psychiatrist gave me that walking stick to build my confidence." Hence, film pairings often acted out the same drama between Hudson's relative psychological stability and the neurotic Other found in star gossip.

As is clear from these last examples, Hudson's normalcy did not operate simply to counterpoint psychoanalytic inflections of masculinity. Randall's remark about his walking stick relied for its humor on the stick's obvious compensatory phallic significance for a character whose neurosis was clearly linked to emasculation. In the post–World War II era, social critics often equated troubled masculinity with weakness, and this weakness, in an ascending spiral of possibilities, could lead to perversion and homosexuality. On a deeper level, Hudson's image represented a "healthy," that is, solidly heterosexual, masculinity

A last minute check of the provisions, and this happy foursome are off on a picnic. George Nader's date for the day is pretty Mara Corday. "Hey, we nearly forgot the lemonade," says George.

Both George and Rock love the desert country, so they decided to have their picnic in a desert oasis. After a short trek they found the perfect spot. Rock's next role is Metro's "Something of Value."

HOLLYWOOD EXPOSÉ

Phyllis made lots of sandwiches and both boys are camera fans, so there was plenty to unload. "We picnic in high style," laughs Rock.

Beating the ants to it, four hungry people demonstrate their hearty appetites as they devour a lunch of sandwiches, chicken, fruit, milk.

HOLLYWOOD EXPOSÉ

Rock Hudson is a movie fan as well as a movie star. Here he shoots his pet subject—wife Phyllis. Rock is great in UI's "Battle Hymn."

You can see George's good boy scout training has stuck as he cleans up. He has just completed filming UI's "Four Girls in Town."

Excerpts from "Hollywood Exposé": The simplicity and sanity of Americana, *Filmland*, April 1957, courtesy of the Academy of Motion Picture Arts and Sciences.

within Cold War perceptions about the deterioration of virility and its implications for national power and familial stability.

Specifically, cultural concerns about male weakness tended to be expressed in relation to two male types: the homosexual and the breadwinner. The homosexual and the family man were subjected to intense scrutiny, always as subjects of a sexual pathology underwritten by anxieties about emasculation. By the end of the war, the continuing assimilation of Freud and the popularity psychiatry had gained after widespread psychiatric screenings of armed forces inductees helped develop notions of sick and healthy behavior that invaded the public consciousness. Further, what was defined as sick often centered on deviations from normative ideals of proper male and female roles.[28] In a culture still uncertain about the success of postwar civilian readjustments and enmeshed in a Cold War that left its powers somewhat in question, the definition of gender roles attained paramount importance, particularly because of their implicit affiliation with social stability. Concomitantly, "failures" at assuming proper gender responsibilities, such as wife and mother or father and breadwinner, caused congressmen, sociologists, psychologists, and other professionals to pathologize deviations and ponder their destructive effects on national security.

As mentioned in chapter 2, homosexuality became much more publicly visible after the war due to an amalgam of factors. These included same-sex experiences during the war, the Kinsey reports which affirmed the prevalence of nonheterosexual behavior, books such as Donald Webster Cory's *The Homosexual in America* and Allen Ginsberg's *Howl*, and an efflorescence of films such as *Rope* (1948), *Tea and Sympathy* (1956), *The Strange One* (1957), and *Cat on a Hot Tin Roof* (1958), which offered barely suppressed representations of homosexuality.

That homosexuality became a demonic pathology through its affiliation with communism at this time is by now a familiar fact. According to John D'Emilio, the link between homosexuality as a pathology and communist ideology was forged in 1950 in a congressional hearing about the loyalty of government employees, which discovered that many dismissed for "moral turpitude" were homosexuals.[29] With the help of a general climate fascinated by both sexual pathologies and the Cold War, Senator Joseph McCarthy escalated this finding into an equation between "moral turpitude," disloyalty, and communist subversion. This series of relationships further demonized communism by aligning it with sexual depravity, at the same time as it heightened anxieties over homosexuality by characterizing it as a serious social menace and threat to national security.

This politicizing of a socially defined pathology had a definite impact on images of masculinity at the time. As Elaine Tyler May has written, "National strength depended on the ability of strong manly men to stand up against communist threats . . . 'perverts' . . . presumably, had no masculine backbone."[30] While Mickey Spillane's Mike Hammer might stand as too extreme a version of this anti-communist macho, concepts of a sound nation were nonetheless inextricably bound to a gender morality that bestowed the imprimatur of virility, incorruptibility, sanity, and patriotism on male heterosexuality. Within this logic, "unmasculine" behaviors such as homosexuality bore the taint of a debilitated moral fiber that made certain individuals susceptible to communist propaganda, and hence, by implication, weakened an entire nation.

The second instance of public anxiety about male weakness, that concerning the breadwinner, was similarly subtended by fears of homosexuality. This time the well-being of the family, always the symbolic subunit of the nation, was the focus.

Psychiatric theory defined adult masculinity strictly in terms of the breadwinner role—the husband and father who earned a living for his family and thus assumed family responsibilities. At best, failure to achieve this role signaled immaturity; at worst, it indicated impaired manhood. In the psychological terms of the time, "immaturity shaded into infantilism, which was, in turn, a manifestation of unnatural fixation on the mother . . . [reaching] its clinical climax in the diagnosis of homosexuality."[31] This perverted family romance led to a series of equations: "I am a failure = I am castrated = I am not a man = I am a woman = I am a homosexual."[32] A refusal of marriage and its attendant commitments often cast dire suspicions, then, on the masculinity of those indulging in such "irresponsible" behavior.

Once men attained the desired status of breadwinner, however, their psychologies were no less subject to the scrutiny of apprehensive professionals. Certainly, the coercive conformity perceived to be at the heart of postwar corporate enterprise raised fears about the loss of rugged individualism and manhood. Best-selling books such as David Riesman's *The Lonely Crowd* (1950) and Sloan Wilson's *The Man in the Gray Flannel Suit* (1955) sounded the alarm about the effects of conformism on society.[33]

But the shrillest analysis of the problems of the family man linked his failure to the looming presence of the "modern woman." According to some contemporary writers, the modern woman enjoyed increased authority in society due to a number of developments. Among these were: changing conceptions of home life that found her sharing housework and decision-making with her husband in a new spirit of democracy, her increased participation in the work force, and her growing prominence as a sexual being with equal right to satisfaction in the bedroom. According to some, the modern woman's emancipation directly and negatively affected the psychology of the U.S. man, who found he had to submit to "petticoat rule."

An article in *Look* magazine called "The American Male: Why Do Women Dominate Him?" revealed this ideology with candor. Citing social scientist David Riesman, anthropologist Margaret Mead, scientist Alfred Kinsey, motivational researcher Ernest Dichter, and other professionals, this essay produced evidence that women's roles were changing in such a way that they had more power, which they often chose to exercise as a series of harmful demands on men. Of particular concern was woman's "new sexual aggressiveness," resulting in the sexual domination of men. Selectively culling facts from the above authors—that women regulated the extent of physical contact, that they made birth control decisions, and that they expected sexual satisfaction on par with their husbands—*Look* defined the impact of this new aggressiveness on men. Men suffered symptoms that ranged from fatigue, passivity, and anxiety (about satisfying women) to impotence and the Freudian "flight from masculinity" that resulted in homosexuality. By exercising her powers, the modern woman could thus "seriously damage his male capacity." Unsexed by failure, the male's potency declines. The author concludes by warning, "We are drifting toward a structure made up of he-women and she-men."[34]

The family man had, then, a difficult double duty to fulfill. On the one hand, he was to be eminently mature and responsible, while on the other, he was to safeguard his family against any imbalance in internal power relations that would threaten proper gender roles and disastrously confuse sexual identity.

In this way, definitions of masculinity were at the center of ideological turmoil over the health of the nation and the family.[35] Through contemporary psychoanalytic thinking, debate obsessively detected a causal relation between new social developments in the Cold War era—from the greater visibility of homosexuals and the modern woman to a business world oriented toward the corporate group—and the emasculation of the U.S. male. In their respective national and familial contexts, the manly man and the responsible patriarch represented militant ideological icons, armed against the subversive infringements on traditional concepts of masculinity signified by male neurosis and its logical terminus in homosexuality.

There were 1950s films that overtly dealt with anticommunist macho (such as *Kiss Me Deadly* [1955]) and the social dangers of weak paternal function (such as *My Son John* [1952]).[36] Hudson's films and star gossip lacked such an explicit Cold War rhetoric. But they nonetheless resonated with reigning definitions of what constituted appropriate masculinity and often the stake of deviation from the desirable norm. For the postwar era, Hudson represented the quintessence of the manly man, the Great Straight Hope in an environment increasingly defined by changing and contested conceptions of manliness.

As U.S. society continued to grapple with sex roles and identities in the 1960s, Hudson's conservative function only sharpened. As Vito Russo has argued in relation to his 1960s films, Hudson's emblematic virility came to be used as a means of ridiculing and supplanting "weaker" versions of masculinity that frequently hinted at homosexuality.[37] The pairings of Hudson with Tony Randall in his three comedies with Doris Day, with Gig Young in *Strange Bedfellows* (1965), or Dick Shawn in *A Very Special Favor* (1965) placed him unequivocally in relation to actors whose physiques and roles conveyed an "impaired" masculinity. Whereas the Stacks, Deans, and Brandos offered attractive images of masculinity with which the Hudson image had to compete, these sex comedies emptied the neurotic male of any sexual allure, pushing his characterization into an unrelieved parody of male capability.

Contrasting characterizations provided one forum for the specter of the feminized male to appear in these sex comedies. But Hudson's characters themselves were also associated with homosexuality. A running gag through *Pillow Talk* finds Hudson mistaken for a man of confused sexual identity by the medical establishment, as he appears in a ladies room, a gynecology and obstetrics waiting room, and as he announces, "I'm going to have a baby," at the end of the film to a doctor who carts him off for observation. In *Lover Come Back*, he has to stroll through a hotel lobby in a mink, the only thing he could find to wear after Doris Day stranded him naked at the seaside. Upon seeing him, two men who had been observing his sexual exploits throughout the film remark, "He's the last guy in the world I would have figured." And in *A Very Special Favor*, Hudson pretends to go off with another man to a love tryst as a means of making Leslie Caron feel guilty about her attempts to emasculate him.

It is debatable, however, whether these plays with Hudson's sexual identity seriously tamper with his established persona. In one sense, the incongruity between his virile persona and the possibility of "compromised" masculinity is responsible for securing the jest, an incongruity already heightened by the overall contrast between Hudson and Randall or Shawn. The jest is carried out, in addition, as a clear case of mistaken or assumed identity, a charade. But perhaps more important, in accord with the *Playboy* ethos, Hudson's new playboy image enabled a depiction of the single male that was so heterosexually fixated that it helped relieve the homosexual implications that had been attached to bachelorhood earlier in the 1950s. Since his bachelor status always terminated at the end of the film with marriage and a passel of kids, the inevitability of heterosexual monogamy as a social norm still held sway. Thus, despite the sexual confusion at the heart of the comedy in these films, Hudson's manliness survived the humor as eminently heterosexual and ultimately family oriented.

While film roles might joke about Hudson's sexual identity, star gossip, almost unequivocally straight in its representation of the actor through the 1960s, left few doubts as to his personification of the manly man. Extra-filmic coverage could attempt to reveal his neuroses (such as stagefright and anger). But, as we have seen, it most often presented him as uncontaminated by traits that might tamper with his healthy manliness. By detailing such things as the Bunyan-esque decor of his home, devoid of any feminine accoutrements, his participation in the small-town, bucolic ritual of the picnic or barbeque, his monogamous disposition, and his difference from "spooky" types like James Dean, star gossip created a male image that was simultaneously distinctly American, traditionally masculine, de-feminized, and antineurotic. The continual presentation of Hudson as beefcake operated to make all this "normality" hyper-virile and sexy.

Characterizations of male stars both in and out of films were often, then, deeply informed by Cold War rhetoric about masculinity. "Is Tony Perkins a Mama's Boy?" and "How Rock Hudson Dodges Dangerous Dames" blared the headlines for one magazine in 1957, indulging once again in contrasts between male types distinctly rooted in sexual disposition.[38] At the same time as the new ultra-emotional, neurotic male star was rewriting the kind of masculine appeal represented by prewar types, he invoked postwar anxieties about the national and social repercussions of maladjusted masculinity.

We can thus regard Hudson's popularity during the 1950s and early 1960s as owing in good measure to the fact that he reinforced notions of "normal" masculinity in the face of growing public evidence that masculinity was under siege. Since, in Cold War terms, this crisis had dire implications for the continuation of the American way of life, Hudson's strong media presence reassured the public through an apparently unchanged and unchangeable facade of exemplary manliness, marked by sanity and status quo sexuality. Hudson was in this sense the veritable "Rock," a sign of the stability of certain old-fashioned notions of the "natural man" uncontaminated by complex social developments.

Star Vehicles and Sirk

What impact could Hudson's social signification have had on Sirk's melodramas? One possible answer to this question concerns the diegetic function of his presence in these films. Genre critics have often seen the depiction of normalcy as intentionally boring and parodic in post–World War II cinema, so much so that it seems to help indict dominant ideological values, rather than salvage them.[39] In addition, the normal operates as an insipid backdrop against which more exciting, dangerously subversive forces take ideological center stage—such as the femme fatale's or neurotic's challenge to the family in film noir and melodrama, respectively. In critical discourse, diabolically flashy characters have tended to overshadow the normal (banal), acting as evidence for the transgressive ideological meaning of these genres.

In this vein, Sirk critics have often treated Sirk's "split" characters such as Robert Stack (Kyle) and Dorothy Malone (Marylee) in *Written on the Wind*, as charismatic signifiers of the subversive politics of his films. "Split" characters have a kind of schizophrenia, an internal divisiveness that fuels the emotional complexity of the family melodrama (such as Kyle's desire for paternal respect which is undone by his alcoholic compulsions). This divisiveness leads to violent confrontations with familial and social orders that Sirk critics have read progressively as ideological critique. The "split" character's counterpart is the one-dimensional, relatively uncomplicated, "immovable" character, played frequently by Rock Hudson, who acts as a dull foil to the former's fascinating destructiveness.[40]

However, if we consider how strongly Hudson's image was freighted with the *appeal* of the normal, how the normal in turn was posed as such a crucial defense against shifting sexual tides, and how the abnormal itself, though exciting, could conjure up the specter of social disaster, we could imagine a different ideological chemistry between "split" and "immovable" characters in these films. In this revised chemistry, the latter would attain a strong degree of parity with the former, qualifying the ideological impact of what critics have seen as the overpowering presence of the misfit.

When placed more fully within historical context, though, we can see that the significance of Hudson's image was not that it totalized the meaning of Sirk's films in some new way. Rather, his star semiosis joined a number of other ideological meanings circulating around and through these melodramas during the 1950s. It was the particular social function of Hudson's image to embody reactionary protest against postwar transformations in male sexuality, while giving the normal a certain persuasive attractiveness. But, as I have argued in chapter 2, the crazed or sexy character had a charisma of its own, invoking voyeuristic pleasures focused on the objectification of the female body and on the sensationalizing of intimate stories. Whether we examine the climate of sexual display or Cold War anxieties about masculinity, Hudson's case continues to suggest that films serve as sites for the confluence of various, sometimes contradictory, ideological concerns. Sirk's films could at the same time act as a forum for the titillation of psychological and sexual excess and as a commentary on the virtues of sanity and normative gender identity.

But the diegetic implications of Hudson's image do not exhaust his impact on the film experience. As we have seen in previous chapters, extra-filmic, social productions of meaning create modes of engagement with films that digress from the narrative proper.[41] Whether through the publicity of sexuality, consumer items, or, in this case, stars, the intertextual network surrounding films and spectators adds a significant dimension to viewing that is not driven solely by film dynamics. As Miriam Hansen so aptly writes in her work on Valentino, "By activating a discourse external to the diegesis, the star's presence enhances a centrifugal tendency in the viewer's relation to the film text. The star's performance weakens the diegetic spell in favor of a string of spectacular moments that display the essence of the star."[42] Hence, the extra-filmic presentations of the star's body, background, personality, etc. inspire a rapture with the image that takes the viewer beyond the horizons of the narrative, encouraging a spectacle-driven sensibility that derives pleasure in a sporadic, alinear, anarrative manner.

When reconsidering the presence of the "strapping" Hudson body in Sirk's films in this light, we can suppose that it created a series of tableaus of desire for the viewer, attracted to the essence of healthy masculinity that Hudson's persona and physical representations in his publicity signified. For the female fan at least, to whom Hudson's publicity was largely addressed, his image could serve as a catalyst for a series of extra-filmic adventures of the imagination that related his diegetic presence to the lore offered by the publicity machine. In this process, his filmic presence offered an arena of fantasy and pleasure for the viewer, rooted in the vision of the virile boy-next-door. Through these viewing dynamics Sirk's films were truly reduced to star vehicles, contexts for the exercise of a sensibility fixed on the appearance and subsequent imaginary romance with a star who typified certain masculine ideals.

1964–1984: Beyond Popularity

As I mentioned at the outset of the chapter, I am focusing on two decades here—the 1950s and the 1980s—since they were the periods in which Hudson attained his greatest social and media prominence. While I do not have the space to analyze the intervening years in detail, I would like to give the reader some sense of what transpired in his career during this time before turning to the 1980s.

After the spate of highly successful comedies Hudson did with Doris Day, his popularity diminished substantially. His reign as number one at the box office ended in 1964, and by 1967, he had completely dropped off the Film Buyer's box-office attraction chart. Hudson continued to make a few comedies, and notably John Frankenheimer's drama *Seconds* (1966), but his comedies fizzled, and his dramatic roles dwindled in number. By the late 1960s, Hudson tended to appear in action genres that underscored a more authoritative, less romantic status. These included *Tobruk* (1967), a war film; *Ice Station Zebra* (1968), a Cold War thriller; and *The Undefeated* (1969), a western. In these, he played a veteran overseeing a "world of men," that is, casts made up almostly exclusively of male characters. In *Ice Station Zebra*, Hudson starred with Ernest Borgnine, Patrick MacGoohan, football player Jim Brown, and Lloyd Nolan. Similarly, in *The Undefeated*—set after the Civil War with Hudson and John Wayne cast, respectively, as Confederate and Union colonels—other actors included grizzly old-timer Ben Johnson and more football players—this time Merlin Olsen and Roman Gabriel. The combination of male action genre, his status as protagonist/commander, and the wide world of sportsmen in which he often found himself, further reified his association with a straight brand of masculinity. While no doubt subtended by the latent homosexuality implicit in the "buddy" film (an impression magnified by our present knowledge of Hudson's sexual preference), Hudson's image grew more overtly "macho."

Hudson's fortunes in the 1970s lay with television, particularly his role in "McMillan and Wife" (1971–1976) and "McMillan" (1976–1977). He played Stewart McMillan, a police commissioner in San Francisco married, until the 1976/1977 season, to Susan St. James. This series blended the comedy of marriage with crime detection, combining aspects of his prior roles from romantic comedies with his status as patriarch accrued from his post-1950s performances. But this period also saw Hudson entering the definitive "has-been" stage of his film career. During the 1970s, he appeared in an exploitation/horror film, *Embryo* (1976) and producer Roger Corman's disaster film, *Avalanche* (1978). In 1980, he starred in *The Mirror Crack'd*, from an Agatha Christie story that played self-reflexively on aged stars of the 1950s. Hudson was cast as Jason Rudd, a movie director married to Elizabeth Taylor. Besides recalling Hudson's pairing with Taylor in *Giant*, the film featured two other big stars of the 1950s, Kim Novak and Tony Curtis. The exploitation films and the Agatha Christie appearance, both legendary forums for has-been stars, signified the demise of Hudson's film career, his inability to draw all but the most marginal audiences as a leading man.

With one exception, extra-filmic coverage of Hudson during this period was sparse. The exception was the rumor of Hudson's secret wedding to Jim Nabors in 1971. This created the first major public rift in Hudson's ultra-heterosexual image. The story was picked up by the press and caused such a stir that Hudson had to publicly denounce it as false. CBS canceled Nabor's variety show, but Hudson's career and "McMillan and Wife" remained untouched. While magazines might later casually broach the issue of sexual preference in stories on Hudson, as *People* magazine did in 1982, they mainly resorted to more conventional topics in their reportage on the star.[43]

Like 1950s sources, the press continued to write about Hudson's personality and lifestyle, but with a particular emphasis on him as an expert on classic Hollywood, able to provide behind-the-scenes information on what it was like to be a studio star in the past. In these stories, we still find biography and character portraits confirming his unassumingness and generosity, accompanied by photos of him with dogs in nature. But we also discover that he is freer now that he is out from under the control of the studios—in his language, dress, and behavior.[44] Among other things, Hudson debunked the cherished myth of the star discovery (such as Lana Turner sitting in a drugstore), discussed his resistance to roles he was forced to play (such as *Taza, Son of Cochise*), and commented on the difference between film and television.[45] By treating Hudson as a seasoned Hollywood veteran, the press transformed him into a kind of historical artifact—in keeping, as we have seen, with the 1970s nostalgic interest in Old Hollywood. Thus, between the 1950s and 1980s, Hudson's image entertained some flux without any serious constitutional changes, despite the Nabors incident. While his social centrality diminished substantially, he was quietly enshrined as a piece of Hollywood history.

The 1980s: Reversal

The issue of Hudson's sexuality was dramatically resolved on July 25, 1985. French publicist Yanou Collart announced that Hudson was in Paris for AIDS treatment, having been diagnosed more than a year earlier in June 1984. What followed was a furor that one writer compared to the media melee during the Beirut hostage crisis.

The impact of this announcement was dramatic, but not only because of the controversial nature of AIDS. The virus was suddenly connected to a sensational case of celebrity image-reversal, as well as to the issue of representativeness. That is, on the one hand, the announcement precipitated a vertiginous reversal of Hudson's image as a public emblem of masculinity and celebratory hetero-sexuality. As *People* magazine put it,

> As the first public figure to announce his affliction with acquired immune deficiency syndrome, Hudson had stunned the world and shattered an image cultivated over three decades . . . for fans who knew him onscreen it was hard to reconcile the image of the indestructible and quintessential '50s movie star with that of the insidious and quintessential '80s disease.[46]

On the other hand, because a star (a super-human, invulnerable type) had gotten the disease, the implications were that anyone could be susceptible: "If a wealthy celebrity can get it, who's safe?"[47] And it was not just any celebrity. With Hudson's diagnosis, it appeared as though "the disease was affecting even all-American types."[48]

It would be hard to underestimate the impact the Hudson announcement and his death a few months later in October had on public awareness of AIDS. Although the AIDS virus had been named in 1984, this breakthrough had been followed by a paucity in media attention, due to the press's continued hesitancy to address "sensitive" homosexual matters. But, as James Kinsella, analyst of the media coverage of AIDS, has documented, Hudson's public admission precipi-tated a 270 percent increase in AIDS reporting by the end of 1985. Because Hudson was an old friend of the Reagans, AIDS "crept onto the agenda of the national political reporters," giving it a bona fide place in journalism and focus-ing unprecedented medical attention on the disease. In addition, Hudson's case even affected national policy. While the Reagan administration had been plan-ning a $10 million cut in the AIDS budget, they now increased it by $100 million.[49]

Hudson thus became the definitive icon of the disease. AIDS hotline callers in Los Angeles referred to it as the "Rock Hudson disease," magazines like *Newsweek* featured cover photos of an emaciated Hudson to accompany issues de-voted to AIDS,[50] and pieces on Hudson's ordeal were accompanied by articles on "regular" people searching for treatment. In addition, *People* magazine's spe-cial issue on twenty people who had defined the 1980s featured Hudson, stating that, "it seemed impossible that one man's fatal infection could transform the public image of AIDS from an alien four-letter word into a shared emergency. But it did."[51]

The social impact of Hudson's death spread in two directions. First, as we have just seen, it mobilized serious and broader media attention on the disease. It was responsible, as one AIDS official commented, "for moving the fight against AIDS ahead more in three months than anything in the past three years."[52] Part of this advance took the form of government spending, as well as AIDS fundraisers, such as Elizabeth Taylor's massive benefit in Hudson's honor, and Hudson's own donations to medical research through his AIDS foundation. While he certainly did not resolve the many problems AIDS victims had to endure because of social prejudice and ignorance, part of the media blitz about Hudson's case helped raise public consciousness. In the process, he became a new kind of hero, a "tragic trailblazer," martyr for a real-life cause.

However, Hudson's affliction and death bred a second response that was not so charitable. In an essay titled "The Media and AIDS Panic: The Post-Hudson Syndrome," Geoffrey Stokes labeled this response "media hysteria," commenting that before Hudson AIDS was nowhere, "now it's everywhere."[53] *The New York Post* ran features titled "AIDS Hits More Hollywood Stars" and "School Cook Dies of AIDS," while the July 1985 issue of *Life* announced, "No One Is Safe from AIDS," and *Newsweek* ran the cover "Fear of AIDS" in September 1985. Journalists proliferated articles about the possibilities of infection in public places—on campus, in prisons, in Hollywood, in the military, and in the work place.

This media hysteria helped generate a "moral panic" over contamination. This panic often arose in relation to concerns over both sexual behavior and professionals who came into contact with blood, such as doctors, dentists, and morticians. But just as frequently, fears of contamination were incited by confusion over the facts of transmission. Sometimes simple contact was perceived as a danger. Thus, bus drivers worried that they might contract the disease from paper bus transfers, social workers were afraid to handle papers from people with AIDS, and patrons stopped going to restaurants with gay waiters.[54]

As AIDS historians and critics tell us, the particular power waged by AIDS contamination fears has its roots in long-standing cultural attitudes toward disease. What Cindy Patton has called "germophobia" in this culture, an irrational, visceral response to the contamination possibilities of germs, was only worsened by the epidemic proportions, sexual origins, and the marginality and "otherness" of those most associated with AIDS (such as homosexuals, IV drug users, prostitutes, and Caribbean nationals). Thus it was that bus drivers, social workers, restaurant patrons, etc. reacted with disgust and paranoiac alarm at the very thought of the most quotidian contact.

But more important, the discourse of contagion served a powerful political ideology. Like both the plague and venereal disease before it, the fear AIDS instilled because of its potential for invasion into the general populace was accompanied by a moralizing discourse that used disease as a means to justify and sustain social differences.[55] This was no more apparent in the contemporary setting than in the New Right's commentary on AIDS, which blamed homosexuality and the modern, sexually liberal society that encouraged it for a new potential apocalypse. From this perspective, AIDS was a just punishment visited on the unjust, a revenge on homosexuality and the sexual revolution. At the same time, its presence ratified the New Right's pro-family platform, the return to "traditional values."

As in the 1950s, right-wing interpretations of homosexuality branded it with the taint of invasive disease that had implications for catastrophic national subversion. Like the "Commie" homosexual, the otherness of AIDS victims seemed to convey the message that *difference* was the problem. It was difference that caused "diseases which have the power to leap social barriers." This logic dictated that the answer to diseased difference would be for individuals "to conform to rigid, traditional standards in order to protect the health of the whole society."[56] Thus, frenzy over contamination fears suited an agenda bent on eradicating social and sexual otherness, while implicitly confirming the rightness and importance of the white, middle-class, nuclear family.

The panicked media response to Hudson's illness, then, helped set off a rhetoric of contamination with historical roots and ideological ramifications. While the sensationalistic coverage of AIDS developed in relation to otherwise legitimate medical and ethical questions raised by the Hudson case, particularly those concerned with transmission and disclosure, it used these issues as a means of profitably capitalizing on cultural paranoia toward disease and nonconformity.

The much-publicized "Dynasty" kiss between Hudson and Linda Evans stands as a case in point. For nine episodes during the 1984–85 season, Hudson appeared on "Dynasty" as Daniel Reece, a wealthy rancher update of his *Giant* image. Although at this point he knew he had AIDS, when the script called for him to kiss Evans, he did, with very little information available about the transmission of the disease and without telling Evans about his diagnosis. This occasion prompted coverage of the means of transmission of AIDS (in this case saliva and non-sexual contact) and the tension between disclosure and the privacy rights of AIDS victims.

"Yellow" presses like *The Enquirer* fixated on the moment of the Hudson/Evans kiss by displaying large, color, cover photos of their embrace which strongly imbued the moment with a sense of deadly contagion and pseudo-ethical outrage. Marc Christian's lawsuit against Hudson's estate for failing to disclose his diagnosis inflamed the disclosure issue substantially, at the same time as it

The much-publicized "Dynasty" kiss.

heightened the sensationalistic aspects of Hudson's personal life. This type of press coverage promoted Hudson as antithetical to heroism, binding Hudson-the-homosexual to a fear of contagion.[57] The fact that this fear was so linked with the kiss, the cornerstone of the major Hollywood convention of heterosexual romance, caused reverberations in the film industry; actresses were reportedly fearful of playing opposite gay actors, and a "legion of actors were facing a groundswell of paranoia."[58]

In both his heroic and plague-associated images, Hudson's social impact in the 1980s rivaled his significance to the 1950s, encouraging liberal and reactionary sentiments alike around a crucial national health crisis. Also, as one might expect, it inspired alterations of his 1950s image. Intertwined with press coverage of Hudson as a medical and ethical subject were the inevitable revisionist biographies designed to reconsider his Hollywood image.

Revising the Image

The 1980s press rewrote Hudson's past according to the revelation that he had always been homosexual. Revisionist forms included the first television docudrama on Hudson telecast in January of 1990,[59] talk shows featuring his friends and ex-lovers, magazine stories, and an authorized biography. The format of these reports recalled 1950s biographies in that the press covered his early childhood, the beginning of his career with Henry Willson, and his rise to fame, accompanied by photos from each period. However, biographies were substantially altered to emphasize his "hidden" life as a gay person; they focused on how the studio protected Hudson by planting stories in fan magazines that emphasized his heterosexuality, by arranging his marriage to Phyllis Gates, and by encouraging his own successful secrecy about his private life.

In keeping with traditions of celebrity journalism, these pieces juxtaposed Hudson's "real" and "reel" lives. But this time they acted not to support the screen image, but to savor the contrast, bringing out the artificiality of classic Hollywood and the romantic roles Hudson played in light of his true sexual orientation. *People*'s cover promised "the other life of Rock Hudson" in a story titled "Rock Hudson: On Camera and Off." The first line of the story read, "The tragic news that he is the most famous victim of an infamous disease, AIDS, unveils the hidden life of a longtime Hollywood hero." The magazine explained that from the start, "Hudson projected one image in front of the camera and another away from it—he has always been gay."[60]

More explicit revisionist work took place outside the framework of magazine publishing. Rock Hudson and Sara Davidson's *Rock Hudson: His Story*, an authorized biography published in 1986, rewrote his history in candid detail.[61] This book follows Hudson through the various stages of his career, concentrating on his homosexual lifestyle and, ultimately, on the details of his affliction with AIDS. We find that it was his first lover in California, Ken Hodge, who urged him to try acting, not truck driver friends as fan magazines had reported, and that Henry Willson was a "notorious homosexual." The story of how Hudson got his name undergoes a similar radical shift. Davidson reports that Hudson's name was coined at a gay party—"Rock" for strength and "Hudson" out of the phone book. In addition, the story of how he got to keep his job in *Magnificent Obsession* after a broken collarbone threatened to keep him off the set involves a liaison with an influential male executive at Universal.

While Hudson's image-reversal is dramatic, I should note that it is not without relation to certain conventions of press coverage of stars. Around the same time that the press was reporting on Hudson and AIDS, it was also doing stories on Ann Jillian's bout with breast cancer, as it had on previous occasions with Happy Rockefeller, Betty Ford, and Jill Ireland. One has only to think of John Belushi's drug overdose, Len Bias's death from cocaine, or Drew Barrymore's drug addiction to realize how prevalent such star coverage was during this period, and continues to be with more recent examples such as Michael Landon's death from cancer and Magic Johnson's diagnosis with HIV. Hudson was very much a part of the "sick star" convention by which the media elaborated social problems via celebrities. Similarly, sensationalistic exposés of stars' private lives are a publishing mainstay. From the "kiss and tell" accounts of Shelly Winters or Zsa Zsa Gabor to biographies detailing Cary Grant's bisexuality, the exposé is part of a publicity machine focused on celebrities.

But even given these commonplaces of star stories, Hudson's case is especially powerful because its obliteration of his 1950s identity afforded more than just a revealing glimpse into Hollywoodiana. It was inextricably bound to a shared, and in some people's minds scandalous, health crisis. Whereas Grant's bisexuality could actually suit his suave image of the 1940s and 1950s, Hudson's homosexuality directly affronted the public's conception of him as a romantic (that is, heterosexual) icon. Hudson's image-reversal was not only associated with sexual behavior still at the center of social debate, but with the relation between that behavior and an incendiary disease which, as we have seen, tapped strongly reactive public sentiment.

Given the substantial revision of Hudson's image from "healthy" heterosexual to "stricken" homosexual, how can we conceive of the impact such a transformation might have on the signification of his past screen roles? Following the cues of press coverage, I offer some tentative hypotheses on this subject.

The Politics of Clashing Codes

Extra-filmic material can often instigate what Richard Dyer has referred to as a "clash of codes" in star signification; this clash is produced from a severe disalignment of on- and off-screen images.[62] According to Dyer, Charles Eckert, and others, the star image typically functions to manage or resolve contradictions within ideology. The fusion of role and "real" person creates the impression of seamlessness within this process. We can see such a function for Hudson's image in the 1950s, when his roles and extra-filmic depictions created and sustained a notion of an ideal, "old-fashioned" masculinity at a time when masculine types were becoming more socially rebellious and sexually ambiguous.

However, this typical operation of ideological management is no longer applicable when we consider the 1980s. Star gossip in this period introduced a substantial conflict between the semiotics of Hudson's past roles and extra-filmic information, resulting in a paradigmatic instance of a "clash of codes." Rather than managing social turmoil by asserting the status quo, the later rewriting of Hudson's image *produces* ideological tension in relation to his screen roles in the 1950s. The contemporary press created fundamental doubt about his on-screen romantic heterosexual image by underscoring the contradictory "facts" of Hudson's private life as a homosexual. The overall impact of this tension lends an artifice to Hudson's roles by directing attention to the apparatus of deceit on which the "magic" of Hollywood is based, as well as to its primary convention, heterosexual romance. A self-reflexive and distancing element is thus introduced into the spectatorial experience of these films. As a result, Sirk's films were most likely "made strange" in ways totally unforeseeable by him or his critics. Press accounts suggest that this awareness of artifice could operate in a number of different ways.

Like Judy Garland, whose MGM image of the girl-next-door was smashed by press coverage of her suicide attempt and personal problems,[63] extra-filmic knowledge converted Hudson into a tragic figure. The press constituted him as a tragic hero, not only because of his public admission and death from AIDS, but because of the duplicitous existence he was forced to lead as a Hollywood star. For liberal readers, Hudson's films become evidence of the compulsory heterosexuality of the film industry and society. His films act as testimony to a schizophrenic relation between public/straight image and private/gay reality, underscoring the price that social mores extract from nonheterosexuals.

Awareness of this kind of schizophrenia is closely related to a camp aesthetic. Camp has always been affiliated with a heightened sense of style as well as role—a theatricalization of the person who affronts social conventions of appearance whether embodied in a "camp" person (such as Oscar Wilde, Andy Warhol) or projected as a sensibility on an image (such as Jayne Mansfield, Victor Mature). While to my knowledge there is no record of a camp canonization of Hudson,[64] the clash of codes characterizing his image creates a situation ripe for this kind of reaction by its dramatic unmasking of heterosexist presumptions, a key facet of the camp aesthetic of identity.

As I mentioned in the preceding chapter, reviewers have sometimes recognized the camp values apparent in Sirk's melodramas, especially in their excesses of color and mise-en-scène. Because of the commentary on gender it produces, Hudson's image offers another potential source for camp reaction to these films.

The Sirk melodrama is so highly structured by the romantic entanglements characteristic of the genre that Hudson's reversed image produces a keen sense of the social constructedness of sex roles. The disjuncture between his homosexuality and the necessary heterosexuality defining his screen roles undermines the apparent naturalness of the sexual conventions of Hollywood cinema and society, reconstructing them as artificial impositions on conduct. Such artifice, as Jack Babuscio comments, makes fun of "the whole cosmology of restrictive sex roles and sexual identification which our society uses to oppress its women and repress its men, including those on the screen."[65]

When viewed from this perspective, romance in Hudson's Sirk melodramas or Day comedies no longer operates as a point of complicit identification of the audience with the emotional center of the film. It appears, rather, as a kind of role-playing demanded by a system that obliterates contradictions in sexual identity and defines the world heterosexually. In this way, Hudson's romantic narratives are injected with heightened artifice around roles, undermining the compulsory heterosexuality that forms the core of the Hollywood film. Extra-filmic knowledge ultimately operates to *ironicize* sex roles, making the Sirk melodrama into a showcase for tragic and humorous recognition of the contrasts between the heterosexual rule over Hudson's public life and the contradictory private facts.

On the other end of the political spectrum, the incongruity can produce reactionary responses as it did in the press. We can consider again for a moment the rewriting of the "Dynasty" kiss between Hudson and Evans from a scripted, dramatic, romantic moment of transgression against marital bonds to a profound example of AIDS contamination and threat. The kiss, shown on television and in print media as one of the emblems of the dangers of undisclosed AIDS, sparked reevaluation of a major institution within the cinema and other media that signifies heterosexual romance—the kiss—but not in a progressively self-reflexive way. The press showed it as contamination, a negative routing of a screen convention where homosexuality makes an unwelcome appearance. In addition, the "Dynasty" kiss often appeared with similar images of romantic involvement from Hudson's previous films, seeming to suggest that these images too were somehow compromised. Hudson's screen kisses thus cease to represent the height of romantic commitment and desire, as the aura of contamination reaches back to redefine even distant screen embraces.

We find an awareness of artifice here that, like liberal camp, undermines steadfast romantic conventions and their heterosexist presumptions. This response, however, materializes as a sort of "retro-camp," where privileged knowledge of the contrasts between role and private life results in a reactionary, homophobic reading. Such a response transforms the screen embrace into a moment of horror or a moment of hilarity. This may very well be the reason students in a classroom will now howl at the line in *All That Heaven Allows* where Hudson tells Jane Wyman that he wishes she were more like a man, or in *Written on the Wind*, when he insists to nymphomaniac Dorothy Malone that he could never satisfy her. Extra-filmic knowledge thus converts romantic scenes into parodies of intended conventions, without the slightest hint of sympathetic political sentiment or awareness.

I have tried to show in this chapter how Rock Hudson's star image functioned filmically and socially in the 1950s, and how through changes in extra-filmic information, that image attained new functions profoundly different from its initial design. Hudson's persona evolved from an affirmation of Hollywood and heterosexual myths to their demystification some thirty years later. By this later period, the authority Hudson's image exercised over reception was magnified, as his mere presence almost guaranteed a confounding of the original design of many of the films in which he appeared. I speculated on how definitions of masculinity may have affected the terms under which Sirk films are received by their audiences, arguing once again how networks of meaning work and rework texts historically—and how difficult it would be to proclaim the meaning of a text once and for all against such unpredictable historical flux.

While we have begun to see the importance of camp in relation to Sirk's melodramas, we have not yet fathomed its full impact on the reception of these films. This will be the focus of the last chapter.[66]

Rock Hudson: Film, Television, and Theater Performances

Films and Directors

1948:	*Fighter Squadron*, Raoul Walsh
1949:	*Undertow*, William Castle
1950:	*Peggy*, Frederick de Cordova
	I Was a Shoplifter, Charles Lamont
	One-Way Street, Hugo Fregonese
	Winchester '73, Anthony Mann
	The Desert Hawk, Frederick de Cordova
	Shakedown, Joseph Pevney
1951:	*Tomahawk*, George Sherman
	The Iron Man, Joseph Pevney

   Air Cadet, Joseph Pevney
   The Fat Man, William Castle
   Bright Victory, Mark Robson

1952: *The Lawless Breed*, Raoul Walsh
   Horizons West, Budd Boetticher
   Has Anybody Seen My Gal?, Douglas Sirk
   Bend of the River, Anthony Mann
   Scarlet Angel, Sidney Salkow

1953: *The Sea Devils*, Raoul Walsh
   The Golden Blade, Nathan Juran
   Seminole, Budd Boetticher
   Back to God's Country, Joseph Pevney
   Gun Fury, Raoul Walsh

1954: *Taza, Son of Cochise*, Douglas Sirk
   Magnificent Obsession, Douglas Sirk
   Bengal Brigade, Laslo Benedek

1955: *Captain Lightfoot*, Douglas Sirk
   One Desire, Jerry Hopper
   All That Heaven Allows, Douglas Sirk

1956: *Never Say Goodbye*, Jerry Hopper
   Giant, George Stevens
   Battle Hymn, Douglas Sirk

1957: *Something of Value*, Richard Brooks
   A Farewell to Arms, Charles Vidor
   Written on the Wind, Douglas Sirk

1958: *Twilight for the Gods*, Joseph Pevney
   Tarnished Angels, Douglas Sirk

1959: *This Earth Is Mine*, Henry King
   Pillow Talk, Michael Gordon

1961: *The Last Sunset*, Robert Aldrich
   Lover Come Back, Delbert Mann
   Come September, Robert Mulligan

1962: *The Spiral Road*, Robert Mulligan

1963: *A Gathering of Eagles*, Delbert Mann

1964: *Man's Favorite Sport?*, Howard Hawks
   Send Me No Flowers, Norman Jewison

1965: *A Very Special Favor*, Michael Gordon
   Strange Bedfellows, Melvin Frank

1966: *Blindfold*, Phillip Dunne
   Seconds, John Frankenheimer

1967: *Tobruk*, Arthur Hiller

1968: *Ice Station Zebra*, John Sturges

1969:   *A Fine Pair*, Francesco Maselli
           The Undefeated, Andrew V. McLaglen

1970:   *Darling Lily*, Blake Edwards
           Hornet's Nest, Phil Karlson

1971:   *Pretty Maids All in a Row*, Roger Vadim

1973:   *Showdown*, George Seaton

1976:   *Embryo*, Ralph Nelson

1978:   *Avalanche*, Corey Allen

1980:   *The Mirror Crack'd*, Guy Hamilton

1986:   *The Ambassador*, shown only on television

Television Shows

1971–76:	"McMillan and Wife"	1981:	"World War III"
1976–77:	"McMillan"		"The Starmaker"
1978:	"Wheels"	1982:	"The Devlin Connection"
1979:	"The Martian	1984:	"Las Vegas Strip Wars"
	Chronicles"	1984–85:	"Dynasty"

Theater

1973–75:	*I Do! I Do!*	1977:	*Camelot*
1976:	*John Brown's Body*	1979:	*On the Twentieth Century*

5

Mass Camp and the Old Hollywood
Melodrama Today

Camp is a form of historicism viewed histrionically.
Philip Core[1]

C AMP, THE LAST province of meaning I discuss, departs from the topics of prior
chapters insofar as it is not as completely affiliated with institutional practices as academic essays, studio advertising, reviews, or star discourse. Indeed,
camp appropriations of films seem much more a product of individual or subcultural investments that lie outside mainstream supervision. The best way of
studying camp, then, would seem to be through empirical, ethnographic methods aimed at the person, rather than through historiographical methods focused
on large social networks.

I include a discussion of camp here for two reasons. First, camp appears to
have a staunch place in the reception of Sirk's melodramas. We can detect its
existence, on the one hand, in the critical disavowals that attempted to expunge
it from consideration. In the 1970s, Paul Willemen treated camp as a "willful
misreading . . . of Sirk's films by . . . nostalgia freaks," while Andrew Sarris and
James Harvey defended the artificial mise-en-scène in *Imitation of Life* against
possible camp appropriation. The film, Sarris claimed, was "too relentlessly reflective," to warrant such responses; Harvey simply cautioned that Sirk must be
taken "seriously and *not* campily."[2] In each case, critics were well aware that
Sirk's films attracted a humorous popular reception. However, in order to establish Sirk as a serious, self-reflexive, Brechtian filmmaker, they had to discredit
such apparently frivolous reactions. But even as critics attempted to dismiss camp,
their denials registered its nagging presence.

On the other hand, beyond its absent presence in Sirk criticism, camp has
been more positively addressed as a bona fide reaction to his melodramas. In
chapter 3 we saw how Jonathan Rosenbaum, a reviewer for the *Soho Weekly
News*, questioned the unresolved "split" he had observed between left-wing and

132

camp readings of Sirk films, implying that academics should come to terms with Sirk's characteristic camp reception. J. Hoberman of the *Village Voice* took the legitimacy of camp one step further by analyzing *Written on the Wind* through an aesthetic trained on its absurd plot twists and hyperbolic Technicolor style.[3]

The point is that whether denying or affirming camp, critics and reviewers have recorded it as a significant popular response to Sirk's melodramas. In this sense, the affiliation between camp and Sirk seems an issue too important to ignore in a study focused on the vicissitudes of meaning that have defined his films historically. The fact that this affiliation remains enigmatic—observed, but so little analyzed, even within recent work that has confirmed the strong relationship between melodrama and camp—makes it an additionally intriguing area of inquiry.[4]

My second reason for treating camp is that the phenomenon may not be as divorced from institutional influences as it might initially seem. There are varieties of camp response that are distinctly gay or otherwise subcultural. But there are also forms of camp born from mainstream mass cultural conditions affecting the general population. Since the 1960s, a combination of social and media developments have caused an efflorescence of camp in the culture at large, making it a sensibility available to many. This more institutionalized form of camp or mass camp has produced a major set of dynamics influencing how classic Hollywood films, including melodramas, appear within a contemporary setting.

The connection between the mass media and camp attitudes toward the cinema is visible at the very least in the number of forums that have customarily spoofed films and their stars. Such forums include "The Tonight Show" (1962–), "The Carol Burnett Show" (1967–1979), "Saturday Night Live" (1975–), "Second City TV" (1977–1981), and, more recently, the Nickelodeon channel and the Comedy Channel's "Mystery Science Theater 3000." These and other popular manifestations of camp attitudes have led to a greater awareness of prior conventions through parody, creating an intricate relation between convention and parody that affects the manner in which audiences presently view films from the past. Mass camp, that is, has encouraged a sensibility that views past Hollywood films as inadvertent campy send-ups. This sensibility is probably part of the reason why students laugh during classroom screenings of classic Hollywood films, and why professors have to work so hard to redirect student responses through theoretical, critical, or historical argument.

By concentrating on mass camp in this chapter, I do not mean to somehow displace subcultural or gay camp from importance. It is simply that the mass variation of camp is most suitable for the present study's focus on institutional modes of meaning production. In addition, by recognizing camp's pervasiveness in culture beyond its subcultural association, I hope to speculate usefully on how its broad presence affects the routine appropriation of Hollywood melodramas by mass audiences today.

I will begin by briefly surveying how theorists have defined camp. This will help clarify the phenomenon itself, particularly its traditional relationship with subcultures, thereby providing some necessary context for recharacterizing camp as a mass practice. Next, I will discuss the developments that led to a more widespread camp response, examining how these developments generally affected the perception of studio era Hollywood films. Finally, I will suggest why film melodramas are particularly susceptible to mass camp appropriation, offering some tentative hypotheses or "notes" on the complicated issue of how Sirk's films mean in a contemporary, popular cultural context.

Defining Camp

Cultural critics tend to define camp by discussing three of its aspects: camp taste, camp practitioners, and camp politics. From one of its major origins in the cult of the dandy in nineteenth-century England through Marcel Duchamp's ready-mades in the 1920s to the rise of pop culture in the 1960s, the camp sensibility has mocked and opposed high culture aesthetics. Critics have consistently described camp as a kind of "counter-taste" that vies brashly with truisms about good taste to establish the validity and special worth of that which appears to be vulgar. As Susan Sontag wrote in 1966, camp is based on "the great discovery that the sensibility of high culture has no monopoly upon refinement . . . that there exists, indeed, a good taste of bad taste. . . . The discovery of the good taste of bad taste can be very liberating. . . . Here camp taste supervenes upon good taste as a daring and witty hedonism.[5] Camp represents a gleeful alternative to repressive cultural canons circumscribed by respectability, a way in which certain individuals can "drop out" of society and flex their aesthetic muscles in unconventional ways.

As an exercise of countertaste, camp can appear in the form of self-presentation (such as the dandy, cross-dressing) or as a vision projected by an artist on his or her artwork (such as ready-mades, pop art). It can also occur through the viewer's conversion of diverse objects into camp (such as Tiffany lamps, Godzilla movies, Victor Mature). The camp viewer gravitates toward images that self-consciously demonstrate exaggeration, stylization, and tackiness, such as pop art or a John Waters film, as well as those more "naive" images that unintentionally represent excess and bad taste, such as Victor Mature's hypermasculinity or the phony special effects of a Japanese horror movie. In this vein, Michael

Bronski writes that camp is a particular "reimagining of the material world . . . which transforms and comments upon the original. It changes the 'natural' and 'normal' into style and artifice."[6] Whatever its specific manifestations, camp operates as an aggressive metamorphosizing operation, attacking norms of behavior, appearance, and art to revel in their inherent artifice. Camp taste is thus distinctly antinatural, eschewing beauty and realism in favor of the patently gilded.

While critics agree on the relation of camp taste and artifice, consensus fails on the issue of who practices camp. Some identify camp as primarily a gay phenomenon. In *Gays and Film* Jack Babuscio argues that "camp describes those elements in a person, situation or activity which express or are created by a gay sensibility." For Babuscio "any appreciation of camp expresses an empathy with typical gay experience."[7] For many in this community, camp emerges as a means of celebrating group solidarity through the exercise of shared aesthetic codes, whether in the form of Judy Garland adoration or enthusiasm about "Dynasty." It also offers the potential to materialize an alternative voice through the willful conversion of mainstream standards and ideals.

Camp has proven to be a particularly effective aesthetic for gays, because its desire to probe mainstream cultural assumptions has included substantial attention to gender. Gays have often used the disaffected qualities of camp to provoke reconsideration of the social distinctions between masculine and feminine. From transvestism to stars who parody or defy normative definitions of gender, including Mae West, Marlene Dietrich, Victor Mature, and Johnny Weismuller, gay camp has been attracted to styles and objects that could illuminate the inherent constructedness of presumed natural categories of gender. Mae West's exaggerated femininity and Marlene Dietrich's androgyny confirmed, respectively, the contrived character of sexual identity and the innate bisexuality of individuals. When focused on gender, camp's proclivity toward excess and artifice could produce a host of iconoclastic sexual spectacles for enjoyment by a community whose own sexual identities lie outside social convention.

Other critics such as Susan Sontag and Andrew Ross address the links between camp and intellectuals. The requisite components of camp are still in force—a penchant for lowbrow tackiness, hyperbole, and artifice over nature—but it appears as a specialized mode of interpretation available primarily to those schooled in culture. That is, only those who are familiar with a broad range of aesthetic offerings, who understand the conventions of good taste well enough to enjoy deposing them, and who have the time to reconstitute themselves and/or objects in extravagant new ways, are liable to pursue the highly self-conscious and omnivorous art of camp. More significantly, however, camp became a vehicle by which some intellectuals could grant themselves cultural power.

Both Sontag and Ross agree that, with the fading of the official aristocracy and rise of a democratizing mass culture in the twentieth century, camp emerged for certain groups as a means of salvaging an aristocratic posture through the exercise of taste. Camp, on the one hand, "offered a negotiated way by which this most democratic of cultures could be partially 'recognized' by intellectuals."[8] On the other hand, it enabled intellectuals to create for themselves an aristocratic identity based on a privileged style of taste not shared by cultural members at large. By canonizing Zsa Zsa Gabor's *Queen of Outer Space* (1958), Flash Gordon comics, and *National Enquirer* headlines, intellectual groups situated themselves between the masses, who allegedly took their mass culture straight, and high culture intellectuals, who reviled such products. As camp proponents often reclaimed objects from the dung heap of mass culture, they created an odd connoisseurship that signified their superior, culturally privy, hip status. By creating a dissident set of aesthetics, camp practitioners assumed a self-proclaimed stance within culture as a minority elite.

Still other writers tend to avoid an exclusive equation between gays, intellectuals, and camp. For example, Philip Core describes how the camp personality cuts across sexual choice, being defined instead by a kind of spiritual isolation induced by an offbeat or eccentric lifestyle, appearance, or artistic practice. In the camp person, this sense of isolation is accompanied by a desire to display his or her affectations, à la Mick Jagger, Andy Warhol, or Grace Jones, to make a mark on culture, as well as to create a small world permeated with his or her own character.[9] In this case, camp defines those who assert their marginality and difference through theatrical style.

But whether elaborating the gay or intellectual or spiritually isolated identities of the camp aesthete, theorists underscore the definitive relation between social marginality and camp. Camp acts as a form of expressive rebuttal to the values of dominant culture for those on the margins. This alternative position raises the issue of camp politics.

For Babuscio and Bronski, camp is eminently political, a means to personal liberation and empowerment because it enables gay men a voice in an adversarial culture. This voice both creates the conditions for group solidarity as gays share common aesthetic codes, and provides a valuable means of subverting mainstream culture.[10] On the opposite end of the spectrum, Sontag assumes that camp is "disengaged, depoliticized—or at least apolitical" because its obsession with style overrides concern for content (p. 277). Mark Booth develops this line of thought further when he remarks that, based on its strong parodic aspects, camp "is a self-mocking abdication of any pretensions to power."[11] And Andrew Ross elaborates how the camp intellectual, in contrast to Gramsci's organic intellectual, withdraws from class conflict through an essential nonalliance with any dominant social group (p. 11).

Thus, while Bronski and Babuscio emphasize the potential of camp to act as a kind of epistemological weapon in the battle between subcultures and the world, Sontag, Booth, and Ross doubt its ability to extend beyond a concern with, respectively, style, parody, and marginalized pseudo-aristocratic taste to materialize a substantive cultural critique or motivate change.

Theories of camp, then, once they leave the arena of taste, vary on whom they identity as practitioners and on the political value of the camp enterprise. These definitions are subject to an even greater variation when considering the phenomenon of mass camp, a type of response facilitated by developments in mass culture, and more widely available to the middle class than its more marginalized relatives.

Mass Camp

Due to a diverse assortment of circumstances from the 1950s forward, camp could no longer be considered a solely sectarian practice; it became pervasive. As I mentioned in chapter 3, the 1950s saw a great "democratizing" of culture, wherein the mass production and dissemination of media texts for the public brought a fearful reaction from many intellectuals about the general lowering of cultural standards. This democratizing, which blossomed in subsequent years, led to the audiences' preference for "mediocre" mass media products over the more distinguished offerings of high culture. Because of this shift, which granted television shows, genre films, and paperback novels a certain status, the proclamations of the superiority of low art, which had always defined camp taste for its more marginalized audiences, gradually became part of a mass aesthetic. The expansion of mass culture dramatically aided camp's potential for a crossover into mainstream society.

As observers of contemporary camp have pointed out, camp attitudes and artifacts were increasingly enshrined by the popular media in the 1960s and 1970s. Besides the publication of Sontag's essay on camp in 1966, which helped pioneer the contemporary currency of the term, pop art, rock music, television, and film of this era made camp an intimate and very visible feature of mass culture. The pop revolution celebrated objects of mass culture as a direct attack on high art pretensions. By extracting these objects from their mundane or ritualized settings, à la Andy Warhol's Campbell soup can and Marilyn Monroe or

Roy Lichtenstein's takeoffs on soap operas and comic strips, they attained a fetishistic, surrealistic glow that denatured them in camp fashion. Despite, or perhaps because of, its high culture baiting, pop art was eventually canonized as a
form of modernism in art museums and offered to the public as part of our national aesthetic heritage.

Rock music similarly contributed to a growing public awareness and proliferation of a camp aesthetic and sensibility. Camp attitudes and dress began appearing in successful rock music trends. Glam rock and punk found musical stars
such as the Kinks, David Bowie, Mick Jagger, and Lou Reed adopting dandyism
and cross-dressing for their look. The presence of camp in the pervasively popular forum of rock helped produce a broader-based cultural attraction to and
acceptance of the phenomenon. While not without its conservative critics, rock
music made one of camp's potentially most volative issues, transgressive sexual
identity, into a public spectacle that sold. As countercultural movements, particularly feminism and gay liberation, created an awareness of gender roles and
their adherence to constraining social norms, the expression of feminine and
masculine identity in the media began to be brought to the forefront of public
discussion.

Television and film greatly enhanced this general expansion of camp. These
developments both saturated the viewer with a body of timeworn conventions
and instilled a self-conscious, often parodic attitude toward them. As Robert Ray
has persuasively argued, the broadcast of "old" movies on television in the
1950s, the mimicry of successful cinematic generic formulae by television genre
shows (particularly westerns), and the growth of revival houses during the 1960s
helped to familiarize viewers with the narrative and formal lingo of earlier
films.[12]

The awareness of conventions on the part of media producers and audiences
alike created a climate ripe for a reflective commentary on these conventions.
Hence, films of the New American Cinema of the 1960s and 1970s, such as
Bonnie and Clyde (1967) and *McCabe and Mrs. Miller* (1971) offered their audiences reworked versions of original genres, escalating the violence and self-
conscious historical importance of the gang in the gangster film or questioning
the myth of the potent, capable hero in the western. Other forms served to
overtly parody established formulae. Besides the aforementioned "The Carol Burnett Show" and "Saturday Night Live," television shows such as "Get Smart"
(1965–1970) and "Batman" (1966–1968), as well as films such as *Cat Ballou*
(1965) and *High Anxiety* (1977), parodied traditional genres (the spy movie, fantasy adventure, western, and Hitchcock thriller, respectively), cashing in on the
audiences' conversancy with conventions to create self-reflexive comedies from

dramatic remains. Each form of recycling past artifacts—revivals, generic invention, and parody—helped circulate a vast body of Hollywood formulae. At the same time, the latter two precipitated an awareness of ritualized generic, narrative, and stylistic conventions (down to camera movements and nondiegetic film music in *High Anxiety*), as well as the mythologies they embodied about heroism, gender, and romance.

The postwar explosion in media recycling thus encouraged a campy perspective on classic Hollywood films by creating an audience schooled in convention and primed by parodies to discover the inherent artifice of the more "naive" products of the film industry. Moreover, as the postwar years wore on, the "aristocratic" privileges of a college education and leisure time were extended to middle-class youth as a whole, giving them the background and the opportunity to recognize and relish savvy plays with convention. Within the interplay of media reflection and educated hipness, audiences were encouraged not to take their classic Hollywood films "straight." Through a modern, reflexive lens, these films could appear rather as unintentionally exaggerated and over-conventionalized.

Thus, mass camp emerged from a relationship between social developments and media events. These included a growing egalitarian spirit in mass culture, consciousness-raising about gender and sexuality, more widely available educational and leisure opportunities, pop art's canonization of mass culture, pop music's questioning of gender categories, and television and film's emphasis on reflexivity and parody. Within this demarginalization of camp, mass cultural artifacts found their way into public aesthetics, sexual ambiguity became commercially successful, and audiences became highly aware of the artifice of conventions. Remarking on these changes, Booth found that in the 1980s camp had become fully "democratized," no longer "the prerogative of an economic elite, but the birthright of all" (*Camp*, p. 175). This democratizing process was enabled not only by camp's explicit visibility in the media, but by general cultural conditions that helped to demarginalize it. Camp thus exceeded its sectarian origins to become a more commonplace reaction to cultural goods. The mass camp sensibility entered mainstream culture ready to adore the mediocre, laugh at the overconventionalized, and critique archaic sex roles.

In democratized or mass camp, we can perceive continuities with subcultural camp, particularly in the former's flagrant disregard of traditional aesthetics and heightened consciousness of conventional sex roles. But there are also important differences stemming from mass camp's availability to more people as an aesthetic choice. If camp in mass culture remains a way of dissenting from staid and repressive social conventions concerning dress, behavior, and art, it has

become an especially popular manner of doing so, from Madonna and her fashion clones to late night television shows spoofing old horror and science fiction
films. In addition, whereas the earliest dandies and gay men practiced their camp
attitudes and styles at some palpable risk of social censure, mass camp tends to
be less directly risky. Mass camp can certainly invoke mainstream protest, as
rock styles like punk or heavy metal have demonstrated. But its frequent lack of
sexual marginality, as well as its embrace as a trendy style by institutions like
the fashion industry, have given it a mainstream chicness that can protect against
serious vilification. This contemporary attitude still can be a sign of social hipness and superiority, without the "stigma" of subcultural affiliation.

Mass camp's popularity and general lack of danger is nowhere more apparent than in the exercise of camp taste. Camp taste can continue to confirm an
aristocratic posture that eschews the notion of sincere consumption by high culture and cultural Neanderthals alike. But there may be less use of camp as a
means of solidifying embattled group identity, as in the case of gays and Sontag's
apolitical intelligentsia both, and more of a tendency to embrace what is perceived as mediocrity for a transient, disinterested form of recreation without
group affiliation or political bite. Diverse viewers can tune into the Nickelodeon
channel's campy rebroadcasts of "The Donna Reed Show" (1958–1966) without
regarding their experience as pointedly countercultural, as a form of privy bond-
ing in the face of a hostile society. These spectacles exist, rather, as a routine
class of entertainment, fun comedies for the enlightened masses.

While mass camp neutralizes the risk and transforms the sectarian nature of
subcultural camp, it wholeheartedly embraces one of its cardinal principles. It is
this principle that has perhaps the greatest bearing on understanding the relation
between mass camp and Hollywood cinema. The camp sensibility has always
gravitated toward objects from the past—the Greta Garbos, *King Kongs*, and
Casablancas of the film world, for example. This penchant implicitly relies on
the historical otherness of the designated objects, their indelible difference from
standards of the present, which makes them completely susceptible to transformation through the camp imagination. Ross clarifies the dynamics behind
camp's preference for the past, when he writes that the camp effect "is created
not simply by the change in the mode of cultural production . . . but rather when
the products (stars . . .) of a much earlier mode of production, which has lost
its power to produce and dominate cultural meanings, become available in the
present for redefinition according to contemporary codes of taste" (p. 5). Sheer
historical difference does not produce camp; camp results from an imposition
of present standards over past forms, turning them into the outdated.

Mass camp has made this hegemony of the present over the disempowered past into its most emphatic principle. The special effects in *King Kong* (1933) or the high-pitched melodramatic moments from *Mildred Pierce* (1945) can be so prone to camp response, because they appear "hokey" by contemporary standards. When measured, respectively, against the special effects technology of a *Star Wars* (1977) or the more apparently realistic situations of *Terms of Endearment* (1983), classic horror films and melodramas seem anachronistic. Displacing the fact that such forms had been shaped by their own industrial and social conditions of production, mass camp fixes on their anachronisms as a place to register their quaint overconventionality, their excesses in comparison to present representational systems that appear to have greater verisimilitude.

Given its pervasiveness in culture, mass camp acts as a particularly significant manner of appropriating texts from bygone eras. Responding to a difference between past and present conventions, mass camp renegotiates the meaning of films according to modern standards. In so doing, its impact is at the same time profoundly historical and ahistorical. Camp is historical insofar as it represents a means of both circulating and preserving the past, like the Nickelodeon channel, by soliciting affections for forms that might otherwise appear, given the outdatedness of their conventions, as inaccessible. As I have quoted Philip Core in this chapter's epigraph, "Camp is a form of historicism viewed histrionically." That is, camp resurrects past artifacts, not to reconstruct their original meaning in some archaeological sense, but to thoroughly reconstitute them through a theatrical sensibility that modifies them by focusing on their artifice.

But this process of reconstitution reveals camp's ahistoricism as well. As Lotte Eisner cautioned about a similar tendency of rewriting common to kitsch, such contemporary responses tend to "negate the historical context" in which cultural artifacts once had "non-kitsch" meanings.[13] Camp can recognize certain general historical aspects, such as the claustrophobia of traditional sex roles in the 1950s in "The Donna Reed Show." But even so, the very conditions of camp oblige a certain annulment of a text's historicity, the status it may have had in past modes of production and reception. Camp characteristically operates in opposition to this status, choosing to turn a film or television show into something *else* far removed from its original design. In the mass camp sensibility, the old media readily become the historical Other because they are so patently out of tune with contemporary social and aesthetic values. So many media products qualify for camp enjoyment because they exhibit the necessary exaggerated exotica in their historical outdatedness in everything from dress, behavior, and dialogue to representations of gender, romance, and marriage.

The more "democratic" form of camp acts, then, as a mode of aesthetic appropriation with historical ramifications: things from the past lose the specifics of their origins, and appear rather in terms of their incongruous relations to contemporary mores and conventions. In this sense, mass camp is distinct from another prevalent response to old Hollywood films as "classics," which seeks to restore and mythologize the circumstances of their production (a tendency vividly represented by the American Movie Channel).

As we shall see in the case of melodrama, mass camp's process of transformation does not necessarily result in a coherent rereading of a film. Rather, mass camp is a "hit-and-run" sensibility insofar as its collision with a text is dramatic in effect, yet momentary. Mass camp gains its pleasures in a sporadic manner, dipping in and out of the text, selecting those moments for response that seem especially antiquated to the contemporary eye. In what follows, I will begin to explore those generic and filmic categories most likely to set off this reaction in relation to the Sirk melodrama.

Mass Camp and Melodrama

Although perhaps not as frequently as horror and science fiction, melodrama has been the target of reflexive play, especially by television. Two situation comedies, "Soap" (1977–1981) and "Mary Hartman, Mary Hartman" (1975–1978), were explicit satires of melodramatic situations and conventions, while the prime-time soap "Dynasty" (1981–1989) was so outrageously indulgent in its story lines and style that critics and fans regarded it as a camp extravaganza. Along with a continuous diet of daytime and other nighttime soap series, such forums made melodramatic conceits very much a part of the contemporary viewing experience.

If the mass camp sensibility emerges from a satiety with convention and thrives additionally on outdatedness, genre films provide a site rich in possibilities for its exercise. Recycled classic Hollywood melodramas offer many areas particularly conducive to this kind of response: these include its subject matter, dramatic logic, mise-en-scène, music, depiction of romance, and representations of gender.

Generally, film melodrama tends to emphasize the social mores of its time, as well its styles and fashions. Hence, melodramas from the earliest days of cinema through the 1960s are liable to appear as keenly "disempowered" in a contemporary context due to the sheer force of social change. Further, melodrama typically demonstrates an exaggerated dramatic logic and style that, through the passage of a few decades, can appear so in excess of contemporary realist norms that it attracts the camp penchant for the absurdly fantastic. In addition, some of melodrama's most definitive elements—its concentration on romance and male/female roles—are likely to register as camp, due to the effects of gender consciousness-raising through feminism and gay liberation. Through these kinds of historical incongruities, one decade's affecting emotional and visual experience serves to elicit a later period's parodic reflexes. This is not to say that old melodramas do not ever successfully produce emotional catharsis for their audiences; when they fail in this regard, however, a mass camp sensibility is probably to blame.

On the surface, it would appear that melodramatic subject matter is the generic aspect most likely to wear with time. From the Victorian ethos surrounding an illegitimate birth in D. W. Griffith's *Way Down East* (1920) to the anti-marijuana hysterics of *Reefer Madness* (1936) to Dorothy Malone's nymphomania in Sirk's *Written on the Wind* (1957), what represents one era's supreme scandal can strike a future generation's funny bone. This kind of metamorphosis is partially due to a loss in social urgency through the passage of time and the ascension of different crises (such as the issue of illegitimate birth, now a more or less accepted social standard, which presently pales in comparison to concerns about dysfunctional families and child abuse). Since the crisis-ridden structure of melodrama often gravitates toward flagrant violations of propriety, it follows that the course of social progress would render these violations old-fashioned to those in more "advanced" value systems. But subject matter does not have to be scandalous for this effect to take place. The fervent espousal of an anonymous, selfless kind of charity in *Magnificent Obsession* (1954) or the embrace of Walden life aesthetics in *All That Heaven Allows* (1955) can strike the same chord, encouraged particularly by the preachiness with which these philosophies are delivered as platforms.

However, upon closer examination, we would have to concede that melodrama's situations are not totally without contemporary currency. Melodramas still strongly center, for example, on sexual indiscretion and intrigue. Viewers who fail to consume studio era melodramas seriously may be partially motivated by the sheer lack of relevance of the topic at hand. But they are equally affected by the style through which these affairs are delivered. That is, melodrama's situations may age badly due to social progress, but this effect also owes strongly to the genre's employment of certain expressive codes. The campy appreciation of melodrama has, in fact, everything to do with how perceptions of its expressive codes as outdated undermine any purported original credibility the genre may once have had—any, that is, "uncampy" meaning.

In terms of dramatic structure, melodramatic plots are particularly focused on the heights of dramatic conflict and the emotional affect such conflicts can arouse on the part of the spectator. Situations such as the moral plunge of a character through alcohol abuse, the travails of star-crossed lovers, or the destructive impact of infidelity on a family are manipulated to produce intense em-

All That Heaven Allows (1955): Walden life aesthetics as outdated subject matter.

Cary Scott (Jane Wyman) discovers Thoreau's *Walden*.

Ron Kirby (Rock Hudson) with a recurring symbolic deer.

pathetic emotions in the viewer. However, like the opera, a form prone to camp appreciation, the anguished machinations characteristic of such plots can appear so excessive as to create the kind of clash with plausible dramatic logic enjoyed by the camp practitioner. Melodrama's inherent commitment to extreme emotion, dramatic crescendoes, and irrational twists of fate portrayed through reversals and coincidences yields a sense of exaggeration now that may alter the original desired effect.

Sirk's films epitomize this kind of "crazy" dramatic logic. *Magnificent Obsession*, for example, relies on a series of remarkable coincidences. First, Bob Merrick (Rock Hudson) indirectly causes the death of Helen Phillips's husband, a prominent and respected doctor at a nearby hospital. Merrick, an irresponsible playboy, needs to use Phillips's artificial respirator after a careless boating accident, while the doctor dies from a heart attack for want of the same device. Next, as Merrick surreptitiously leaves the hospital before he is officially released, his weakened condition causes him to tumble down a hill just as Helen Phillips (Jane Wyman) drives by him. This coincidence allows the two protagonists to meet, at the same time as it delivers the irony of Phillips unwittingly helping the man indirectly responsible for her husband's death. Later, Merrick crashes his car into a tree, which just happens to be near the house of Dr. Phillips's spiritual mentor, Mr. Randolph. Upon this fateful meeting, Merrick learns of the secret charitable system the doctor had been using to help people for many years. Merrick initially plans to emulate this system as a means of winning Helen Phillips's favor. At this point, Merrick inadvertently causes her blindness, as his unwanted attentions force her into the street in front of an oncoming car. This series of events acts as a prelude to the rest of the film, which describes the medical training Merrick undertakes so that he can cure Helen, and his romantic pursuit of her under an assumed identity.

Similarly, a reversal occurring in the denouement of *All That Heaven Allows* involves Cary Scott (Jane Wyman) finally deciding to forget about social convention and marry the younger, lower-class gardener Ron Kirby (Rock Hudson). She arrives at his house to deliver the good news, but leaves when she discovers he is not home. Meanwhile, Ron has been on a cliff overlooking his house, gesticulating wildly and unsuccessfully to get her attention. He falls off the cliff and is seriously injured. Unaware, Cary drives on. Thus, there is a vertiginous reversal of fortune when the narrative turns from a long-awaited reunion scene between the film's central couple to a dramatic accident that incapacitates the male lead.

The slew of coincidences in *Magnificent Obsession* and the reversal in *All That Heaven Allows* represent a type of dramatic logic that may have once worked for its audiences, but now appears contrived. These devices seem forced,

The reversal toward the end of *All That Heaven Allows*. At the moment of their potential reunion, Ron falls off a cliff while Cary drives away unaware.

tools of narrative expediency and emotional exploitation, rather than of persuasive verisimilitude. As the stories thus lose purchase on contemporary emotions, they appear to the camp viewer as a series of dramatic manipulations, introducing a reflexive and distancing dimension to the spectator's comprehension of the genre.

Melodrama's visual and aural style supports the contrived appearance of the plot. The genre's mise-en-scène has a characteristic flamboyance that has often attracted camp appreciation—as in the case of the highly stylized sets and costumes in *Queen Christina* (1933) or Von Sternberg's expressive lighting of Marlene Dietrich in *Shanghai Express* (1932). With its Technicolor richness, luxurious mise-en-scène, and lush symphonic musical scores, the 1950s melodrama similarly provides a spectacle of startling exotica when compared with contemporary modes of production, the more "realistic" color schemes and sets of, say, *Fatal Attraction* (1987) or *Fried Green Tomatoes* (1992). The historical difference in style between then and now, in everything from wardrobe to color process, gives these films a sense of foreignness that the viewer assimilates as camp.

Written on the Wind and *Imitation of Life* (1959) are two of Sirk's most opulent films. As J. Hoberman points out in his review, the former film's brilliant Technicolor surface magnifies the overstated colors which symbolize wealth and sexual malaise (including bright yellow and red sports cars, scarlet phones and flowers, and swirling pink negligees). Visually, the film thus attains a lurid, trashy feel, sending its style and characterizations "over the top." Besides the campy excess found in the general look of Sirk's melodramas, mise-en-scène is subject to another historical rewriting. Melodramatic mise-en-scène tends to sport the latest fashions or interior decors. Since decor and fashion are intimately connected to the evolution of trends, they are elements of film design highly susceptible to being viewed as anachronistic. Universal originally sold the fashions and accessories in *Imitation of Life* as high fashion in an attempt to attract the consumer impulses of female patrons in an era focused on expanding the domestic market. Over thirty years later, this element of the film no longer has the same purchase on middle-class female desire, which has since moved on to other consumer fantasies. Lora Meredith's (Lana Turner) noveau riche house in the mountains or pink, fur-trimmed, dressing gown and turban or bleached blonde hair thus appear ostentatious, unbelievable, hilarious. In this way, the archaic status of color and aspects of melodramatic mise-en-scène render style as recognizable artifice, as something that makes these films bizarrely fantastic.

The effects of film music in soliciting comedic readings of melodrama cannot be overestimated. Critical moments in classic melodramas are usually accompanied by dramatic music that is so emphatic that it appears naively exaggerated. Part of the reason the charity theme in *Magnificent Obsession* strikes the camp viewer as so corny, is that its espousal by various characters is almost always accompanied by a heavenly chorus of voices on the soundtrack, which makes the theme's religious associations too explicit. Two moments from *Written on the Wind* stand out in a similar way. The first, accompanied by a surge in string instruments, finds Marylee (Dorothy Malone) weeping in poignant recollection of her childhood romance with Mitch (Rock Hudson) on a tree inscribed with a heart displaying their initials. The second is the blaring jazz rendition of "Temptation" that accompanies her wild dance and her father's heart attack on the stairs. In each case, film music underscores the emotion in these scenes to such an extent that it appears as an entertaining instance of the dramatic ineptitudes of previous forms—their failure to exercise verisimilar restraint and to indulge instead in rampant overdramatization.

Along with structure and style, melodrama's customary preoccupation with heterosexual romance figures importantly in its contemporary reception. The audience laughs at the line in *Casablanca* (1942), "Was it the cannon fire or is my heart pounding?" and the charged moment at the end of *Now Voyager* (1942) when Paul Henreid lights two cigarettes in his mouth and passes one to Bette Davis, because such instances appear as clichéd examples of romantic exchange. The same is true of the romances that captivated the original audiences of Sirk's *Magnificent Obsession* and *All That Heaven Allows*. In the latter film, for example, gardener Ron Kirby (Rock Hudson) invites Cary Scott (Jane Wyman) to come and see the silver-tipped spruce he is growing at his house, a thinly veiled romantic invitation equivalent in the mass camp imagination to asking a woman to come up and see your etchings as a seductive ploy. Later, after having accepted Ron's invitation, Cary is in the process of ascending a staircase in the old mill on his property when a bird suddenly flies past her, causing her to scream and fall into Ron's arms. Ron kisses her and the end of the segment lingers on a cooing pigeon on the stairs. This "surprise" method of bringing together the romantic leads for their initial encounter is such a stock element that it seems to parody itself. The contentedly cooing pigeon only adds to the sense that the film plays up its romantic situations to such an extent that the romance itself loses purchase on audience identification.

As I mentioned in chapter 4, the 1980s revelation of Rock Hudson's gay identity has a powerful impact on how Sirk's films are presently seen, particularly in relation to romantic situations. His very appearance on screen in these films unfortunately elicits laughter, as do specific moments or dialogue that seem

Romance as cliché in *All That Heaven Allows*.

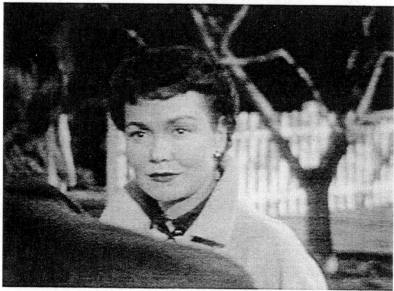

Ron's invitation to Cary to come over to his place and see his silver-tipped spruce.

to bring out the ironies of his position in relation to conventions of heterosexual romance. *All That Heaven Allows* is full of such moments. Some examples include: when Cary says to Ron, "And you want me to be a man?"; when Cary, concerned about whether Ron thinks he will ever find the "right girl," asks, "Or don't you think you're susceptible?"; and when, to explain why her children won't accept him, Ron tells Cary that "I'm not like their father. If you were marrying the same kind of man . . . " The droll response that accompanies these moments confirms the fact that camp audiences may be cognizant of the substantial artifice behind romantic conceits and gender roles in the melodrama without necessarily developing such awareness in progressive directions. Mass camp recognition simply translates this "incongruity" in sexual preference into the ridiculous. This recognition thus paradoxically disturbs screen and social conventions around courtship without inspiring political consciousness.

As part of the fallout from seeing romance as parody, gender roles stand in relief. From the vantage point of more liberal audiences, the film industry and society have often manipulated these roles according to traditional values, now seen as objectionable. Given the presence of stock, strong, silent masculine types such as Hudson and John Gavin, and extremes of femininity represented by Jane Wyman's passivity, Sandra Dee's innocence, Dorothy Malone's femme fatale, and Lana Turner's blonde bombshell, Sirk's melodramas lend themselves to a kind of exposé of gender stereotypes. In *Imitation of Life* when Susy (Dee) runs out on a balcony to proclaim to her mother and their party guests, "Oh, mama, look! A falling star!", or when Marylee responds to her brother's accusation that she is a filthy liar with "I'm filthy, period," the roles of virginal and debauched women, respectively, reach the level of caricature.

There are also moments in Sirk's films that seem particularly sexist to a postfeminist world. In *All That Heaven Allows*, a friend comments to Ron about Cary, "She doesn't want to make up her own mind. No girl does. She wants you to make it up for her." In *Tarnished Angels* (1958), Laverne (Dorothy Malone) parachutes from a plane as her dress blows up and conveniently reveals her lower torso for an extended period of time. Mass camp audiences interpret such moments as clear instances of common patriarchal attitudes about women's lack of self-determination and her existence as spectacle for men. Through stereotypes and attitudes, Sirk's melodramas also offer the liberal consciousness a place to exercise its political awareness about gender.

Thus, the camp transformation of each of these generic areas—subject matter, dramatic logic, style, romance, and gender—consistently relies on a comparative historical effect, supported by a post-1960s parodic mentality about vintage Hollywood forms. Audiences view melodrama's various aspects through the

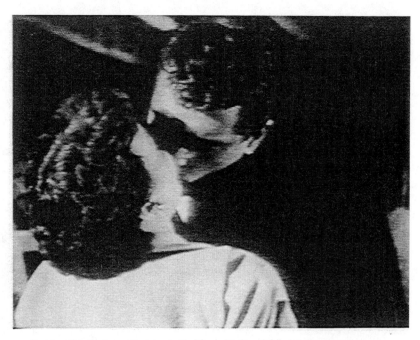

Once at Ron's place, Cary is startled by a bird and falls into Ron's arms as a prelude to their first kiss.

genre's narrative and stylistic differences from contemporary modes of production that appear to have greater verisimilitude, as well as through the genre's ideological differences from more "sophisticated" contemporary value systems. Convention savvy audiences, primed through television rebroadcasts of old movies, film spoofs, soap satires, and consistent, sometimes outrageous, soap programming, experience this historical divergence at some expense to the object in question, transforming it into the ridiculous.

There is, however, more than a little irony in this process. To the contemporary eye, more recent melodramas such as the ones I have already mentioned—*Terms of Endearment, Fatal Attraction,* and *Fried Green Tomatoes*—exhibit a dramatic realism that upholds their emotional thrust. The irony here is that these melodramas do not essentially differ from their predecessors. They demonstrate their own vertiginous reversals and coincidences (such as the successive train accidents in *Fried Green Tomatoes*), and underscore moments of dramatic intensity with an unrestrained visual and musical emphasis (for example, the cross-cutting involving the bunny boiling in the pot on the stove in *Fatal Attraction*). They are also far from free of romantic and gender stereotypes. It is

Unexpected ironies of sexual identity in *All That Heaven Allows*: "And you want me to be a man."

simply that these films have the power of currency and immediacy, due largely to their contemporary stars, settings, situations, dialogue, and subscription to a familiar filmmaking style, that helps prevent the distance necessary for mass camp appropriation.

Before concluding, it is also important to point out that many of my observations about melodrama and camp seem to accord with long-standing arguments about Sirk within the academy. These arguments have held that Sirk was a master at using the cliché as a means of undercutting romance and assaulting melodrama's typical emotional affect. In other words, his films represent a self-conscious trash aesthetic aimed ultimately at generic auto-critique. However, even if we grant the intentionality of campy excess in Sirk's melodramas, we cannot guarantee that these intentions will impress themselves on various viewing factions. As I have argued in previous chapters, Sirk's intentions have not played a role in other institutional, historical, and social provinces of meaning outside the academy. The imperatives of sensationalism and sex or realism and mass culture anxiety in the 1950s, for example, do not associate his films with a self-conscious aesthetic.

Perceived sexism in *All That Heaven Allows*: Ron's friend tells him that Cary "doesn't want to make up her own mind. No girl does. She wants you to make it up for her."

While Sirk's films may appear to some camp practitioners as knowing camp today, the mass camp sensibility often tends to assume the supreme naiveté of the dated objects within its purview. As representing disempowered modes of production, old films appear as simple, even simpleminded, to a sensibility that considers itself sophisticated and "hip" to convention. Without access to knowledge of Sirk's or other directors' intentions, the mass camp viewer approaches these films as naive examples of camp, *unconscious* reflections of past conventions and social values. As mentioned, mass camp's historical myopia, privileging the immediate over the distant, aids the process whereby original circumstances of production and meaning are effaced.

Mass camp responses to melodrama may thus recognize the same elements that were once intended as self-conscious artifice by Sirk. But, in the absence of this information, these elements become examples instead of an unwitting style that confirms the outdated conventionality of the past. Outdatedness may ultimately provoke a Sirkian distanciation from the tenets of melodrama; the mass camp viewer may grasp the constructedness of romance and gender roles, for instance. But this awareness does not necessarily connect with a larger association between film and ideology; it may simply rest on a sense of superiority to the past that remains essentially self-congratulatory vis à vis one's superior spectatorial skills, one's ability to spot vintage corn. Given mass camp's availability to many as a sensibility, how spectators read the artifice of the past depends substantially on their already established, heterogeneous, lived political positions. With a Sirk film, they may respond homophobically to Hudson, with a postfeminist consciousness to gender, or with uncommitted enjoyment of cinematic anachronisms. In this way, the contemporary ideological meaning of Sirk's films is far removed from his intentions; it is dependent on the whims of the mass camp imagination as a specific kind of social and historical vision.

Mass camp represents, then, our most contemporary example of a historical operation that affects the social meaning of Sirk's films. To the potent and pervasive sensibility of mass camp, the products of the Hollywood studio system have become ancient relics whose relevance to culture as anything more than amusing instances of outdated values and conventions has long since passed.

Conclusion

Cinema, Ideology, History

IN THIS BOOK I have tried to demonstrate how different historical, cultural, and institutional contexts produced meaning and ideological significance for Douglas Sirk's melodramas from the 1950s to the 1990s. In the 1950s alone, we have seen how varied this melodramatic identity could be. The film industry classified Sirk's films as stylishly "adult" in response to a number of industrial and social developments, including revisions in censorship, the cultural climate of sexual display, and postwar affluence. By emphasizing sexual intrigue combined with a luxurious mise-en-scène, the industry aligned the 1950s melodrama with patriarchal and bourgeois ideologies of the time. These included the objectification of female sexuality on screen and the definition of female subjectivity through a middle-class, consumerist mentality.

For journalists operating within the constraints of the "realist" canon, Sirk's melodramas fell short of this aesthetic by representing slick Hollywood illusionism and the banalities of soap opera plotting. Within intellectual debate, soap operas represented mass culture's totalitarian potential to act as a form of social control, leveling cultural production and creating passive, feminized audiences. For the review establishment, soaps represented the worst mass culture had to offer, threatening cultural hierarchies of value and refined audience sensibilities through their sheer popularity and embodiment of bad taste.

Along with their exhibition of sexuality, affluence, and bad taste, Sirk's melodramas offered reassuring images of masculinity to 1950s audiences. Filmic and extra-filmic sources defined Rock Hudson's brand of masculinity as sane, healthy, and traditional in sexual desire. This characterization occurred within a cultural framework bursting at the seams with anxieties over the "perversion" of male sexuality and behavior through homosexuality, female domination, corporate pressures, and communism. The image of Hudson in Sirk's melodramas struggled to affirm the attractive appeal of the "normal" in the face of socially disturbing developments around masculinity. In the context of the 1950s, then, institutions defined Sirk's melodramas in response to a variety of different social ideologies from sexual voyeurism and acquisitiveness to fears about mass culture and masculine potency.

Later contexts added new dimensions and even more complexity to the ideological meaning of Sirk's melodramas. In the 1970s and 1980s, academic auteurists, in conjunction with the "textual politics" project, various critical developments, and procedures of canon formation, enshrined Sirk's melodramas as transgressive of 1950s bourgeois and patriarchal ideology. Around the same time, many reviewers confirmed the social criticism inherent in his films. But frustrated by the torturous politics of the 1970s as well as its corporate, commercial culture, reviewers had a larger agenda. They routinely touted studio era films as evidence of Old Hollywood's superior aesthetic culture and simpler values in comparison with the corporately controlled New American Cinema. Here, Sirk's films were valued as subversive, while they also served the reactionary agenda of nostalgia—that is, its characteristic rejection of new social developments through the enthusiastic creation of a better past.

In the 1980s, given Hudson's declaration of his homosexuality and affliction with AIDS, Sirk's films became vehicles of dissonant gender values. Rather than simply confirming Hollywood's portrayals as it had in the 1950s, star coverage revealed the industry's deceptive gender machinations. These melodramas thus came to express the clash between Hudson's heterosexual roles and homosexual private life, potentially provoking progressive as well as homophobic responses to his appearance on screen. Last, for contemporary audiences savvy to convention, studio era melodramas appeared as "camp," as outdated forms that exuded artifice in everything from narrative structure to depictions of romance. As we have just seen in the preceding chapter, while mass camp uniformly converted old films into comedies of inept conventions, it varied in political reactions to its self-reflexive discoveries about representation.

Within a more contemporary framework, institutions once again identified Sirk's films through a number of different ideologies. His melodramas signified transgression to the dominant ideology, a reactive, nostalgic refuge from 1970s politics and corporately produced art, and an exposé of both Hollywood's heterosexual masculinity and the artifice of past systems of representation that could serve opposing political positions.

This historical journey bears centrally on reconsiderations of authorship, genre, and meaning. Critics affected by developments in academia constructed Sirk as an author; outside of this sphere of influence his "personality" and intentions had very little bearing on how his films were exhibited and otherwise defined for consumption. His became a small voice in a wilderness of other discursive forces, from the sexual display to camp. This particular author, then, often lost "control" of the meaning of his films through their relationship to social and historical developments that dominated the terms of their reception. Similarly, his melodramas were constantly subsumed under various categories as they circulated through culture. They were classified and reclassified through a succession of labels, including the adult film, realism, the sophisticated family melodrama, and camp. Each of these categories offered different accounts of the definitive features of these films, respectively: risqué sexual content, cheap formulaic artifice, ironic devices, and naive parodies of conventions. As a result of their relationship to such cultural classifications, these genre films were liable to dramatic reversals of semantic fortune, serving divergent, even contradictory ideological purposes.

This interaction between melodrama and context helps us observe a dynamic historical process that continuously transformed the significance and value of Sirk's films. My study has demonstrated that there has been nothing stable about the meaning of his melodramas; they have been subject at every cultural turn to the particular *use* to which various institutions and social circumstances put them. In this process, meaning itself becomes something we cannot determine "once and for all," but a volatile, essentially *cultural* phenomenon that shifts with the winds of time. This volatility has further ramifications for conceptualizing cinema's relationship to ideology, history, and the spectator.

Sirk's case suggests that the relation between film and ideology cannot be conceived of as isomorphic. Comolli and Narboni postulated a one-to-one relationship between these two terms in their influential essay, "Cinema/Ideology/Criticism," which failed to grasp the complexity of the medium's situation in the social formation. As I have tried to show, films do not have a singular association with cultural norms, nor do periods have singular ideological identities. Treating the 1950s as indicative, historical eras are characteristically full of different, sometimes conflicting social ideas, rather than uniform principles. Similarly, films respond to a number of coexisting, sometimes oppositional value systems, rather than carry a single message. Further, the historiographic analysis of Sirk reveals, contra Comolli and Narboni, that films themselves do not determine their own ideological pedigree; rather, they serve as sites of confluence for diverse cultural concerns during particular eras and through time.

This potential diversity and changeability make it difficult for us to label individual films as reactionary or progressive. The perspective of this study is that labeling films one way or the other potentially short-circuits recognition of the repertoire of social functions a text may serve. By locating the multiple liaisons texts have with different cultural values, we are better able to identify the social discourses and ideological interests that vie for control over meaning during reception. This alternative procedure does not throw the question of ideological status into a polymorphous, postmodern flux of meaning, but attempts to specify the multiple historical significances a text has for its audiences.

In addition, I have argued that reception is affected by variables external to the film or the person of the viewer. As opposed to text-oriented and reader-oriented approaches which hold, respectively, that textual features or the reader's psychology determine the interpretation of the text, I have shown how historical and intertextual environments shape meanings that circulate during the time of reception. My analysis of these environments is not intended as a blanket polemic against other methods that take the text or the viewer as the point of departure for reception study. I do contend, however, that an understanding of reception is incomplete without coming to terms with the relationship between textual features and the social universe in which they exist, between reader-response and larger social agencies acting on the audience's experience of a film.

More specifically, historical understanding of Sirk's films suggests that institutional and historical forces frequently activate modes of reception that operate simultaneously with the spectator's usual work of decipherment and comprehension. But, unlike these latter two processes, the institutional promotion of such factors as sexual sensationalism, consumerism, star fetishism, and camp provokes a spectacle-driven sensibility that freezes and emphasizes certain moments in a film, deriving culturally cultivated pleasures that may be set off, but not contained, within the progress of the narrative. Placing films within larger discursive and cultural frameworks thus suggests that the viewing experience is partially negotiated by antilinear dynamics that ceaselessly puncture the film body, relating its elements to external discursive and cultural systems.

Within all of these various reconsiderations, it becomes clear, finally, that regarding meaning as a fluid transaction between cinema and culture has certain implications for aesthetics. In order to come to terms with cinema's cultural existence, we are obliged to relinquish certain aesthetic presumptions about timeless textual integrity and "real" meaning. Aesthetic presumptions about textual worth are traditionally based on assertions that *this* meaning and no other is valid; and, further, that we can prove this meaning by close analysis of a text's internal organization and features. By contrast, historical analysis tells us that there is a certain fluidity to meaning, that textual characteristics are routinely subject to cultural rewriting, that there is nothing sacred about textual boundaries.

In the case of film melodrama, a contextualist perspective would qualify enthusiasm about the ipso facto subversiveness of the "sophisticated family melodramas" of Sirk, Minnelli, and Ray—or any film—by regarding this aesthetic status as an *effect* of institutional, academic agendas, rather than as a transcendent characteristic of the films themselves. This qualification does not mean that melodramas do not serve certain ideological functions. As we have seen, in the course of their social histories, melodramas are strongly valued for their subversive or reactionary content, and may come to polarize their audiences about issues of sexuality and gender, among other things. But these values are a product of certain strategic, historically specific negotiations between these films and their cultural contexts. They do not describe a permanent state of affairs or provide accounts of some definitive textual status.

In this sense, my findings would support Tony Bennett's statement that retention of the concept of the objective, self-determining text is "not necessary and has no political implications for the practical conduct of criticism."[1] That is, cultural criticism has nothing to gain by maintaining a sense of the authority of the text; an appeal to this authority usually harbors an aesthetic stake that interferes with the serious consideration of alternative textual identities by invalidating them as "incorrect." Although analyzing a text's social use, "its perpetual remaking and transformation, in the light of its inscription into a variety of different material, social, institutional and ideological contexts" represents an assault on aesthetics, it provides a significant means to historicize the study of media phenomena.[2]

Historically, there does not appear to be "the one, true, text," but a text continually in the throes of transformation. If we were to insist otherwise by claiming that a film's intrinsic features resist barbarous treatment or misinterpretation at the hands of various nonacademic social institutions, we could well miss the rich and varied ideological functions cinema serves in society, functions at the very heart of unlocking the continuing mysteries of cinema's relation to culture and its values.

Notes

Introduction

1. V. N. Vološinov, "The Latest Trends in Linguistic Thought in the West," *Bakhtin School Papers*, Noel Owens, trans. (Oxford: RPT Publications, 1983), 32.

2. To complete the biography, Sirk left the United States at the height of his career in 1959, allegedly tired of Hollywood filmmaking. He settled in Switzerland, staged some theater in Germany, and supervised the making of three film shorts while he was teaching at the Munich Academy of Film and Television. He died in 1987.

3. Thomas Elsaesser, "Tales of Sound and Fury," *Monogram* 4 (1972): 2–15.

4. Christine Gledhill, "The Melodramatic Field: An Investigation," in Christine Gledhill, ed., *Home Is Where the Heart Is: Studies in Melodrama and the Woman's Film* (London: The British Film Institute, 1987) 7. See also John Fletcher, "Introduction—Melodrama," *Screen* 29.3 (Summer 1988): 43–70, especially 46–48; and Jane Feuer, "Melodrama, Serial Form and Television Today," *Screen* 25.1 (Jan./Feb. 1984): 4–16.

5. As a sign of Sirk's accepted equation with the genre, two recently published books on melodrama play off of his film titles to represent their projects: Marcia Landy's anthology *Imitations of Life: A Reader on Film and Television Melodrama* (Detroit: Wayne State University Press, 1991); and Jackie Byars's *All That Hollywood Allows: Re-Reading Gender in 1950s Melodrama* (Chapel Hill: University of North Carolina Press, 1991).

6. Jane Tompkins, *Sensational Designs: The Cultural Work of American Fiction 1790–1860* (New York: Oxford University Press, 1985), 3–39; Charles J. Maland, *Chaplin and American Culture: The Evolution of a Star Image* (Princeton: Princeton University Press, 1989); Robert E. Kapsis, "Hollywood Filmmaking and Reputation Building: Hitchcock's *The Birds*," *Journal of Popular Television and Film* 15.1 (Spring 1987): 5–15 and "The Historical Reception of Hitchcock's *Marnie*," *Journal of Film and Video* 40:3 (Summer 1988): 46–63. These two essays are included in Kapsis's recent book *Hitchcock: The Making of a Reputation* (Chicago: University of Chicago Press, 1992).

7. Peter Brooks, *The Melodramatic Imagination: Balzac, Henry James, Melodrama, and the Mode of Excess* (New Haven: Yale University Press, 1976), xiii.

8. Lea Jacobs, *The Wages of Sin: Censorship and the Fallen Woman Cycle, 1928–1942* (Madison: University of Wisconsin Press, 1991); Jeanne Thomas Allen, "Fig Leaves in Hollywood: Female Representation and Consumer Culture," in Jane Gaines and Charlotte Herzog, eds., *Fabrications: Costume and the Female Body* (New York: Routledge, 1990), 122–33; Maria LaPlace, "Producing and Consuming the Woman's Film: Discursive Struggle in *Now, Voyager*," in Christine Gledhill, ed., *Home Is Where the Heart Is*, 138–66.

9. A step in this direction is Lucy Fischer's *Imitation of Life* (New Brunswick: Rutgers University Press, 1991), which not only supplies historical information about the contexts in which Sirk's film was originally received, but also resurrects the film's critical history. However, since Fischer's book is intended as a collection of essays that have been written about the film, her object is not to analyze fully the implications of the film's history for understanding its changing relation to culture and ideology.

10. Paul Willemen, "Towards an Analysis of the Sirkian System," *Screen* 13.4 (1972/73): 128–34.

11. See, for example, Mike Budd, "The Moments of Caligari," in Mike Budd, ed., *The Cabinet of Dr. Caligari: Texts, Contexts, Histories* (New Brunswick: Rutgers University Press, 1990), 7–119; and Jane Gaines, "The Queen Christina Tie-Ups: Convergence of Show Window and Screen," *Quarterly Review of Film and Video* 11.1 (1989): 35–60.

12. In this sense her position parallels that of cultural studies scholar Tony Bennett. His theory of reading formations calls for the study of "the operation of those interdiscursive and intertextual processes that bear most specifically and most closely on the process of reading" ("Texts in History: The Determinations of Readings and Their Texts," *The Journal of the Midwest Modern Language Association* 18.1 [1985] 9). See also Bennett and Janet Woollacott's *Bond and Beyond: The Political Career of a Popular Hero* (New York: Methuen, Inc., 1987), which attempts a book-length application of reading formation theory. Unlike Staiger, Bennett and Woollacott's approach is compromised at times by lapses into traditional, text-based interpretation that contradicts reading formation theory (in their chapter "Bonded Ideologies," for example).

13. Janet Staiger, *Interpreting Films: Studies in the Historical Reception of American Cinema* (Princeton: Princeton University Press, 1992) 81.

14. Example of attempts in this direction would be Bennett and Woollacott, Kapsis's work on Hitchcock, and Maland's work on Chaplin. Staiger's position also strongly encourages a diachronic dimension to historical reception studies, but her case studies tend to focus on reviews within the original contexts of reception.

15. This is a tendency in Robert Kapsis's work, particularly in his essay on *Marnie*. While he emphasizes how meaning for Hitchcock's films has been constituted by such things as his biographical legend, he contradicts the historiographical premise of his position by, at times, disputing the legitimacy of certain critical readings, either by referring to "textual evidence" or the authority of the biographical legend itself. See particularly, Kapsis, "The Historical Reception of Hitchcock's *Marnie*," 52–53, 58.

1. The "Progressive" Auteur, Melodrama, and Canonicity

1. Fred Camper, "The Films of Douglas Sirk," *Screen* 12.2 (1971): 44.

2. Jane Tompkins, *Sensational Designs: The Cultural Work of American Fiction, 1790–1860* (New York: Oxford University Press, 1985), 36–37.

3. Barbara Herrnstein Smith, *Contingencies of Value: Alternative Perspectives for Critical Theory* (Cambridge: Harvard University Press, 1988), 30–53.

4. See, for example, David Bordwell, *Making Meaning: Inference and Rhetoric in the Interpretation of Cinema* (Cambridge: Harvard University Press, 1989). Bordwell demonstrates how apparently diverse interpretive enterprises are actually underwritten by the same set of principles and protocols, thus attacking the idea that theories and theoretical developments radically affect interpretation. Sirk criticism could certainly be analyzed according to Bordwell's model; approaches to Sirk tend to employ symptomatic interpretations that call on certain semantic fields and schemata, such as reflexivity and the personification of the author, respectively. However, while these particular terms will prove useful to my examination of Sirk criticism, to show how a fixed set of interpretive moves has governed forty years of criticism would result in a more static sense of history and a more passive sense of the role of theory than is useful for my project here. While I agree that theoretical and critical shifts are themselves not responsible for determining interpretations, Douglas Sirk's case suggests that movements within a field have a definite heuristic value for studying meaning production. As we shall see, such movements can play a role in motivating specific meanings (or semantic fields) over others, defining interpretive positions as legitimate or illegitimate and creating sympathetic communities of practitioners at particular moments in academic history. Thus, such shifts are valuable in ascertaining some of the dynamics involved in the march of meaning over time.

5. There have been numerous lengthy studies of various stages of the discipline's development. See, for example, D. N. Rodowick's work on the major influences, concerns, and limitations of 1970s theory in *The Crisis of Political Modernism: Criticism and Ideology in Contemporary Film Theory* (Urbana and Chicago: University of Illinois Press, 1988).

6. For a cultural contextualization of the work of the French auteurists see John Hess, "La Politique des auteurs: Part One: World View as Aesthetic," *Jump Cut* 1 (May–June 1974): 19–22, and, to a lesser extent, "La Politique des auteurs: Part Two: Truffaut's Manifesto," *Jump Cut* 2 (July–August 1974): 20–22.

7. For the impact of *Cahiers* on later criticism, see Jim Hillier's introduction to Jim Hillier, ed., *Cahiers du cinéma: The 1950s* (Cambridge: Harvard University Press, 1985), 11–12.

8. See, for example, Edward Buscombe, "Ideas of Authorship," *Screen* 14.3 (Autumn 1973): 75–85.

9. See William Horrigan, "An Analysis of the Construction of an Author: The Example of Douglas Sirk," Ph.D. diss., Northwestern University, 1980. Horrigan's study was a groundbreaking attempt to reconsider Sirk's status as an auteur in both early French and British periods of criticism from a Foucauldian perspective. My research on these periods concurs strongly with several of Horrigan's key findings, including *Cahiers'* lack of unanimity about what Sirk's films signified and the centrality of the Sirk interviews to resolving this question. Horrigan also provides a useful counterpoint to my treatment of these two periods by concentrating on the role played by editorial policies in shaping differences between key journals' conceptions of auteurism and subsequent constructions of Sirk as an auteur.

10. Phillippe Demonsablon, "Portrait d'un honnête homme," *Cahiers du cinéma* 49 (1955): 48–50.

11. Louis Marcorelles, "Le film gratuit," *Cahiers du cinéma* 69 (1957): 49.

12. Luc Moullet, "Re-création par la récréation," *Cahiers du cinéma* 87 (1958): 56.

13. François Truffaut, *The Films in My Life*, Leonard Mayhew, trans. (New York: Simon and Schuster, 1978), 149.

14. Jean-Luc Godard, *Godard on Godard*, Tom Milne, trans., (New York: Viking Press, 1972), 134–39. *Screen* also featured this essay in its special issue on Sirk as "Tears and Speed," Susan Bennett, trans., *Screen* 12.2 (Summer 1971): 96–97. The essay appeared originally as "Des larmes et de la vitesse," *Cahiers du cinéma* 94 (April 1959): 51–54.

15. On this point, see James Naremore, "Authorship and the Cultural Politics of Film Criticism," *Film Quarterly* (Fall 1990): 14–22.

16. Andrew Sarris, "The American Cinema," *Film Culture* 28 (Spring 1963): 1–68; *The American Cinema: Directors and Directions, 1929–68* (New York: E. P. Dutton, 1968).

17. Sarris, *The American Cinema*, 109–110.

18. Horrigan, "The Construction of an Author," 21.

19. Bordwell, *Making Meaning*, 1–70.

20. On this point see Kevin McDonnell and Kevin Robbins, "Marxist Cultural Theory: The Althusserian Smokescreen," in Simon Clarke, Victor Seidler, et al., eds., *One Dimensional Marxism: Althusser and the Politics of Culture* (New York and London: Allison & Busby, 1980), 172.

21. Antony Easthope, "The Trajectory of *Screen*, 1971–79," in Francis Barker, Peter Hulme, et al., eds., *Essex Conference on the Sociology of Literature (July 1982): The Politics of Theory* (Colchester: University of Essex, 1983), 121.

22. *Cahiers du cinéma* 189 (April 1967): Serge Daney and Jean-Louis Noames, "Entretien avec Douglas Sirk," 19–25; Jean-Louis Comolli, "L'aveugle et le miroir," 14–18; and Patrick Brion and Dominique Labourde, "Biofilmographie," 26–29.

23. Jon Halliday, *Sirk on Sirk: Interviews with Jon Halliday* (New York: Viking Press, 1972). All subsequent references appear in the text. On this connection, see also Horrigan, 27.

24. Robert Ray, "The Bordwell Regime and the Stakes of Knowledge," *Strategies* 1 (Fall 1988): 171.

25. Camper, "The Films of Douglas Sirk," 44.

26. Donald Spoto, *The Dark Side of Genius: The Life of Alfred Hitchcock* (New York: Ballantine Books, 1983); Robert Kapsis, *Hitchcock: The Making of a Reputation* (Chicago: University of Chicago Press, 1992).

27. This is what Bordwell has referred to as the necessary "personification of the filmmaker" underlying almost all auteur criticism. Bordwell, *Making Meaning*, 158.

28. Along these lines, it is interesting to note that, on the one hand, Sirk insisted on rewriting Halliday's interview before publication, while, on the other, he later admitted that he didn't know what a moment or object in his films meant until Halliday suggested it to him. See James Harvey, "Sirkumstantial Evidence," *Film Comment* (July–Aug. 1978): 52–59.

29. In his editorial to *Screen*'s special issue on Sirk, Sam Rohdie laments the "confusion in method" in the issue, ascribing it to the "difficulty in Britain of trying to establish a film and critical culture" and the "lack of ideological, intellectual, or critical agreement even among a small group of film critics and film educationists." Rohdie, *Screen* 12.1: 5–6.

30. Fred Camper, "The Films of Douglas Sirk," and David Grosz, "*First Legion*: Vision and Perception in Sirk," *Screen* 12.2 (Summer 1971): 44–62, 99–117, respectively; Tim Hunter, "*Summer Storm*," Mike Prokosh, "*Imitation of Life*," and Jean-Loup Bourget, "Sirk's Apocalypse," in *Douglas Sirk*, Jon Halliday and Laura Mulvey, eds. (London: Edinburgh Film Festival in association with the National Film Theatre and John Player and Sons) 31–40, 89–94, 67–78, respectively.

31. Camper, "The Films of Douglas Sirk," 2. All subsequent references appear in the text.

32. Jon Halliday, "*All That Heaven Allows*," in *Douglas Sirk*, Jon Halliday and Laura Mulvey, eds., 61.

33. Fassbinder's frequently reprinted essay on Sirk's films contained some political insight; however, his essay chiefly served other functions in the rhetoric of author construction, which I shall treat in a later chapter. (Rainer Werner Fassbinder, "*Imitation of Life*," in *Fernsehen und Film* 2 (Feb. 1971): 8–13. This essay is better known as "Six Films by Douglas Sirk," Thomas Elsaesser, trans., in Halliday and Mulvey, *Douglas Sirk*, 95–107).

34. For an overview of the repercussions of May 1968 on film intellectuals, see Sylvia Harvey, *May '68 and Film Culture* (London: British Film Institute, 1978).

35. Sam Rohdie, *Screen* 12.1: 4–5.

36. Paul Willemen, "Remarks on *Screen*, Introductory Notes for a History of Contexts," *Southern Review* 16.2 (July 1983): 297. For a discussion of the post–World War II political background that shaped the British New Left, see Perry Anderson, "The Left in the Fifties," *The New Left Review* 29 (Jan.–Feb. 1965): 3–18. For a more sweeping history of Marxism that chronicles its turn to theory in an academic setting as a retreat from political practice, see Anderson, *Considerations of Western Marxism* (London: NLB, 1976), 42.

37. On this point, see Antony Easthope, *British Post-Structuralism since 1968* (London and New York: Routledge, 1988), 34–35.

38. Bertolt Brecht, *Brecht on Theatre*, John Willett, trans. (New York: Hill and Wang, 1964).

39. Easthope, *British Post-Structuralism since 1968*, 34.

40. Jean Comolli and Jean Narboni, "Cinema/ideologie/critique I," *Cahiers du cinéma* 216 (October 1969): 11–15; "Cinema/Ideology/Criticism," trans. Susan Bennett, *Screen* 12.1 (1971): 27–36.

41. Interestingly enough, Willemen analyzes the drift toward theoreticism as a direct result of reactionary political developments of the 1960s in England, particularly continuous financial attacks on educational institutions, job security, and career opportunities for intellectuals, in "Remarks on *Screen*": 299. In this threatening climate, theory became a "safer" expression of political ideals than activist political practice.

42. Paul Willemen, "Distanciation and Douglas Sirk," *Screen* 12.1 (Spring 1971): 63–67,

and "Towards an Analysis of the Sirkian System," *Screen* 13.4 (1972–73): 128–34. All subsequent references appear in the text.

43. Thomas Elsaesser, "Tales of Sound and Fury," *Monogram* 4 (1972): 2–15. All subsequent references appear in the text.

44. Camper, "The Films of Douglas Sirk," 61.

45. There is a more detailed discussion of the shared characteristics of these types of films in my " 'Cinema/Ideology/Criticism' Revisited: The Progressive Text," *Screen* 25.1 (Jan.–Feb. 1984): 30–44.

46. See Ellen Keneshea, "Sirk: *There's Always Tomorrow* and *Imitation of Life*," *Women and Film* 2 (1972): 51–55. Keneshea stresses Sirk's portrayal of a stifling middle class, but she focuses more particularly on the way the films represent the oppressive conditions for women in the postwar United States. In this, both she and Molly Haskell presage later feminist treatments of Sirk as a director of the "woman's film," who subtly attacks the ideological place of women. See also, Molly Haskell, *From Reverence to Rape: The Treatment of Women in the Movies* (New York: Penguin Books, 1974), 271–76.

47. Stanley Fish, *Is There a Text in This Class? The Authority of Interpretive Communities* (Cambridge: Harvard University Press, 1980), 303–321. See also his more recent defenses of this concept in *Doing What Comes Naturally: Change, Rhetoric, and the Practice of Theory in Literary and Legal Studies* (Durham and London: Duke University Press, 1989), 141–62.

48. A later chapter will treat the film reviews associated with retrospectives and screenings in greater detail.

49. See, for example, James Harvey, "Sirkumstantial Evidence," *Film Comment*; Michael Stern, "Interview with Douglas Sirk," *Bright Lights* 2.2 (Winter 1977–78): 29–34; and Mathias Brunner and Kathryn Bigelow, "Douglas Sirk," *Interview* (July 1982): 50–51.

50. See, for example, Michael Stern, *Douglas Sirk* (Boston: Twayne Publishers, 1979); and Jean-Loup Bourget, *Douglas Sirk* (Paris: Edilig and the Toulouse Cinematheque, 1984). A more traditional stance is also taken by many of the essayists in the special issue on Sirk in *Bright Lights* 2.2 (Winter 1977–78).

51. See James McCourt's "Melo-Maestro," *Film Comment* 11.6 (Nov.–Dec. 1975): 19–21. For an earlier treatment of Sirk in this source see Michael McKegney, "*Imitation of Life*," *Film Comment* 8.2 (Summer 1972): 71–73.

52. Louis Althusser, "Ideology and Ideological State Apparatuses (Notes towards an Investigation)," *Lenin and Philosophy and Other Essays*, Ben Brewster, trans. (New York: Monthly Review Press, 1971): 127–86.

53. Stephen Heath, "Film and System: Terms of an Analysis I," *Screen* 16.1 (Spring 1975): 7–77; Christian Metz, "The Imaginary Signifier," *Screen* 16.2 (Summer 1975): 14–83; Laura Mulvey, "Visual Pleasure and Narrative Cinema," *Screen* 16.3 (Autumn 1975): 6–18.

54. Laura Mulvey, "Notes on Sirk and Melodrama," *Movie* 25 (1977–78): 56.

55. Peter Brooks, *The Melodramatic Imagination: Balzac, Henry James, Melodrama, and the Mode of Excess* (New Haven: Yale University Press, 1976).

56. While *Screen*-oriented approaches served as a major means of access to melodrama, analyses closer to the traditional auteurist school also employed psychoanalysis. See, for example, Michael Stern, "Patterns of Power and Potency, Repression and Violence: An Introduction to the Study of Douglas Sirk's Films of the 1950s," *The Velvet Light Trap* 16 (1976): 15–21. See also, George Robinson, "America, Sex, and Sirk," *The Filmmaker's Review* 1.5 (March 18, 1976): 3.

57. Steve Neale, quoted in Griselda Pollock, "Report on the Weekend School," *Screen* 18.2 (1977): 107.

58. Mulvey, "Notes on Sirk and Melodrama," 54, 56. All subsequent references appear in the text.

59. The editors of Cahiers du cinéma, "Young Mr. Lincoln, texte collectif," Cahiers du cinéma 223 (Aug. 1970): 29–47, trans. in Screen 13.3 (Autumn 1972): 5–44; Roland Barthes, S/Z, trans. Richard Miller (New York: Hill and Wang, 1974); Stephen Heath, "Film and System: Terms of an Analysis I", Screen 16.1 (Spring 1975).

60. Along with Molly Haskell, Mulvey was an important influence on explicitly feminist considerations of Sirk's melodramas. For other feminist treatments of Sirk during this era, see Janie Place and Julianne Burton, "Feminist Film Criticism," Movie 22 (1976): 53–62. This is mainly a review of feminist literature on film, but it uses Sirk's melodramas as an example of the possibility of gender role critique in the Hollywood cinema. The authors cite Sirk's use of artifice, mirrors, and objects in the mise-en-scène as creating a formal subversion of complacent views on middle-class, married life typically offered by mainstream cinema. For a dissident feminist reading of Sirk that argues how reactionary his films are, see Brandon French, On the Verge of Revolt: Women in American Films of the Fifties (New York: Frederick Ungar Publishing Co., 1978), 92–104. French's chapter on All That Heaven Allows is titled "Oppression in Sheep's Clothing."

61. Geoffrey Nowell-Smith, "Minnelli and Melodrama," Screen 18.2 (1977): 117. All subsequent references appear in the text.

62. Steve Neale, "Douglas Sirk," Framework 5 (1976–77): 17. For a more systematic critique of the whole concept of Sirk as auteur outside the main line, see Jean-Loup Bourget, "Situation de Sirk," Positif 137 (April 1972): 35–46, reprinted as "Sirk and the Critics," Eithne Bourget, trans., in Bright Lights 2.2 (Winter 1977–78): 6–10, 19. Bourget cites the significant and consistent contributions of other personnel to Sirk's films.

63. Stern, "Patterns of Power and Potency, Repression and Violence," 21.

64. Christopher Orr, "Closure and Containment: Marylee Hadley in Written on the Wind," Wide Angle 4.2 (1980): 29–34.

65. D. N. Rodowick, "Madness, Authority and Ideology: The Domestic Melodrama of the 1950s," The Velvet Light Trap 19 (1982): 40–45.

66. Thomas Schatz, Hollywood Genres: Formulas, Filmmaking, and the Studio System (New York: Random House, 1981) 245–60. For another prominent example of criticism in this phase, see Chuck Kleinhans, "Notes on Melodrama and the Family under Capitalism," Film Reader 3 (1978): 40–46. Kleinhans relies on, but dimensionalizes, preceding discussions by arguing how tied melodrama is to personal experience.

67. Herrnstein Smith, Contingencies of Value, 23. All three of my critical examples demonstrate the conditions and exigencies of such a reproduction of value. At the time the first two essays were written, Orr and Rodowick were graduate students, challenged to establish their membership in film academia by showing their conversancy with and mastery of past interpretations of their chosen subject. The textbook also tends to reproduce value, since its mission as a genre of publication is often to distill the essence of knowledge about a particular area in a field.

68. James Harvey, "A Thalia Series," 54; Charles Affron, Cinema and Sentiment (Chicago and London: University of Chicago Press, 1982) 156.

69. Mary Ann Doane, "Caught and Rebecca: The Inscription of Femininity as Absence," Enclitic 5.2 and 6.1 (1981–82): 75–89; Linda Williams, "Something Else besides a Mother": Stella Dallas and the Maternal Melodrama," Cinema Journal 24.1 (1984): 2–27.

70. This kind of shift is evident in Screen's 1980 change in editorial policy, as Paul Willemen writes, to "reconnect in a more responsibly interventionist manner with the culture within which it exists" ("Remarks on Screen: 298). For broader accounts of the impact of cultural studies on 1970s theory and criticism, see Larry Grossberg, "The Formations of Cultural Studies: An American in Birmingham," Cultural Studies 2 (1989): 114–47.

71. Richard de Cordova's "A Case of Mistaken Legitimacy: Class and Generational Differ-

ence in Three Family Melodramas," in *Home Is Where the Heart Is: Studies in Melodrama and the Woman's Film*, Christine Gledhill, ed. (London: British Film Institute, 1987), 255–67.

72. See also Marcia Landy, ed., *Imitations of Life: A Reader on Film and Television Melodrama* (Detroit: Wayne State University Press, 1991), 20–21. For similar canonical revivals outside the format of the anthology, see Jane Feuer, "Melodrama, Serial Form, and Television Today," *Screen* 25.1 (Jan.–Feb. 1984): 4–16, and John Fletcher, "Introduction—Melodrama," *Screen* 29.3 (Summer 1988): 2–12.

73. Steve Neale, "Melodrama and Tears," *Screen* 27.6 (1986): 6–23; Fletcher, "Versions of Masquerade," *Screen* 29.3 (1988): 43–70, especially 46–48.

74. Marina Heung, "What's the Matter with Sara Jane? Daughters and Mothers in Douglas Sirk's *Imitation of Life*," *Cinema Journal* 26.3 (1987): 35.

75. Michael Selig, "Contradiction and Reading: Social Class and Sex Class in *Imitation of Life*," *Wide Angle* 10.4 (1988): 13–23.

76. While updates are primarily associated with either the audience or woman's film trend, contemporary essays do not always fall comfortably within either category. See, for example, Bruce Fairley, "Sirk and Bach: Fugal Construction in *Written on the Wind, CineAction!* 8 (1987): 65–68.

77. Lucy Fischer, ed., *Imitation of Life* (New Brunswick: Rutgers University Press, 1991). Unlike a great deal of other writing on this film, Fischer provides a historical and institutional context for understanding its significance by including commentaries on Lana Turner's star construction, the status of working and black women in the postwar era, and a production history, among other things. For other work on race, women's issues, and melodrama, see Jane Gaines, "*The Scar of Shame*: Skin Color and Caste in Black Silent Melodrama," in Landy, 331–48; and, on the 1930s Stahl version of *Imitation of Life*, Lauren Berlandt, "National Brands/National Body: *Imitation of Life*," in Hortense J. Spillers, ed., *Comparative American Identities: Race, Sex, and Nationality in the Modern Text* (New York: Routledge, 1991), 110–40.

78. Christine Saxton appears to reflect in a similar way by reconsidering ideas of Sirk's authorship via Foucault in "The Collective Voice as Cultural Voice," *Cinema Journal* 26.1 (1986): 19–30. But, in fact, her essay is entirely focused on textual structures.

79. This is the same conclusion reached by David Bordwell in *Making Meaning*, 247–74. Bordwell tends to see this "inertia" in interpretation as a product of several factors, among them, the continual application of a limited set of interpretive protocols and schemata to new semantic fields and the dominance of ideological theory over criticism since 1968. While I ultimately ascribe the static quality of criticism in Sirk's case to the gridlock effect of canonicity, like Bordwell, I see the role a schemata such as the author's personification and certain paradigms of ideological theory such as the progressive text can play in creating repetitive meanings for films. Similarly, as the design of my book would suggest, I concur strongly with his statement that "to make all films mean the same things by applying the same critical procedures is to ignore the rich variety of film history" (p. 267). However, my stake in this critique is not to suggest that we overhaul how we approach films in the discipline to rid ourselves of conventional interpretive efforts; I am not sure that any new research paradigm can escape the ritual effects of the institution. Rather, in recognizing academic interpretation as a particular activity, shaped by specific critical, historical, and institutional dynamics, I hope to reframe its procedures as relative, rather than authoritative. In so doing, academic criticism may be considered an important part of a text's history and placed in relation to its other meanings as an equal, rather than a better. In addition, I am less interested in deposing ideological theory—if anything, it is the institution's use of theory more than the theories themselves that creates inertia—than in arguing for a mutation of ideological theory that could more effectively address historical issues of meaning production.

80. Janet Staiger, "The Politics of Film Canons," *Cinema Journal* 24.3 (Spring 1985): 4–23.

81. Fletcher, "Versions of Masquerade," 47–48; Heung, "What's the Matter with Sara Jane?" 35–36.

82. Herrnstein Smith, *Contingencies of Value*, 40–41.

2. Selling Melodrama

1. L. P. Hartley, *The Go-Between* (London: Hamish Hamilton, 1953) 9.

2. I should point out that I will be concentrating on aspects of the film's national, rather than local, campaign. While campaigns designed by local exhibitors were still a part of advertising, Universal's ad policies for their high-quality films became particularly focused on preselling on the national level in the 1950s. Ad executives explained this emphasis on long-term, wide-scale promotion as a means of enhancing their ability to recapture lost audiences—those consumers no longer attending movies in an era of television saturation. In addition, television, like radio before it, provided a sterling opportunity to expand media coverage. Because of the importance of this level of advertising, I will focus on appeals made to mass audiences, rather than the more specialized ones used by local advertising. For a general examination of how and why national advertising became a widespread industry practice after the 1930s, see Janet Staiger, "Announcing Wares, Winning Patrons, Voicing Ideals: Thinking about the History and Theory of Film Advertising," *Cinema Journal* 29.3 (Spring 1990): 12–14.

The national ad campaign for *Written on the Wind* was implemented from August 1956 through January 1957. Three Technicolor "teaser" trailers and the regular trailer began running three weeks before the film's premiere. Interviews with the stars of the film—Rock Hudson, Dorothy Malone, and Robert Stack—appeared on network and syndicated television and radio and in national and fan magazines three months before the film's release. A record national and Sunday supplement magazine advertising campaign for the November, December, and January issues ran in nineteen publications (including *Life, Look* and *Colliers*), having a combined circulation of forty million and an estimated readership of 125 million. Besides numerous radio ads, 400 television trailers, shown in thirty-five markets with a viewing range of sixteen million sets, started to air in early November. Television advertising also included a special tie-in with the CBS television and radio show "Strike It Rich." And last, promotion featured the title song (written by Sammy Cahn and sung by The Four Aces) and the soundtrack album, which was released in January of 1957. My information on Universal's exhibition strategies comes from the advertising files for *Written on the Wind*, Special Collections, Doheny Library, the University of Southern California, Los Angeles. Sources relating specifically to policy decisions include studio meeting reports and "News to U from U-I," a Univeral publication concerned with advertising and publicity disseminated throughout the organization and to exhibitors.

3. Joe Morella, Edward Z. Epstein, and Eleanor Clark, *Those Great Movie Ads* (New Rochelle: Arlington House, 1972), 88.

4. *Variety*, Sept. 5, 1956: 8–9.

5. *Variety*, Dec. 5, 1956: 19.

6. Hy Hollinger, "Sticks Now on 'Hick Pix' Kick," *Variety*, Dec. 5, 1956: 1.

7. Steve Neale, "Art Cinema as Institution," *Screen* 22.1 (1981): 32–33.

8. For a fuller discussion of censorship and *The Outlaw*, see Mary Beth Haralovich, "Film Advertising, the Film Industry, and the Pin-Up," *Current Research in Film*, 143–51.

9. *Variety*, Dec. 5, 1956: 1, 86.

10. Joseph Burstyn, Inc. vs. Wilson, 343 U.S. 475 (1952).

11. Morella et al., *Those Great Movie Ads*, 77.

12. From Universal-International's "News to U from U-I," *Written on the Wind* files, Doheny Library. It is worth noting that *Written on the Wind* was not the only Sirk melodrama promoted as adult. Although *Magnificent Obsession, All That Heaven Allows*, and *Imitation of Life* were primarily advertised as women's films, that is, as romances, each of their trailers and

many of their newspaper advertisements also emphasized shocking content. *Tarnished Angels* most closely compares to *Written on the Wind* for its strong promotion as adult.

13. *Variety*, Sept. 20, 1956; *Film Daily*, Sept. 20, 1956. All of the trade reviews for *Written on the Wind* appeared in September 1956 as a result of special advance screenings for trade journal critics and are documented in the *Written on the Wind* files, Doheny Library.

14. Unless otherwise indicated, all of the materials discussed in this section were found in the *Written on the Wind* files, Doheny Library. This library holds the largest collection of materials that I found for this film, including studio inter-office communications, extensive documentation of their market research on and national campaign for the film, advertising suggestions for local exhibitors, press books, posters, trailer transcripts, and other documents. Throughout this chapter, I have of necessity synthesized this material, selecting types of ads to analyze that best represent the spirit and content of the campaign's general thrust. For a broader view of ad materials, see my dissertation, "Cinema and Social Process: A Contextual Theory of the Cinema and Its Spectators," Ph.D. diss., University of Iowa, 1986. While the Doheny had the most extensive holdings on *Written on the Wind*, other archives also provided rich resources. In this case, posters and newspaper ads were also available under the name of the studio, the film, and the director at The New York Public Library/Theater for the Performing Arts and The Museum of Modern Art Film Archive, New York.

15. Trailer, teaser trailer, and television trailer transcripts for this film and all of Sirk's major 1950s melodramas were found in a collection called "Universal Pictures Company Collection—Trailer Scripts" at the Academy of Motion Picture Arts and Sciences, Margaret Herrick Library. The main trailer can also be found at the Doheny Library. I did not find in either archive a significant variation in trailers for *Written on the Wind*. There is, however, a "Northern" and "Southern" trailer for *Imitation of Life* at the Academy.

16. *Film Daily*, Sept. 20, 1956; *Harrison's Report*, Sept. 24, 1956.

17. Janet Staiger discusses the overall importance of market research for studios in the post–World War II era in "Announcing Wares, Winning Patrons, Voicing Ideals," 12–14. See also Susan Ohmer, "Measuring Desire: George Gallup and Audience Research in Hollywood," *Journal of Film and Video* 43.1–2 (Spring–Summer 1991): 3–28.

18. Sindlinger and Company, "Movie Market Trends," Nov. 17, 1956. This publication was a monthly report containing statistics charting audience numbers and patterns of attendance.

19. Richard Dyer, *Heavenly Bodies: Film Stars and Society* (New York: St. Martin's Press, 1986), 19–66.

20. John D'Emilio, *Sexual Politics, Sexual Communities: The Making of a Homosexual Minority in the United States, 1940–70* (Chicago: University of Chicago Press, 1983), 23–39.

21. Michael Bronski, *Culture Clash: The Making of Gay Sensibility* (Boston: South End Press, 1984), 79–88.

22. For more on lesbian pulp fiction see Fran Koski and Maida Tilchen, "Some Pulp Sappho," in Karla Jay and Allen Young, eds., *Lavender Culture* (New York: Jove, 1979), 262–74. For a discussion of the paperback publication background of *Howl*, see Kenneth C. Davis, *Two-Bit Culture: The Paperbacking of America* (Boston: Houghton Mifflin Company, 1984), 269.

23. For discussions of both beatniks and "sick" comics as incipient forms of the more developed countercultures of the 1960s, see Marty Jezer, *The Dark Ages: Life in the United States 1945–1960* (Boston: South End Press, 1982), 258–90.

24. John D'Emilio and Estelle B. Freedman, *Intimate Matters: A History of Sexuality in America* (New York: Harper & Row, 1988), 239–74.

25. Elaine Tyler May, *Homeward Bound: American Families in the Cold War Era* (New York: Basic Books, 1988), 116.

26. D'Emilio and Freedman, *Intimate Matters*, 277.

27. See Haralovich, "Film Advertising," 134–42.

28. For a detailed discussion of the pernicious relation of *Playboy* to images of the family

and women in the 1950s, see Barbara Ehrenreich, *The Hearts of Men: American Dreams and the Flight from Commitment* (New York: Anchor Press, 1983), 42–51.

29. For a discussion of paperback covers and obscenity problems, see Davis, *Two-Bit Culture*, 135–41, 216–47.

30. Thomas Peterson, *Magazines in the Twentieth Century* (Urbana: University of Illinois Press, 1964), 304; for his account of the success of exposé magazines in the 1950s, see 379–82.

31. While this does not prove the effectiveness of the advertising campaign, exhibitor's statistics for major urban areas show that while 70 percent of the matinee audience for *Written on the Wind* was female, evening showings were equal in gender distribution.

32. Tony Bennett and Janet Woollacott, *Bond and Beyond: The Political Career of a Popular Hero* (New York: Methuen, 1987), 81. See also Steve Neale's call for a historicizing of generic definitions in "Questions of Genre," *Screen* 31.1 (Spring 1990): 45–46.

33. Bennett and Woollacott, *Bond and Beyond*, 81.

34. Jeanne Allen, "Fig Leaves in Hollywood: Female Representation and Consumer Culture," *Fabrications*, Jane Gaines and Charlotte Herzog, eds. (New York: Routledge, 1990), 122–33; Jane Gaines and Charlotte Herzog, " 'Puffed Sleeves before Tea-Time': Joan Crawford, Adrian, and Women Audiences," *Wide Angle* 6.4 (1985): 24–33; and Diane Waldman, "From Midnight Shows to Marriage Vows: Women, Exploitation and Exhibition," *Wide Angle* 6.2 (1984): 40–48.

35. Writers have particularly emphasized how the strong interrelation between the industry and consumer culture flourishing by the 1920s helped define and sharpen the industry's treatment of film style as material spectacle. See Charles Eckert, "The Carole Lombard in Macy's Window," *Quarterly Review of Film Studies* 3.1 (1978): 1–21; and Jeanne Allen, "The Film Viewer as Consumer," *Quarterly Review of Film Studies* 5.4 (Fall 1980): 481–99.

36. For more on Universal's history in relation to prestige picture production, see the Universal sections in Thomas Schatz, *The Genius of the System: Hollywood Filmmaking in the Studio Era* (New York: Pantheon Books, 1988).

37. Review of *Written on the Wind*, *Film Daily*, Sept. 20, 1956.

38. Unlike posters and trailers, the public status of press book copy is less certain. It is unknown in the case of *Written on the Wind* whether the stories in the press books were actually published in newspapers and magazines. However, I would argue that whether or not press book copy actually appeared publicly, analyzing it can reveal how Universal designed its campaign to sell style, like genre, to appeal to public predilections.

39. Press books were located at the Doheny Library, the New York Public Library/Theatre for the Performing Arts, and the Museum of Modern Art.

40. See David Bordwell, Janet Staiger, and Kristin Thompson, *The Classical Hollywood Cinema* (New York: Columbia University Press, 1985), 99–101.

41. David Bonyard, "WOW is Lavish," *The Los Angeles Herald and Express*, Dec. 26, 1956.

42. *Variety*, Mar. 7, 1956.

43. Steve Neale, *Cinema and Technology: Image, Sound, Color* (Bloomington: Indiana University Press, 1985), 139.

44. Ibid., 151–55.

45. Information about the tie-in comes from the *Written on the Wind* files, Doheny Library.

46. Information courtesy of CBS Audience Services, New York. There is a further description of the show in *The Complete Directory to Prime Time Network TV Shows: 1946–Present*, Tim Brooks and Earle March, eds. (New York: Ballantine Books, 1981), 720–21.

47. Several episodes of the show featuring a burn victim, a poor, illiterate farmer, and a blind women's choir as contestants were available for viewing at the UCLA Film and Television Archive, Los Angeles.

48. Douglas T. Miller and Marion Nowak, *The Fifties: The Way We Really Were* (New York: Doubleday & Company, 1977), 118–19.

49. Paul Baran and Paul Sweezy, *Monopoly Capital* (New York: Monthly Review Press, 1966), 115.

50. Jezer, *The Dark Ages*, 120.

51. See May, *Homeward Bound*, 16–36, 162–82.

52. George Lipsitz, *Time Passages: Collective Memory and American Popular Culture* (Minneapolis: University of Minnesota Press, 1990), 44.

53. Ibid., 50–52.

54. For work on women and consumption in the early 1900s, see, for example, Judith Mayne, "Immigrants and Spectators," *Wide Angle* 5.2 (1982): 32–41, or Kathy Peiss, *Cheap Amusements: Working Women and Leisure in Turn-of-the-Century New York* (Philadelphia: Temple University Press, 1986). For the 1920s, see Stuart Ewen, *Captains of Consciousness: Advertising and the Social Roots of the Consumer Culture* (New York: McGraw-Hill, 1976), 159–84.

55. The preoccupation with presenting women as domestic, consuming beings during the 1950s is of course widely and diversely manifested during this period. For example, Michael Renov discusses how a number of media constituted the female image to serve the historical exigencies of war and postwar eras in the 1940s (from a patriotic, job-oriented image to one focused exclusively on consumption for the home and child-rearing) in "Advertising/Photojournalism/Cinema: The Shifting Rhetoric of Forties Female Representation," *Quarterly Review of Film and Video* 11.1 (1989): 1–21.

56. Betty Friedan, *The Feminine Mystique* (New York: Dell Publishing Co., 1974).

57. Ibid., 199.

58. May, *Homeward Bound*, 167.

59. Mary Ann Doane, *The Desire to Desire* (Bloomington: Indiana University Press, 1987), 30–31.

3. Tastemaking

1. Pierre Bourdieu, *Distinction: A Social Critique of the Judgment of Taste*, Richard Nice, trans. (Cambridge: Harvard University Press, 1984), 7.

2. Jean-Louis Comolli and Jean Narboni, "Cinema/Ideology/Criticism," Susan Bennett, trans., *Screen* 12.1 (Spring 1971): 34.

3. In his work on film audiences of the late 1940s, Leo Handel found that reviews ranked third in importance, after hearsay and trailers, among sources influencing the attendance of moviegoers at certain pictures, in *Hollywood Looks at Its Audience* (Urbana: University of Illinois Press, 1950), 69.

4. Robert C. Allen and Douglas Gomery, *Film History: Theory and Practice* (New York: Alfred A. Knopf, 1985), 90. See also Mike Budd, "The National Board of Review and the Early Art Cinema in New York: *The Cabinet of Dr. Caligari* as Affirmative Culture," *Cinema Journal* 26.1 (Fall 1986): 3–18.

5. For a thorough analysis of the origins and concerns of the earliest film reviews, see Myron Lounsbury, *The Origins of American Film Criticism, 1909–1939* (New York: Arno Press, 1973).

6. James Agee, *Agee on Film* (New York: McDowell, Obolensky Inc., 1958). This book reprinted Agee's criticism during the 1940s in *The Nation, Time,* and *Life.* Arthur Knight, *The Liveliest Art: A Panoramic History of the Movies* (New York: MacMillan, 1957). Gilbert Seldes, *The Seven Lively Arts* (1924; New York: Sagamore Press Inc., 1957); *The Great Audience* (New York: Viking Press, 1951); and *The Public Arts* (New York: Simon and Schuster, 1956). Robert Warshow, *The Immediate Experience: Movies, Comics, Theatre and Other Aspects of Popular*

Culture (New York: Doubleday & Company, 1962). This book collected Warshow's criticism from his writings in the 1940s and 1950s in *Commentary* and *Partisan Review*.

7. In the 1960s, Andrew Sarris placed many of these directors in his "Less Than Meets the Eye" category. Filmmakers in this category had "reputations in excess of inspiration," and lacked a "personal signature" (*The American Cinema: Directors and Directions* [New York: E. P. Dutton, 1968], 155). While it later influenced critical opinion to reject these overt humanists, Sarris's position had little relevance to the critical atmosphere of the 1950s. Although at the time some reviewers, such as *The Nation's* Manny Farber, railed against what they saw as the superficial seriousness of films such as *High Noon*, the realist aesthetic predominated in reviews of dramas.

8. For further discussion of the impact of war documentaries and Italian neo-realism on Hollywood, see David Cook, *A History of Narrative Film* (New York: W. W. Norton and Company, Inc., 1990), 454–79. See also Janet Staiger, who explicitly argues that the critical success of art films such as *Open City* helped orient the critical agenda in the postwar era toward bitter, shocking, frank, realistic, "sexy" message films (*Interpreting Films: Studies in the Historical Reception of American Cinema* [Princeton: Princeton University Press, 1992], 184). For further discussion of post–World War II developments in theater that resulted in a new naturalism, see Barnard Hewitt, *Theater U.S.A. 1668–1957* (New York: McGraw-Hill Book Company, 1959), 453.

9. Bosley Crowther, *The New York Times*, Mar. 16, 1952; *The New York Times Encyclopedia of Film*, Gene Brown, ed. (New York: Times Books, 1985).

10. Edwin Locke, *Films*, Spring 1940, *American Film Criticism: From the Beginnings to Citizen Kane*, Stanley Kauffmann, ed. (New York: Liveright, 1972), 385.

11. Franz Hollering, *The Nation*, Dec. 30, 1939, *American Film Criticism*, 370–71.

12. Gilbert Seldes, *Esquire*, Aug. 1941, *American Film Criticism*, 419.

13. Bosley Crowther, *The Great Films: Fifty Golden Years of Motion Pictures* (New York: G. P. Putnam's Sons, 1967), 9–10. See also Crowther's *Vintage Films* (New York: G. P. Putnam's Sons, 1977).

14. Arthur Knight, *The Saturday Review*, Dec. 29, 1956: 22–24.

15. *Newsweek*, Dec. 17, 1956: 106.

16. Bosley Crowther, *The New York Times*, Dec. 13, 1957: 35.

17. Moira Walsh, *America*, Sept. 27, 1958: 679.

18. Philip T. Hartung, *Commonweal*, Sept. 26, 1958: 637.

19. Questions of plausibility were also connected to the exercise of censorship. See Chon Noriega, "SOMETHING'S MISSING HERE! Homosexuality and Film Reviews during the Production Code Era, 1934–1962," *Cinema Journal* 30.1 (Fall 1990): 20–41.

20. Philip T. Hartung, *Commonweal*, Mar. 2, 1956: 569.

21. Crowther, *The New York Times*, Oct. 27, 1955: 28.

22. Lee Rogow, *The Saturday Review*, July 31, 1954: 36; Arthur Knight, *The Saturday Review*, Jan. 25, 1958: 27, and April 11, 1959: 28. See also, for example, Pauline Kael's later very qualified praise of *Tarnished Angels* as "it's the kind of bad movie that you know is bad—and yet you're held by the mixture of polished style and quasi-melodramatics achieved by the director," in *5001 Nights at the Movies* (New York: Holt, Rinehart and Winston, 1982), 580.

23. James Agee, *Agee on Film* (New York: McDowell, Obolensky, Inc., 1958), 105. Originally appeared in *The Nation*, July 22, 1944.

24. Bosley Crowther, *The New York Times*, Feb. 29, 1956: 35; *Time*, Mar. 26, 1956: 104.

25. Philip T. Hartung, *Commonweal*, July 23, 1954: 388.

26. "*All That Heaven Allows*," *Monthly Film Bulletin*, Oct. 1955: 151; "*Written on the Wind*," *Monthly Film Bulletin*, Nov. 1956: 139; "*Imitation of Life*," *Monthly Film Bulletin*, May 1959: 55.

27. Bosley Crowther, *The New York Times*, Jan. 12, 1957: 12.

28. *Newsweek*, Apr. 13, 1959: 118; Moira Walsh, *Catholic World*, Aug. 1959: 154–55.

29. John McCarten, *The New Yorker*, Aug. 14, 1954: 59.

30. See, for example, Patrice Petro, "Mass Culture and the Feminine: The Place of Television in Film Studies," *Cinema Journal* 25.3 (Spring 1986): 5–21.

31. Richard H. Pells, *The Liberal Mind in a Conservative Age: American Intellectuals in the 1940s and 1950s* (Middletown, Conn.: Wesleyan University Press, 1989), 218.

32. Andrew Ross, *No Respect: Intellectuals and Popular Culture* (New York: Routledge, 1989), 53–54.

33. Joseph Wood Krutch, "Is Our Common Man too Common," *The Saturday Review*, Jan. 10, 1953: 8.

34. D. W. Brogan, "The Taste of the Common Man," *The Saturday Review*, Jan. 28, 1953: 50.

35. Brogan, 48; Krutch, 36.

36. Edward C. Linderman, "The Common Man as Reader," *The Saturday Review*, May 9, 1953: 11–12, 47–48; Gilbert Seldes, "Radio, Television, and the Common Man," *The Saturday Review*, Aug. 29, 1953: 11–12, 39–41.

37. Theodor Adorno and Max Horkheimer, "The Culture Industry: Enlightenment as Mass Deception," *Dialectic of Enlightenment* (1944; New York: Herder and Herder, 1977), 152, 126, 144.

38. Bernard Rosenberg and David Manning White, eds., *Mass Culture: The Popular Arts in America* (Glencoe, Ill.: The Free Press, 1957), 9.

39. Paul Lazarsfeld and Robert Merton, "Mass Communication, Popular Taste, and Organized Social Action," *Mass Culture* (Rosenberg and White), 464–66.

40. Seldes, "Radio, Television, and the Common Man," 39–40.

41. Nora Sayre, "Films That Still Have the Power to Panic," *The New York Times*, July 31, 1977: 85.

42. Robert B. Ray, *A Certain Tendency of the Hollywood Cinema, 1930–1980* (Princeton: Princeton University Press, 1985), 247–95.

43. Michiko Kakutani, "Garson Kanin Recalls Hollywood's High Times," Nov. 18, 1979, *The New York Times Encyclopedia of Film*, Gene Brown, ed. (New York: Times Books, 1985).

44. Richard Corliss, "The New Conservatism," *Film Comment*, Jan.–Feb. 1980: 34–35 and 45.

45. Roger Angell, *The New Yorker*, Dec. 31, 1979: 52.

46. David Ehrenstein, "Melodrama and the New Woman," *Film Comment*, Sept.–Oct. 1978: 59.

47. Russell Baker, quoted by Richard Corliss in "The Seventies," *Film Comment*, Jan.–Feb. 1980: 34.

48. Walter Goodman, "The Man Who Would Be Hitchcock," *The New York Times*, Aug. 8, 1976: II, 11.

49. Andrew Sarris, *The Village Voice*, July 26, 1977: 41; June 11, 1964: 13; July 18, 1977: 37.

50. For a source that thoroughly discusses the nature of the phenomenon of nostalgia and its different historical manifestations, see David Lowenthal, *The Past Is a Foreign Country* (New York: Cambridge University Press, 1985).

51. Fred Davis, "Nostalgia, Identity, and the Current Nostalgia Wave," *The Journal of Popular Culture* 11.2 (Fall 1977): 421.

52. Peter Clecak, *America's Quest for the Ideal Self: Dissent and Fulfillment in the 60s and 70s* (New York: Oxford University Press, 1983), 43.

53. Ibid., 44.

54. See Fred Davis, *Yearning for Yesterday: A Sociology of Nostalgia* (New York: The Free Press, 1979), 104–107.

55. In *The New York Times Encyclopedia:* Andrew H. Malcolm, "John Huston: I Want to Keep Right On Going," *The New York Times,* Dec. 11, 1979; Vincent Canby, "Nicholas Ray: Still a Rebel with a Cause," *The New York Times,* Sept. 24, 1972A; Morris Dickstein, "It's a Wonderful Life, but . . . ," *American Film,* May 1980: 42–47.

56. "Can a Director Grow on Foreign Soil?" *The New York Times,* May 2, 1976A, *The New York Times Encyclopedia.*

57. Rainer Werner Fassbinder, "Fassbinder on Sirk," Thomas Elsaesser, trans., *Film Comment* 11.6 (1975): 22–24; Andrew Sarris, "Fassbinder and Sirk: The Ties That Unbind," *The Village Voice,* Sept. 3–9, 1980: 37–38.

58. Fassbinder, "Fassbinder on Sirk," 24.

59. George Morris, "Sirk's Imitations of Life," *The Soho Weekly News,* Dec. 13, 1979: 40.

60. Program notes written in conjunction with the various series similarly demonstrated an absorption of academic values, rendered more accessible. The Thalia's notes were composed, for example, by James Harvey, a professor at the State University of New York–Stony Brook, who had previously published work on Sirk in *Film Comment.* Harvey refers to Sirk's "famous ironical sub-text," arguing that although his films elicit ambivalent responses from audiences unsure as to whether they are watching sheer tackiness or a critique of it, the films support an ironical reading through devices like the unhappy end. "A Thalia Series in Honor of Douglas Sirk's First Visit to America in Twenty Years," 1979.

61. Fred Camper, "Sirk's Masterworks," *The Soho Weekly News,* Aug. 5, 1976: 21.

62. Sarris, "Fassbinder and Sirk: The Ties That Unbind," 37–38; see also Sarris, *The Village Voice,* Dec. 17, 1979: 54–55.

63. Sarris, *The Village Voice,* Nov. 21, 1977: 44.

64. Jonathan Rosenbaum, "Sirk's Works," *The Soho Weekly News,* Aug. 27, 1980: 44, 48.

65. J. Hoberman, "Twister," *The Village Voice,* Oct. 27, 1987: 70; reprinted in Hoberman's *Vulgar Modernism: Writing on Movies and Other Media* (Philadelphia: Temple University Press, 1991), 248.

66. Andrew Sarris, *The Village Voice,* Dec. 30–Jan. 5, 1982: 26, 36; see also Molly Haskell's critique of George Lucas as a reactionary in "May the Force Shut Up!" *The Village Voice,* July 4, 1977: 37.

67. J. Hoberman, "Heroes and Villains in the Arts," *The Village Voice,* Dec. 30–Jan. 5, 1982: 26.

68. Haskell, "May the Force Shut Up!" 37.

69. Ibid.; see also on the *Voice's* attitudes toward the mass audience, Andrew Sarris, "Smart Movies, Dumb Audiences," in which he laments the popularity of *The Jerk* over *Pennies from Heaven,* blaming the audience for its lack of discrimination, *The Village Voice,* Dec. 30–Jan. 5, 1982: 36.

4. Star Gossip

1. Edgar Morin, *Les Stars* (Paris: Seuil, 1957).

2. Richard Dyer, *Stars* (London: British Film Institute, 1979), 72; Dyer, *Heavenly Bodies: Film Stars and Society* (New York: St. Martin's Press, 1986), 2.

3. Charles Eckert, "Shirley Temple and the House of Rockefeller," *American Media and Mass Culture: Left Perspectives,* Donald Lazere, ed. (Berkeley: University of California Press, 1987), 164–77; Richard Dyer, *Heavenly Bodies,* 19–66.

4. Richard de Cordova, "Dialogue: Richard de Cordova Responds to Miriam Hansen's 'Pleasure, Ambivalence, Identification: Valentino and Female Spectatorship,'" *Cinema Journal* 26.3 (Spring 1987): 55.

5. Eleanor Harris, "Rock Hudson: Why He's No. 1 Lover," *People,* July 9, 1958: 17–20; Eleanor Harris, "Rock Hudson: Why He's No. 1," *Look,* March 18, 1958: 47–56; "Rock Hud-

son: Hollywood's Most Handsome Bachelor," *Life*, Oct. 3, 1955: 129–32; At the time, *Life* was the most popular magazine in the world with a circulation of eight million.

6. For a discussion of the centrality of the celebrity biography to mass culture, see Leo Lowenthal, "The Triumph of Mass Idols," *Literature, Popular Culture, and Society*, Leo Lowenthal, ed. (Englewood Cliffs, N.J.: Prentice-Hall, Inc., 1961), 109–140.

7. Joe Hyams, "The Rock Hudson Story, Part One," *Photoplay*, Feb. 1957: 90. All further references appear in the text. Some other biographies in fan magazines include: "Home Town Report on Rock Hudson," *Motion Picture*, July 1955; Louis Pollock, "Big Noise from Winnetka," *Modern Screen*, March 1955; and Janet McCutcheon, "Who Is Rock Hudson?" *Movie Star Parade*, March 1957. Magazine stories on Hudson were found either as clippings in The New York Public Library/Theater for the Performing Arts, New York City, or the Margaret Herrick Library, the Motion Picture Academy of Arts and Sciences, Los Angeles. Given the deteriorated condition of some of these clippings from the New York Public Library, I have not always been able to provide page numbers.

8. General circulation biographies could be more critical of Hudson. In *People* and *Look*, Eleanor Harris mildly criticized Hudson for being "the classic example of the created movie star," in "Rock Hudson: Why He's No. 1 Lover," 17–20, and "Rock Hudson: Why He's No. 1," 47–56. Some other general and women's magazine biographies include, "Rock Hudson: Hollywood's Most Handsome Bachelor," *Life*, Oct. 3, 1955; and "Rock Hudson Tells His Own Story," *American Weekly*, March 25, 1956.

9. For a discussion of the comparative depiction of Hudson's body in the 1950s and 1980s, see Richard Meyer, "Rock Hudson's Body," *Inside/Out*, Diana Fuss, ed. (New York: Routledge, 1991), 259–88.

10. Liza Wilson, "How a Hollywood Bachelor Lives," *American Weekly*, May 23, 1954: 13. Some other articles on bachelor status and lifestyle include, "The Simple Life of a Busy Bachelor," *Life*, Oct. 3, 1955: 129–32; Sidney Skolsky, "Lonely Bachelor," *New York Post*, Feb. 6, 1955: M3; Louella Parsons, "Rock Hudson: Teen-Ager's Dream-Boat," *The Sunday News*, April 8, 1956; "King of Movies Always Had a Way with Women," *New York Journal*, Feb. 24, 1958.

11. Essays covering this pivotal shift in his marital identity include Beverly Ott, "The Man Who almost Got Away," *Photoplay*, April 1956: 37, 102; "Hog-Tied and I Couldn't Care Less," *Silver Screen*, Feb. 1957; "Why Rock Had to Get Married," *Motion Picture*, Feb. 1956; "Secrets of Rock Hudson's Most Crucial Year," *Movie Life*, Oct. 1956; and "What Marriage Did to My Son," *Movie Mirror*, May 1957: 25–28.

12. Beverly Ott, "Planning a Heavenly Love Nest," *Photoplay*, Feb. 1956: 44–45.

13. For a detailed exploration of this turn of events, see Denise Mann, "The Spectacularization of Everyday Life: Recycling Hollywood Stars and Fans in Early Television Variety Shows," *Camera Obscura* 16 (Jan. 1988): 49–77.

14. Ott, "Planning a Heavenly Love Nest," 44.

15. Dyer, *Heavenly Bodies*, 12–13.

16. Hyatt Downing, "Give a Man Room to Grow," *Photoplay*, May 1957: 71, 109.

17. Janet McCutcheon, *Movie Star Parade*, March 1957: 35–37, 58–59.

18. *Coronet*, July 1952: 75–79; *Colliers*, Nov. 1, 1952.

19. George Scullin, "James Dean: The Legend and the Facts," *Look*, Oct. 16, 1956: 122.

20. *Coronet*, July 1952: 78.

21. "Zolotow's Twist on Dean," *Variety*, Dec. 5, 1956.

22. "Marlon Brando: World's Worst Lover," *Rave*, Dec. 1953: 1–9.

23. "Moody New Star," *Life*, Mar. 7, 1955: 5.

24. Scullin, "James Dean," 4.

25. Harris, "Rock Hudson: Why He's No. 1 Lover," 18.

26. "Hollywood Exposé," *Filmland*, April 1957: 15, 17.

27. These photos are beautifully reprinted in Richard Schickel, *Hollywood at Home: A Family Album 1950–1965* (New York: Crown Publishers, 1990), 88–89.

28. John D'Emilio, *Sexual Politics, Sexual Communities: The Making of a Homosexual Minority in the United States, 1940–1970* (Chicago: University of Chicago Press, 1983), 17.

29. Ibid., 41.

30. Elaine Tyler May, *Homeward Bound: American Families in the Cold War Era* (New York: Basic Books, 1988), 93.

31. Barbara Ehrenreich, *The Hearts of Men: American Dreams and the Flight from Commitment* (New York: Anchor Press, 1983), 20.

32. Ibid., 25.

33. See also George B. Leonard, "The American Male: Why Is He Afraid to Be Different?" *Look*, Feb. 18, 1958: 95–102. This essay was part of a series on the American male.

34. J. Robert Moskin, "The American Male: Why Do Women Dominate Him?" *Look*, Feb. 4, 1958: 77–80.

35. For another account of the relation of a 1950s star image to a crisis in masculinity with national proportions, see Steven Cohan's excellent "Masquerading as the American Male in the Fifties: *Picnic*, William Holden, and the Spectacle of Masculinity in Hollywood Film," *Camera Obscura* 25/26 (1992): 43–72. In contrast to my interpretation of Hudson's image, Cohan suggests the possibility of a subversive dimension to Holden's image, via contradictions between the sexual presentation of his body in *Picnic* and extra-filmic characterizations of him as a sincere, ordinary, middle-class citizen. Hudson's roles and coverage similarly exploit the erotic charge of his body. However, I argue that since this aspect of his persona is continuously related to boyishness, status quo morality, and an atavistic masculinity, eros operates less to create transgressive pleasures than to make certain norms more attractive and desirable.

36. For further discussion of the links between family ideology and Cold War rhetoric in films, see Michael Paul Rogin, *Ronald Reagan, the Movie, and Other Episodes in Political Demonology* (Berkeley: University of California Press, 1987), 236–71.

37. Vito Russo, *The Celluloid Closet: Homosexuality in the Movies* (New York: Harper & Row, 1987), 160–61.

38. *Movie and TV Spotlight*, May 27, 1957.

39. See, for example, Sylvia Harvey, "Woman's Place: The Absent Family of Film Noir," *Women in Film Noir*, E. Ann Kaplan, ed. (London: British Film Institute, 1978), 22–34.

40. See Sirk on this point, in Jon Halliday, *Sirk on Sirk* (New York: Viking Press, 1972), 98.

41. I have written on this subject at greater length in "Digressions at the Cinema: Reception and Mass Culture," *Cinema Journal* 28.4 (Summer 1989): 3–19.

42. Miriam Hansen, *Babel and Babylon: Spectatorship in American Silent Film* (Cambridge: Harvard University Press, 1991), 246.

43. *People* wrote, "Since no woman's name has been linked seriously to Hudson's since his 1958 divorce, rumors that he is gay have surfaced." *People*, Nov. 15, 1982: 148.

44. "Rock Hudson Finds Fun in Just Hanging Loose," *The New York Post*, Aug. 27, 1977.

45. "Roy Fitzgerald Takes Some Time to Reminisce," *TV Guide*, April 29–May 5, 1972: 24–28; Gordon Gow, "Actors Always Try," *Films and Filming* 22.9 (June 1976): 8–13; and John Kobal, "Interview with Rock Hudson," *Films and Filming* 373 (Oct. 1985): 15–18.

46. "The Long Goodbye: Rock Hudson, 1925–1985," *People*, Oct. 21, 1985: 93.

47. Michael Musto, "Benefits and Backlash: The Reaction to Rock Hudson," *The Village Voice*, Aug. 13, 1985: 24.

48. James Kinsella, *Covering the Plague: AIDS and the American Media* (New Brunswick: Rutgers University Press, 1989), 4.

49. Ibid., 144, 266.

50. "AIDS," *Newsweek* Aug. 12, 1985: cover. See also "AIDS Strikes a Star: Rock Hudson

Plays the Lead in a Real-Life Drama," in *Newsweek's* medical section, Aug. 5, 1985: 68–69. This essay attributes Hudson's case with focusing "new attention on the deadly disease and the experimental drugs being developed to treat it."

51. "Rock Hudson: He Didn't Mean to Make History," *People Extra*, Fall 1989: 65–66. Along the same lines, see "Rock Hudson's Sinister Secret," in a gala retrospective titled "Scandals of the Rich and Famous," *National Enquirer Special*, Fall 1990: 4–6.

52. Quoted in "The Long Goodbye," *People*: 93.

53. Geoffrey Stokes, "The Media and AIDS Panic: The Post-Hudson Syndrome," *The Village Voice*, Oct. 15, 1985: 19.

54. On the extent of these contamination fears, see Dennis Altman, *AIDS in the Minds of America* (Garden City, N.Y.: Anchor Press, 1986), 58–81.

55. Cindy Patton, *Sex and Germs: The Politics of AIDS* (Boston: South End Press, 1985), 51–59. On the ramifications of the use of the plague metaphor see also Susan Sontag, *AIDS and Its Metaphors* (New York: Farrar, Straus and Giroux, 1989); and especially, David Richards, "Human Rights, Public Health, and the Idea of Moral Plague," *Social Research* 55.3 (Autumn 1988): 491–528.

56. Patton, *Sex and Germs*, 58. Patton considers the relation between the right and AIDS more extensively, 83–100.

57. Simon Watney reports that British coverage of Hudson's affliction was even less kind and more moralizing than in the United States. For example, a headline in *The Daily Mail*, showing "before" and "after" pictures of Hudson, read, "The two faces of Hollywood—vibrant, virile . . . dissipated, corrupt, decadent—captured on the two faces of Rock Hudson, the first celebrity victim of AIDS," while *The Sun* later headlined, "Madonna Buys Rock's Plague Palace," quoted from *Policing Desire: Pornography, AIDS, and the Media* (Minneapolis: University of Minnesota Press, 1987), 89–90.

58. Musto, *Benefits and Backlash*, 24.

59. *TV Guide's* article on the show by Susan Littwin is titled "Will America Be Shocked by 'Rock?' " with an insert essay titled "Remembering Rock: Superstar with a Painful Secret," Jan. 6–12, 1990: 14–17.

60. Jeff Jarvis, "Rock Hudson: On Camera and Off," *People* Aug. 12, 1985: 35–36. See also Boze Hadleigh, "Scared Straight," *American Film*, Jan.–Feb. 1987: 47–51.

61. Rock Hudson and Sara Davidson, *Rock Hudson: His Story* (New York: William Morrow and Company, 1986).

62. Dyer, *Stars*, 38.

63. See Dyer, *Heavenly Bodies*, 141–94.

64. Although, on this note, there is a great deal of Hudson memorabilia in the Lester Sweyd collection at the New York Public Library/Theater for the Performing Arts. Lester Sweyd reportedly was a female impersonator.

65. Jack Babuscio, "Camp and the Gay Sensibility," *Gays and Films*, Richard Dyer, ed. (London: British Film Institute, 1977), 46.

66. As this book went to press, I discovered an article in a scandal magazine from the 1950s that made strong intimations about Hudson's homosexuality, although all of its allegations were tempered by chronicles of Hudson's heterosexual dating life ("Why Rock Hudson's Giving Hollywood the Willies," *Uncensored*, Dec. 1955: 34–35, 66–67). The article chides Hudson for liking to make curtains and cook, for once hating women, for having Henry Willson as his agent—an agent with a "reputation for handling unusual talent," and for having Tab Hunter, who was arrested for participating in a " 'pajama party' restricted to boys," as his friend. *Uncensored* was a cut-rate version of the better known scandal magazine *Confidential*, which Universal allegedly bought off to prevent them from running a similar story about Hudson. In any case, what the presence of such an article suggests is that, while the "official" mainstream press continually elaborated Hudson's heterosexual appeal, other more subterranean sources

were not so constrained and at least tried to make doubts about Hudson's sexual identity part of public culture at this time.

5. Mass Camp and the Old Hollywood Melodrama Today

1. Philip Core, *Camp: The Lie That Tells the Truth* (New York: Delilah Books, 1984), 7.

2. Paul Willemen, "Towards an Analysis of the Sirkian System," *Screen* 13.4 (1972–73): 133; Andrew Sarris, *The Village Voice*, Nov. 21, 1977: 44; from James Harvey's program notes for the Thalia Series retrospective on Sirk films in 1979. It is also interesting that the academic appropriation of Fassbinder's commentary on Sirk (in "Six Films by Douglas Sirk") tended to emphasize the political content of his essay and overlook his campy regard for Sirk's melodramas.

3. Jonathan Rosenbaum, "Sirk's Works," *The Soho Weekly News*, Aug. 27, 1980: 40, 48; J. Hoberman, "Twister," *The Village Voice*, Oct. 27, 1987: 70.

4. Most of the work in this area treats the connection between melodrama and camp in terms of gay self-recognition. See, for example, Mark Finch, "Sex and Address in 'Dynasty,'" *Screen* 27.6 (1986): 24–42; Mark Finch and Richard Kwietniowski, "Melodrama and *Maurice*: Homo Is Where the Het Is," *Screen* 29.3 (Summer 1988): 72–83; Richard Dyer, ed., *Gays and Film* (London: British Film Institute, 1977).

5. Susan Sontag, *Against Interpretation* (New York: Farrar, Straus & Giroux, 1966), 291. All further references appear in the text.

6. Michael Bronski, *Culture Clash: The Making of Gay Sensibility* (Boston: South End Press, 1984), 42.

7. Jack Babuscio, "Camp and the Gay Sensibility," *Gays and Film*, Richard Dyer, ed. (New York: New York Zoetrope, 1984), 40, 48.

8. Andrew Ross, "Uses of Camp," *The Yale Journal of Criticism* 2.1 (Fall 1988): 13. All further references appear in the text.

9. Core, *Camp*, 9.

10. For a work that questions the progressive status of camp for gay men, see Andrew Britton, "For Interpretation, Against Camp," *Gay Left* 7 (Winter 1978–79): 11–14.

11. Mark Booth, *Camp* (New York: Quartet Books, 1983), 30.

12. Robert B. Ray, *A Certain Tendency of the Hollywood Cinema, 1930–1980* (Princeton: Princeton University Press, 1985), 257.

13. Gillo Dorfles, *Kitsch* (New York: Bell, 1969), 197–217.

Conclusion

1. Tony Bennett, "Text and Social Process: The Case of James Bond," *Screen Education* No. 41 (Winter/Spring 1982): 7.

2. Ibid., 4.

Filmography

'T was een April (1935)
April, April (1935)
Das Mädchen vom Moorhof (1935)
Stutzen der Gesellschaft (1935)
Schlussakkord (1936)
Das Hofkonzert (1936)
La Chanson du Souvenir (1936)
Zu Neuen Ufern (1937)
La Habanera (1937)
Accord Final (1939)
Boefje (1939) ·
Hitler's Madman (1943)
Summer Storm (1944)
A Scandal in Paris (1946)
Lured/Personal Column (1947)
Sleep, My Love (1948)
Slightly French (1949)
Shockproof (1949)
Mystery Submarine (1950)
The First Legion (1951)
Thunder on the Hill (1951)
The Lady Pays Off (1951)
Weekend with Father (1951)
Has Anybody Seen My Gal? (1952)
No Room for the Groom (1952)
Meet Me at the Fair (1952)
Take Me to Town (1953)

All I Desire (1953)
Taza, Son of Cochise (1954)
Magnificent Obsession (1954)
Sign of the Pagan (1954)
Captain Lightfoot (1955)
All That Heaven Allows (1955)
There's Always Tomorrow (1956)
Battle Hymn (1956)
Written on the Wind (1957)
Interlude (1957)
Tarnished Angels (1958)
A Time to Love and a Time to Die (1958)
Imitation of Life (1959)

Uncredited Directorial Efforts

The Strange Woman (1946), Edgar Ulmer
Lulu Belle (1948), Leslie Fenton
Never Say Goodbye (1956), Jerry
 Hopper

Shorts

Unknown title (1934)
Dreimal Liebe (1934)
Der Eingebildete Kranke (1934)
Sprich Zu Mir Wie Der Regen (1975)
Sylvesternacht (1977)
Bourbon Street Blues (1978)

Bibliography

Adorno, Theodor, and Max Horkheimer. *Dialectic of Enlightenment*. 1944. New York: Herder, 1977.

Affron, Charles. *Cinema and Sentiment*. Chicago: University of Chicago Press, 1982.

Agee, James. *Agee on Film*. New York: McDowell, Obolensky, 1958.

"AIDS." *Newsweek*, Aug. 12, 1985: 20–29.

"AIDS Strikes a Star: Rock Hudson Plays the Lead in Real-Life Drama." *Newsweek* Aug. 5, 1985: 68–69.

Allen, Jeanne Thomas. "Fig Leaves in Hollywood: Female Representation and Consumer Culture," in Gaines and Herzog 122–33.

———. "The Film Viewer as Consumer." *Quarterly Review of Film Studies* 5.4 (Fall 1980): 481–99.

Allen, Robert C., and Douglas Gomery. *Film History: Theory and Practice*. New York: Knopf, 1985.

Review of *All That Heaven Allows*. *Time*, March 26, 1956: 104.

Althusser, Louis. "Ideology and Ideological State Apparatuses (Notes towards an Investigation)." *Lenin and Philosophy and Other Essays*. Ben Brewster, trans. New York: Monthly Review Press, 1971. 127–86.

Altman, Dennis. *AIDS in the Minds of America*. Garden City, NY: Anchor, 1986.

Anderson, Perry. "The Left in the Fifties." *New Left Review* 29 (Jan.–Feb. 1965): 3–18.

———. *Considerations of Western Marxism*. London: NLB, 1976.

Angell, Roger. "Current Cinema." *The New Yorker*, Dec. 11, 1979: 52.

Babuscio, Jack. "Camp and the Gay Sensibility." *Gays and Films*. Richard Dyer, ed. London: British Film Institute, 1977. 40–57.

Review of *Baby Doll*. *Newsweek*, Dec. 17, 1956: 106.

Baran, Paul, and Paul Sweezy. *Monopoly Capital*. New York: Monthly Review Press, 1966.

Barthes, Roland. *S/Z*. Richard Miller, trans. New York: Hill and Wang, 1974.

Bennett, Tony. "Text and Social Process: The Case of James Bond." *Screen Education* 41 (Winter–Spring 1982): 3–14.

———. "Texts in History: The Determinations of Readings and Their Texts." *The Journal of the Midwest Modern Language Association* 18.1 (1985): 1–16.

Bennett, Tony, and Janet Woollacott. *Bond and Beyond: The Political Career of a Popular Hero*. New York: Methuen, 1987.

Berlandt, Lauren. "National Brands/National Body: *Imitation of Life*." *Comparative American Identities: Race, Sex, and Nationality in the Modern Text*. Hortense J. Spillers, ed. New York: Routledge, 1991. 110–40.

Bonyard, David. "WOW Is Lavish." *The Los Angeles Herald and Express*, Dec. 26, 1956.

Booth, Mark. *Camp*. New York: Quartet Books, 1983.

Bordwell, David. *Making Meaning: Inference and Rhetoric in the Interpretation of Cinema*. Cambridge: Harvard University Press, 1989.

Bordwell, David, Janet Staiger, and Kristin Thompson. *The Classical Hollywood Cinema: Film Style & Mode of Production to 1960*. New York: Columbia University Press, 1985.

Bourdieu, Pierre. *Distinction: A Social Critique of the Judgment of Taste*. Richard Nice, trans. Cambridge: Harvard University Press, 1984.

Bourget, Jean-Loup. "Sirk's Apocalypse," in Halliday and Mulvey, 67–78.

———. *Douglas Sirk*. Paris: Edilig and the Toulouse Cinemateque, 1984.

———. "Situation de Sirk." *Positif* 137 (April 1972): 35–46. Rpt. as "Sirk and the Critics." Eithne Bourget, trans. *Bright Lights* 2.2 (Winter 1977–78): 6–10, 19.

Brecht, Bertolt. *Brecht on Theatre*. John Willett, trans. New York: Hill and Wang, 1964.

Brion, Patrick, and Dominique Labourde. "Biofilmographie." *Cahiers du cinéma* 189 (April 1967): 26–29.

Britton, Andrew. "For Interpretation, Against Camp." *Gay Left* 7 (Winter 1978–79): 11–14.

Brogan, D. W. "The Taste of the Common Man." *Saturday Review* Jan. 28, 1953: 10–11, 48–50.

Bronski, Michael. *Culture Clash: The Making of Gay Sensibility*. Boston: South End Press, 1984.

Brooks, Peter. *The Melodramatic Imagination: Balzac, Henry James, Melodrama, and the Mode of Excess*. New Haven and London: Yale University Press, 1976.

Brooks, Tim, and Earle March, eds. *The Complete Directory to Prime Time Network TV Shows: 1946–Present*. New York: Ballantine, 1981.

Brown, Gene, and Harry Geduld, eds. *New York Times Encyclopedia of Film*. New York: Times Books, 1985.

Brunner, Mathias, and Kathryn Bigelow. "Douglas Sirk." *Interview* July 1982: 50–51.

Budd, Mike. "The National Board of Review and the Early Art Cinema in New York: *The Cabinet of Dr. Caligari* as Affirmative Culture." *Cinema Journal* 26.1 (Fall 1986): 3–18.

———. "The Moments of Caligari." *The Cabinet of Dr. Caligari: Texts, Contexts, Histories*. Mike Budd, ed. New Brunswick: Rutgers University Press, 1990. 7–199.

Joseph Burstyn, Inc. vs. Wilson. 343 U.S. 475. 1952.

Buscombe, Edward. "Ideas of Authorship." *Screen* 14.3 (Autumn 1973): 75–85.

Byars, Jackie. *All That Hollywood Allows: Re-Reading Gender in the 1950s Melodrama*. Chapel Hill: University of North Carolina Press, 1991.

Camper, Fred. "The Films of Douglas Sirk." *Screen* 12.2 (1971): 44–62.

———. "Sirk's Masterworks." *Soho Weekly News*, Aug. 5, 1976: 21.

"Can a Director Grow on Foreign Soil?" *New York Times* May 2, 1976A. Rpt. in Brown and Geduld.

Canby, Vincent. "Nicholas Ray: Still a Rebel with a Cause." *New York Times*, Sept. 24, 1972A. Rpt. in Brown and Geduld.

Clecak, Peter. *America's Quest for the Ideal Self: Dissent and Fulfillment in the 60s and 70s*. New York: Oxford University Press, 1983.

Cohan, Steven. "Masquerading as the American Male in the Fifties: *Picnic*, William

Holden, and the Spectacle of Masculinity in Hollywood Film." *Camera Obscura* 25–26: 43–72.

Comolli, Jean-Louis. "L'aveugle et le miroir." *Cahiers du cinéma* 189 (April 1967): 14–18.

Comolli, Jean-Louis, and Jean Narboni. "Cinema/ideologie/critique I." *Cahiers du cinéma* 216 (Oct. 1969): 11–15. Rpt. as "Cinema/Ideology/Criticism." Susan Bennett, trans. *Screen* 12.1 (Spring 1971): 27–36.

Cook, David. *A History of Narrative Film*. New York: W. W. Norton, 1990.

Core, Philip. *Camp: The Lie That Tells the Truth*. New York: Delilah, 1984.

Corliss, Richard. "The New Conservatism." *Film Comment* Jan–Feb. 1980: 34–38.

———. "The Seventies." *Film Comment* Jan.–Feb. 1980: 34–38.

Crowther, Bosley. Review of *All That Heaven Allows*. *The New York Times*, Feb. 29, 1956: 35.

———. *The Great Films: Fifty Golden Years of Motion Pictures*. New York: Putnam, 1967.

———. "Hollywood Accents the Downbeat." *New York Times*, March 16, 1952. Rpt. in Brown and Geduld.

———. Review of *Peyton Place*. *New York Times*, Dec. 13, 1957: 35.

———. Review of *Rebel without a Cause*. *New York Times*, Oct. 27, 1955: 28.

———. "Screen: Sad Psychosis." Review of *Written on the Wind*. *New York Times*, Jan. 12, 1957: 12.

———. *Vintage Films*. New York: G. P. Putnam's Sons, 1977.

Daney, Serge, and Jean-Louis Noames. "Entretien avec Douglas Sirk." *Cahiers du cinéma* 189 (April 1967): 19–25.

Davis, Fred. "Nostalgia, Identity and the Current Nostalgia Wave." *Journal of Popular Culture* 11.2 (Fall 1977): 414–24.

———. *Yearning for Yesterday: A Sociology of Nostalgia*. New York: Free Press, 1979.

Davis, Kenneth C. *Two-Bit Culture: The Paperbacking of America*. Boston: Houghton Mifflin, 1984.

de Cordova, Richard. "A Case of Mistaken Legitimacy: Class and Generational Difference in Three Family Melodramas," in Gledhill, 255–67.

———. "Dialogue: Richard de Cordova Responds to Miriam Hansen's 'Pleasure, Ambivalence, Identification: Valentino and Female Spectatorship.' " *Cinema Journal* 26.3 (Spring 1987): 55–57.

D'Emilio, John. *Sexual Politics, Sexual Communities: The Making of a Homosexual Minority in the United States, 1940–70*. Chicago: University of Chicago Press, 1983.

D'Emilio, John, and Estelle B. Freedman. *Intimate Matters: A History of Sexuality in America*. New York: Harper, 1988.

Demonsablon, Phillippe. "Portrait d'un honnête homme." *Cahiers du cinéma* 49 (1955): 48–50.

Dickstein, Morris. "It's A Wonderful Life, but . . . " *American Film* May 1980: 42–47.

Doane, Mary Ann. "*Caught* and *Rebecca*: The Inscription of Femininity as Absence." *Enclitic* 5.2/6.1 (1981–82): 75–89.

———. *The Desire to Desire*. Bloomington: Indiana University Press, 1987.

Dorfles, Gillo. *Kitsch: The World of Bad Taste*. New York: Bell, 1969.

Downing, Hyatt. "Give a Man Room to Grow." *Photoplay* May 1957: 71.

Dyer, Richard, ed. *Gays and Film*. London: British Film Institute, 1977.

———. *Heavenly Bodies: Film Stars and Society*. New York: Routledge, 1988.

———. *Stars*. London: British Film Institute, 1979.

Easthope, Antony. "The Trajectory of *Screen*, 1971–79." *Essex Conference on the Sociology of Literature (July 1982): The Politics of Theory*. Francis Barker, Peter Hulme, et al., eds. Colchester: University of Essex, 1983. 121–33.

———. *British Post-Structuralism since 1968*. London and New York: Routledge, 1988.

Eckert, Charles. "The Carole Lombard in Macy's Window." *Quarterly Review of Film Studies* 3.1 (1978): 1–21.

———. "Shirley Temple and the House of Rockefeller." *American Media and Mass Culture: Left Perspectives*. Donald Lazere, ed. Berkeley: University of California Press, 1987. 164–177.

Editors of *Cahiers du cinéma*. "Young Mr. Lincoln, texte collectif." *Cahiers du cinéma* 223 (Aug. 1970): 29–47. Editors of *Screen*, trans. *Screen* 13.3 (Autumn 1972): 5–44.

Ehrenreich, Barbara. *The Hearts of Men: American Dreams and the Flight from Commitment*. New York: Anchor, 1983.

Ehrenstein, David. "Melodrama and the New Woman." *Film Comment* 14.5 (Sept.–Oct. 1978): 59–62.

Elsaesser, Thomas. "Tales of Sound and Fury: Observations on the Family Melodrama." *Monogram* 4 (1972): 2–15.

Ewen, Stuart. *Captains of Consciousness: Advertising and the Social Roots of Consumer Culture*. New York: McGraw-Hill, 1976.

Fairley, Bruce. "Sirk and Bach: Fugal Construction in *Written on the Wind*." *Cineaction!* 8 (1987): 65–68.

Fassbinder, Rainer Werner. "Fassbinder on Sirk." Thomas Elsaesser, trans. *Film Comment* 11.6 (1975): 22–24.

———. "*Imitation of Life*." *Fernsehen und Film* 2 (Feb. 1971): 8–13. Rpt. as "Six Films by Douglas Sirk." Thomas Elsaesser, trans., in Halliday and Mulvey, 95–107.

Feuer, Jane. "Melodrama, Serial Form, and Television Today." *Screen* 25.1 (Jan.–Feb. 1984): 4–16.

Film Daily, Sept. 20, 1956.

Finch, Mark. "Sex and Address in 'Dynasty.'" *Screen* 27.6 (1986): 24–42.

Finch, Mark, and Richard Kwietniowski. "Melodrama and *Maurice*: Homo is Where the Het Is." *Screen* 29.3 (Summer 1988): 72–83.

Fischer, Lucy, ed. *Imitation of Life*. New Brunswick: Rutgers University Press, 1991.

Fish, Stanley. *Doing What Comes Naturally: Change, Rhetoric, and the Practice of Theory in Literary and Legal Studies*. Durham and London: Duke University Press, 1989.

———. *Is There a Text in This Class? The Authority of Interpretive Communities*. Cambridge: Harvard University Press, 1980.

Fletcher, John. "Versions of Masquerade." *Screen* 29.3 (Summer 1988): 43–70.

———. "Introduction—Melodrama." *Screen* 29.3 (Summer 1988): 2–12.

French, Brandon. *On the Verge of Revolt: Women in American Films of the Fifties*. New York: Frederick Ungar, 1978.

Friedan, Betty. *The Feminine Mystique*. New York: Dell, 1974.

Fuss, Diana. *Inside/Out*. New York: Routledge, 1991.

Gaines, Jane. "Costume and Narrative: How Dress Tells the Woman's Story," in Gaines and Herzog, 180–211.

———. "The Queen Christina Tie-Ups: Convergence of Show Window and Screen." *Quarterly Review of Film Studies* 11.1 (1989): 35–60.

———. "*The Scar of Shame*: Skin Color and Caste in Black Silent Melodrama," in Landy, 331–48.

Gaines, Jane, and Charlotte Herzog, eds. *Fabrications: Costume and the Female Body*. New York: Routledge, 1990.

———. " 'Puffed Sleeves before Tea-Time': Joan Crawford, Adrian, and Women Audiences." *Wide Angle* 6.4 (1985): 24–33.

Gledhill, Christine, ed. *Home Is Where the Heart Is: Studies in Melodrama and the Woman's Film*. London: British Film Institute, 1987.

———. "The Melodramatic Field: An Investigation," in Gledhill, 5–39.

Godard, Jean-Luc. *Godard on Godard*. Tom Milne, ed. and trans. New York: Viking, 1972.

———. "Des larmes et de la vitesse." *Cahiers du cinéma* 94 (April 1959): 51–54. Rpt. as "Tears and Speed." Susan Bennett, trans. *Screen* 12.2 (Summer 1971): 96–97.

Goodman, Walter. "The Man Who Would Be Hitchcock." *New York Times*, Aug. 8, 1976: 11.

Gow, Gordon. "Actors Always Try." *Films and Filming* 22.9 (June 1976): 8–13.

Grossberg, Larry. "The Formations of Cultural Studies: An American in Birmingham." *Cultural Studies* 2 (1989): 114–47.

Grosz, David. "*First Legion*: Vision and Perception in Sirk." *Screen* 12.2 (Summer 1971): 99–117.

Hadleigh, Boze. "Scared Straight." *American Film*, Jan.–Feb. 1987: 47–51.

Halliday, Jon. *Sirk on Sirk: Interviews with Jon Halliday*. New York: Viking, 1972.

———. "All That Heaven Allows." Halliday and Mulvey, 61.

Halliday, Jon, and Laura Mulvey, eds. *Douglas Sirk*. London: Edinburgh Film Festival, National Film Theatre, and John Player and Sons, 1972.

Handel, Leo. *Hollywood Looks at Its Audience*. Urbana: University of Illinois Press, 1950.

Hansen, Miriam. *Babel and Babylon: Spectatorship in American Silent Film*. Cambridge: Harvard University Press, 1991.

Haralovich, Mary Beth. "Film Advertising, the Film Industry, and the Pin-Up." *Current Research in Film*. Vol. 1. Bruce A. Austin, ed. Norwood, N.J.: Ablex, 1985. 143–51.

Harris, Eleanor. "Rock Hudson: Hollywood's Most Handsome Bachelor." *Life*, Oct. 3, 1955: 129–32.

———. "Rock Hudson: Why He's No. 1." *Look*, March 18, 1958: 47–56.

———. "Rock Hudson: Why He's No. 1 Lover." *People*, July 9, 1958: 17–20.

Harrison's Report, Sept. 24, 1956.

Hartley, L. P. *The Go-Between*. London: Hamish Hamilton, 1953.

Hartung, Philip T. "Through a Glass Darkly." Rev. of *Cat on a Hot Tin Roof*. *Commonweal*, Sept. 26, 1958: 637.

———. "Watermelon and Ham." Rev. of *Picnic*. *Commonweal*, March 2, 1956: 569.

Harvey, James. "Sirkumstantial Evidence." *Film Comment*, July–Aug. 1978: 52–59.

———. "A Thalia Series in Honor of Douglas Sirk's First Visit to America in Twenty Years." Program notes. 1979.

Harvey, Sylvia. *May '68 and Film Culture*. London: British Film Institute, 1978.

———. "Woman's Place: The Absent Family of Film Noir." *Women in Film Noir*. E. Ann Kaplan, ed. London: British Film Institute, 1978. 22–34.

Haskell, Molly. *From Reverence to Rape: The Treatment of Women in the Movies*. New York: Penguin, 1974.

———. "May the Force Shut Up!" *Village Voice*, July 4, 1977: 37.

Heath, Stephen. "Film and System: Terms of an Analysis I." *Screen* 16.1 (Spring 1975): 7–77.

"Here's Brando." *Colliers*, Nov. 1, 1952: 24–26.

Herrnstein Smith, Barbara. *Contingencies of Value: Alternative Perspectives for Critical Theory*. Cambridge: Harvard University Press, 1988.

Hess, John. "*La Politique des auteurs*: Part One: World View as Aesthetic." *Jump Cut* 1 (May–June 1974): 19–22.

———. "La Politique des auteurs: Part Two: Truffaut's Manifesto." *Jump Cut* 2 (July–August 1974): 20–22.

Heung, Marina. "What's the Matter with Sara Jane? Daughters and Mothers in Douglas Sirk's *Imitation of Life*." *Cinema Journal* 26.3 (1987): 21–43.

Hewitt, Barnard. *Theater U.S.A. 1668–1957*. New York: McGraw, 1959.

Hillier, Jim, ed. *Cahiers du cinéma: The 1950s*. Cambridge: Harvard University Press, 1985.

Hoberman, J. "Twister." *Village Voice*, Oct. 27, 1987: 70. Rpt. in *Vulgar Modernism: Writing on Movies and Other Media*. Philadelphia: Temple University Press, 1991. 248.

———. "Heroes and Villains in the Arts." *Village Voice* Dec. 30–Jan. 5, 1982: 26.

"Hog-Tied and I Couldn't Care Less." *Silver Screen*, Feb. 1957.

Hollering, Franz. *The Nation*, Dec. 30, 1939. Rpt. in Kauffmann, 370–71.

Hollinger, Hy. "Sticks Now on 'Hick Pix' Kick." *Variety*, Dec. 5, 1956: 1, 89.

"Hollywood Exposé." *Filmland*, April 1957: 15–19.

"Home Town Report on Rock Hudson." *Motion Picture*, July 1955.

Horrigan, William. "An Analysis of the Construction of an Author: The Example of Douglas Sirk." Ph.D. diss., Northwestern University, 1980.

Hudson, Rock, and Sara Davidson. *Rock Hudson: His Story*. New York: William Morrow and Co., Inc., 1986.

Hunter, Tim. "*Summer Storm*." In Halliday and Mulvey, 31–40.

Hyams, Joe. "The Rock Hudson Story, Part One." *Photoplay*, Feb. 1957: 45, 90–93.

Review of *Imitation of Life*. *Monthly Film Bulletin*, May 1959: 55.

———. *Newsweek*, April 13, 1959: 118.

Jacobs, Lea. *The Wages of Sin: Censorship and the Fallen Woman Cycle 1928–1942*. Madison: University of Wisconsin Press, 1991.

Jarvis, Jeff. "Rock Hudson: On Camera and Off." *People*, Aug. 12, 1985: 35–41.

Jezer, Marty. *The Dark Ages: Life in the United States 1945–1960*. Boston: South End Press, 1982.

Johnson, Grady. "Marlon Brando: Actor on Impulse." *Coronet*, July 1952: 75–79.

Kael, Pauline. *5001 Nights at the Movies*. New York: Holt, Rinehart and Winston, 1982.

Kakutani, Michiko. "Garson Kanin Recalls Hollywood's High Times." *The New York Times*, Nov. 18, 1979. Rpt. in Brown and Geduld.

Kapsis, Robert E. "The Historical Reception of Hitchcock's *Marnie*." *Journal of Film and Video* 40.3 (Summer 1988): 46–63.

———. *Hitchcock: The Making of a Reputation*. Chicago: University of Chicago Press, 1992.

———. "Hollywood Filmmaking and Reputation Building: Hitchcock's *The Birds*." *Journal of Popular Film and Television* 15.1 (Spring 1987): 5–15.

Kauffmann, Stanley, ed. *American Film Criticism: From the Beginnings to Citizen Kane*. New York: Liveright, 1972.

Keneshea, Ellen. "Sirk: *There's Always Tomorrow* and *Imitation of Life*." *Women and Film* 2 (1972): 51–55.

"King of Movies Always Had a Way with Women." *New York Journal*, Feb. 24, 1958.

Kinsella, James. *Covering the Plague: AIDS and the American Media*. New Brunswick: Rutgers University Press, 1989.

Kleinhans, Chuck. "Notes on Melodrama and the Family under Capitalism." *Film Reader* 3 (1978): 40–46.

Klinger, Barbara. " 'Cinema/Ideology/Criticism' Revisited: The Progressive Text." *Screen* 25.1 (Jan.–Feb. 1984): 30–44.

———. "Cinema and Social Process: A Contextual Theory of the Cinema and Its Spectators." Ph.D. diss., University of Iowa, 1986.

———. "Digressions at the Cinema: Reception and Mass Culture." *Cinema Journal* 28.4 (Summer 1989): 3–19.

Knight, Arthur. *The Liveliest Art: A Panoramic History of the Movies*. New York: Sagamore, 1957.

———. "Plenty of Room for More." Review of *Imitation of Life*. *The Saturday Review* April 11, 1959: 28.

———. Review of *Tarnished Angels*. *Saturday Review*, Jan. 25, 1958: 27.

———. "The Williams-Kazan Axis." Review of *Baby Doll*. *The Saturday Review*, Dec. 29, 1956: 22–24.

Kobal, John. "Interview with Rock Hudson." *Films and Filming* 37.3 (October 1985): 15–18.

Koski, Fran, and Maida Tilchen. "Some Pulp Sappho." *Lavender Culture*. Karla Jay and Allen Young, eds. New York: Jove, 1979. 262–274.

Krutch, Joseph Wood. "Is Our Common Man too Common." *The Saturday Review*, Jan. 10, 1953: 8–9, 35–41.

Landy, Marcia, ed. *Imitations of Life: A Reader on Film and Television Melodrama*. Detroit: Wayne State University Press, 1991.

LaPlace, Maria. "Producing and Consuming the Woman's Film: Discursive Struggle in *Now, Voyager*," in Gledhill, 138–166.

Lazarsfeld, Paul, and Robert Merton. "Mass Communication, Popular Taste, and Organized Social Action," in Rosenberg and White, 464–66.

Leonard, George B. "The American Male: Why Is He Afraid to Be Different?" *Look*, Feb. 18, 1958: 95–102.

Linderman, Edward C. "The Common Man as Reader." *Saturday Review*, May 9, 1953: 11+.

Lipsitz, George. *Time Passages: Collective Memory and American Popular Culture*. Minneapolis: University of Minnesota Press, 1990.

Littwin, Susan. "Will America Be Shocked by 'Rock?'" *TV Guide*, Jan. 6–12, 1990: 14–17.

Locke, Edwin. *Films*, Spring 1940. Rpt. in Kauffmann, 385.

"The Long Goodbye: Rock Hudson, 1925–1985." *People*, Oct. 21, 1985: 92–105.

Lounsbury, Myron. *The Origins of American Film Criticism, 1909–1939*. New York: Arno, 1973.

Lowenthal, David. *The Past Is a Foreign Country*. New York: Cambridge University Press, 1985.

Lowenthal, Leo. "The Triumph of Mass Idols." *Literature, Popular Culture, and Society*. Leo Lowenthal, ed. Englewood Cliffs, N.J.: Prentice-Hall, 1961. 109–140.

Maland, Charles J. *Chaplin and American Culture: The Evolution of a Star Image*. Princeton: Princeton University Press, 1989.

Malcolm, Andrew H. "John Huston: I Want to Keep Right On Going." *New York Times*, Dec. 11, 1979. Rpt. in Brown and Geduld.

Mann, Denise. "The Spectacularization of Everyday Life: Recycling Hollywood Stars and Fans in Early Television Variety Shows." *Camera Obscura* 16 (Jan. 1988): 49–77.

Marcorelles, Louis. "Le film gratuit." *Cahiers du cinéma* 69 (1957): 48–49.

"Marlon Brando: World's Worst Lover." *Rave*, Dec. 1953: 1–9.

May, Elaine Tyler. *Homeward Bound: American Families in the Cold War Era*. New York: Basic, 1988.

Mayne, Judith. "Immigrants and Spectators." *Wide Angle* 5.2 (1982): 32–41.

McCarten, John. Review of *Magnificent Obsession*. *The New Yorker*, Aug. 14, 1954: 50.

McCourt, James. "Melo-Maestro." *Film Comment* 11.6 (Nov.–Dec. 1975): 19–21.

McCutcheon, Janet. "Who Is Rock Hudson?" *Movie Star Parade*, March 1957: 35–37, 58–59.

McDonnell, Kevin, and Kevin Robbins. "Marxist Cultural Theory: The Althusserian Smokescreen." *One-Dimensional Marxism: Althusser and the Politics of Culture*. Simon Clarke, Victor Seidler, et al., eds. New York and London: Allison & Bushy, 1980. 157–231.

McKegney, Michael. "*Imitation of Life*." *Film Comment* 8.2 (Summer 1972): 71–73.

Metz, Christian. "The Imaginary Signifier." *Screen* 16.2 (Summer 1975): 14–83.

Meyer, Richard. "Rock Hudson's Body," in *Inside/Out*. Diana Fuss, ed. New York: Routledge, 1991. 259–288.

Miller, Douglas T., and Marion Nowak. *The Fifties: The Way We Really Were*. New York: Doubleday, 1977.

"Moody New Star." *Life*, March 7, 1955: 5.

Morella, Joe, Edward Z. Epstein, and Eleanor Clark. *Those Great Movie Ads*. New Rochelle: Arlington, 1972.

Morin, Edgar. *Les Stars*. Paris: Seuil, 1957.

Morris, George. "Sirk's Imitations of Life." *Soho Weekly News*, Dec. 13, 1979: 40.

Moskin, J. Robert. "The American Male: Why Do Women Dominate Him?" *Look*, Feb. 4, 1958: 77–80.

Moullet, Luc. "Re-création par la récréation." *Cahiers du cinéma* 87 (1958): 54–56.

Movie and TV Spotlight, May 27, 1957.

Mulvey, Laura. "Notes on Sirk and Melodrama." *Movie* 25 (1977–78): 53–56.

———. "Visual Pleasure and Narrative Cinema." *Screen* 16.3 (Autumn 1975): 6–18.

Musto, Michael. "Benefits and Backlash: The Reaction to Rock Hudson." *The Village Voice*, Aug. 13, 1985: 24.

Naremore, James. "Authorship and the Cultural Politics of Film Criticism." *Film Quarterly* 44.1 (Fall 1990): 14–22.

Neale, Steve. "Art Cinema as Institution." *Screen* 22.1 (1981): 11–39.

———. *Cinema and Technology: Image, Sound, Color*. Bloomington: Indiana University Press, 1985.

———. "Douglas Sirk." *Framework* 11.5 (1976–77): 16–18.

———. "Melodrama and Tears." *Screen* 27.6 (1986): 6–23.

———. "Questions of Genre." *Screen* 31.1 (Spring 1990): 45–66.

Newsweek, Dec. 17, 1956: 106.

Noriega, Chon. "SOMETHING'S MISSING HERE! Homosexuality and Film Reviews during the Production Code Era, 1934–1962." *Cinema Journal* 30.1 (Fall 1990): 20–41.

Nowell-Smith, Geoffrey. "Minnelli and Melodrama." *Screen* 18.2 (1977): 113–18.

Ohmer, Susan. "Measuring Desire: George Gallup and Audience Research in Hollywood." *Journal of Film and Video* 43.1–2 (Spring–Summer 1991): 3–28.

Orr, Christopher. "Closure and Containment: Marylee Hadley in *Written on the Wind*." *Wide Angle* 4.2 (1980): 29–34.

Ott, Beverly. "The Man Who almost Got Away." *Photoplay*, April 1956: 37.

———. "Planning a Heavenly Love Nest." *Photoplay*, Feb. 1956: 44–45, 102–104.

Parsons, Louella. "Rock Hudson: Teen-Ager's Dream-Boat." *Sunday News*, Apr. 8, 1956.

Patton, Cindy. *Sex and Germs: The Politics of AIDS*. Boston: South End Press, 1985.

Peiss, Kathy. *Cheap Amusements: Working Women and Leisure in Turn-of-the-Century New York*. Philadelphia: Temple University Press, 1986.

Pells, Richard H. *The Liberal Mind in a Conservative Age: American Intellectuals in the 1940s and 1950s*. Middletown, Conn.: Wesleyan University Press, 1989.

People, Nov. 15, 1982: 148.

Peterson, Thomas. *Magazines in the Twentieth Century*. Urbana: University of Illinois Press, 1964.

Petro, Patrice. "Mass Culture and the Feminine: The Place of Television in Film Studies." *Cinema Journal* 25.3 (Spring 1986): 5–21.

Place, Janie, and Julianne Burton. "Feminist Film Criticism." *Movie* 22 (1976): 53–62.

Pollock, Griselda. "Report on the Weekend School." *Screen* 18.2 (1977): 105–113.

Pollock, Louis. "Big Noise from Winnetka." *Modern Screen*, March 1955.

Prokosh, Mike. "*Imitation of Life*," in Halliday and Mulvey, 89–94.

Ray, Robert B. *A Certain Tendency of the Hollywood Cinema, 1930–1980*. Princeton: Princeton University Press, 1985.

———. "The Bordwell Regime and the Stakes of Knowledge." *Strategies* 1 (Fall 1988): 143–81.

"Remembering Rock: Superstar with a Painful Secret." *TV Guide*, Jan. 6–12, 1990: 14–17.

Renov, Michael. "Advertising/Photojournalism/Cinema: The Shifting Rhetoric of Forties Female Representation." *Quarterly Review of Film and Video* 11.1 (1986): 1–21.

Richards, David. "Human Rights, Public Health, and the Idea of Moral Plague." *Social Research* 55.3 (Autumn 1988): 491–528.

Robinson, George. "America, Sex, and Sirk." *Filmmaker's Review* 1.5 (Mar. 18, 1976): 3–4.

"Rock Hudson Finds Fun in Just Hanging Loose." *The New York Post*, Aug. 27, 1977.

"Rock Hudson: He Didn't Mean to Make History." *People Extra*, Fall 1989: 65–66.

"Rock Hudson: Hollywood's Most Handsome Bachelor." *Life*, Oct. 3, 1955.

"Rock Hudson's Sinister Secret." *National Enquirer Special*, Fall 1990: 4–6.

"Rock Hudson Tells His Own Story." *American Weekly*, March 25, 1956.

Rodowick, D. N. *The Crisis in Political Modernism: Criticism and Ideology in Contemporary Film Theory*. Urbana and Chicago: University of Illinois Press, 1988.

———. "Madness, Authority and Ideology: The Domestic Melodrama of the 1950s." *The Velvet Light Trap* 19 (1982): 40–45.

Rogin, Michael Paul. *Ronald Reagan, the Movie, and Other Episodes in Political Demonology*. Berkeley: University of California Press, 1987.

Rogow, Lee. Review of *Magnificent Obsession*. *The Saturday Review*, July 31, 1954: 36.

Rohdie, Sam. Editorial. *Screen* 12.2 (Summer 1971): 4–6.

Rosenbaum, Jonathan. "Sirk's Works." *Soho Weekly News*, Aug. 27, 1980: 40.

Rosenberg, Bernard, and David Manning White, eds. *Mass Culture: The Popular Arts in America*. Glencoe, Ill.: Free Press, 1957.

Ross, Andrew. *No Respect: Intellectuals and Popular Culture*. New York: Routledge, 1989.

———. "Uses of Camp." *Yale Journal of Criticism* 2.1 (Fall 1988): 1–24.

"Roy Fitzgerald Takes Some Time to Reminisce." *TV Guide*, April 29–May 5, 1972: 24–28.

Russo, Vito. *The Celluloid Closet: Homosexuality in the Movies*. New York: Harper, 1987.

Sarris, Andrew. "The American Cinema." *Film Culture* 28 (Spring 1963): 1–68.

———. *The American Cinema: Directors and Directions, 1929–1968*. New York: Dutton, 1968.

———. "A Devil of a Movie, but Not Diabolical." Review of *Sorcerer*. *The Village Voice*, July 18, 1977: 37.

———. "Fassbinder and Sirk: The Ties That Unbind." *The Village Voice*, Sept. 3, 1980: 37–38.

———. "Musings of a Movie Maven." *The Village Voice*, July 25, 1977: 41.

————. "Regrets for Roads Not Taken." *The Village Voice* Nov. 21, 1977: 44.

————. "Smart Movies, Dumb Audiences." *The Village Voice*, Dec. 30–Jan. 5, 1982: 35.

————. *The Village Voice*, June 11, 1964: 13.

————. *The Village Voice*, Dec. 17, 1979: 54–55.

Saxton, Christine. "The Collective Voice as Cultural Voice." *Cinema Journal* 26.1 (1986): 19–30.

Sayre, Nora. "Films That Still Have the Power to Panic." *The New York Times*, July 31, 1977: 85.

Schatz, Thomas. *The Genius of the System: Hollywood Filmmaking in the Studio Era.* New York: Pantheon, 1988.

————. *Hollywood Genres: Formulas, Filmmaking, and the Studio System.* New York: Random, 1981.

Schickel, Richard. *Hollywood at Home: A Family Album 1950–1965.* New York: Crown, 1990.

Scullin, George. "James Dean: The Legend and the Facts." *Look*, Oct. 16, 1956: 120–26.

"Secrets of Rock Hudson's Most Crucial Year." *Movie Life*, Oct. 1956.

Seldes, Gilbert. *Esquire*, Aug. 1941. Rpt. in Kauffmann, 419.

————. *The Great Audience.* New York: Viking, 1951.

————. *The Public Arts.* New York: Simon and Schuster, 1956.

————. "Radio, Television, and the Common Man." *The Saturday Review*, Aug. 29, 1953: 11–12, 39–41.

————. *The Seven Lively Arts.* 1924. New York: Sagamore, 1957.

Selig, Michael. "Contradiction and Reading: Social Class and Sex Class in *Imitation of Life*." *Wide Angle* 10.4 (1988): 13–23.

"The Simple Life of a Busy Bachelor." *Life*, Oct. 3, 1955: 129–32.

Sindlinger and Company. "Movie Market Trends." Nov. 17, 1956.

Skolsky, Sidney. "Lonely Bachelor." *New York Post*, Feb. 6, 1955: M3.

Sontag, Susan. *Against Interpretation.* New York: Farrar, Straus and Giroux, 1966.

————. *AIDS and Its Metaphors.* New York: Farrar, Straus and Giroux, 1989.

Spoto, Donald. *The Dark Side of Genius: The Life of Alfred Hitchcock.* New York: Ballantine Books, 1983.

Staiger, Janet. "Announcing Wares, Winning Patrons, Voicing Ideals: Thinking about the History and Theory of Film Advertising." *Cinema Journal* 29.3 (Spring 1990): 12–14.

————. *Interpreting Films: Studies in the Historical Reception of American Cinema.* Princeton: Princeton University Press, 1992.

————. "The Politics of Film Canons." *Cinema Journal* 24.3 (Spring 1985): 4–23.

Stern, Michael. *Douglas Sirk.* Boston: Twayne, 1979.

————. "Interview with Douglas Sirk." *Bright Lights* 2.2 (Winter 1977–78): 29–34.

————. "Patterns of Power and Potency, Repression and Violence: An Introduction to the Study of Douglas Sirk's Films of the 1950s." *Velvet Light Trap* 16 (1976): 15–21.

Stokes, Geoffrey. "The Media and AIDS Panic: The Post-Hudson Syndrome." *Village Voice*, Oct. 15, 1985: 19.

Tompkins, Jane. *Sensational Designs: The Cultural Work of American Fiction, 1790–1860*. New York and Oxford: Oxford University Press, 1985.

Truffaut, François. *The Films in My Life*. Leonard Mayhew, trans. New York: Simon & Schuster, Inc., 1978.

Variety, March 7, 1956; Sept. 5, 1956; Dec. 5, 1956; Dec. 20, 1956.

Vološinov, V. N. "The Latest Trends in Linguistic Thought in the West." *Bakhtin School Papers*. Noel Owens, trans. Oxford: RPT Publications, 1983. 31–49.

Waldman, Diane. "From Midnight Shows to Marriage Vows: Women, Exploitation and Exhibition." *Wide Angle* 6.2 (1984): 40–48.

Walsh, Moira. Review of *Cat on a Hot Tin Roof*. *America*, Sept. 27, 1958: 679.

———. Review of *Imitation of Life*. *Catholic World*, May 1959: 154–55.

Warshow, Robert. *The Immediate Experience: Movies, Comics, Theatre, and Other Aspects of Popular Culture*. New York: Doubleday, 1962.

Watney, Simon. *Policing Desire: Pornography, AIDS, and the Media*. Minneapolis: University of Minnesota Press, 1987.

"What Marriage Did to My Son." *Movie Mirror*, May 1957: 25–28.

"Why Rock Had to Get Married." *Motion Picture*, Feb. 1956.

Willemen, Paul. "Distanciation and Douglas Sirk." *Screen* 12.2 (1971): 63–67.

———. "Remarks on *Screen*: Introductory Notes for a History of Contexts." *Southern Review* 16.2 (July 1983): 292–311.

———. "Towards an Analysis of the Sirkian System." *Screen* 13.4 (1972–73): 128–34.

Williams, Linda. " 'Something Else besides a Mother': *Stella Dallas* and the Maternal Melodrama." *Cinema Journal* 24.1 (Fall 1984): 2–27.

Wilson, Liza. "How a Hollywood Bachelor Lives." *American Weekly*, May 23, 1954: 13.

Review of *Written on the Wind*. *Film Daily*, Sept. 20, 1956.

———. *Harrison's Report*, Sept. 24, 1956.

———. *Monthly Film Bulletin*, Nov. 1956: 139.

———. *Variety*, Sept. 20, 1956.

"Zolotow's Twist on Dean." *Variety*, Dec. 5, 1956: 4.

Index

Adorno, Theodore, 81, 82, 95
Adult film: as genre, 37–41, 55–57, 66–67, 157
"Adventures of Ozzie and Harriet," 38
Agee, James, 71, 77
Ali, Fear Eats the Soul (Fassbinder), 90
All That Heaven Allows (Sirk), xi, xviii; academic criticism and, 13, 19, 21; reviews of, 77–78, 90; and Rock Hudson, 98–100, 109, 129; and camp, 145, 149, 151; and Universal Pictures, 170–171n12. *Illustrations*, 144, 146–147, 150, 152–153, 154, 155
Allen, Jeanne, xiv, 57
Allen, Robert, 70
Althusser, Louis, 13, 19
America, 71, 75
American Cinema, 5, 9, 92, 138
And God Created Woman (Vadim), 38
Avalanche (Allen), 119

Babuscio, Jack, 128, 135, 136, 137
Baby Doll (Kazan), 40, 75
The Bad Seed (LeRoy), 37, 40, 47
Bacall, Lauren, 41, 50, 58, 60, 97
Baran, Paul, 64
Barthes, Roland, 22, 25
"Batman," 138
Battle Hymn (Sirk), 98
Battle of San Pietro (Huston), 72
Bend of the River (Mann), 99, 100
Bennett, Tony, xvi, 55, 161, 164nn12,14
Bigger Than Life (Ray), xii, 56, 75
Booth, Mark, 136–137, 139
Bordwell, David, 6, 31, 164n4, 166n27, 169n79
Bourdieu, Pierre, 69n1, 70, 95–96
Brando, Marlon, 99, 104, 105–106, 115
Brecht, Bertolt, 8, 11, 14, 15, 17, 19, 25, 30, 132
Bridge on the River Kwai (Lean), 72
Bronski, Michael, 134–135, 136, 137
Brooks, Peter, xiii, 19–20

Cahiers du cinéma, 1, 2–5, 7–8, 11, 14, 32; editors of, 17
Camp: and mass camp, xv, xix, 137–142, 158, 159; subcultures and, xix, 132, 134–137, 139–140; in review journalism, 92–93, 132–133; and Rock Hudson, 127–129, 145, 149, 151, 156; Sirk critics and, 132–133, 180n2; and the politics of reception, 127–129, 134, 136–137, 139–140, 149, 151, 155–156, 158. *See also* Film reviews; Hudson, Rock
Camper, Fred, 1, 6, 9, 11–12, 15, 17, 20, 92
Canon-formation: and academia, xviii, 27–29, 31, 32–35; and Sirk criticism, 2, 27–28, 29, 31, 32–35, 158; and review journalism, xviii, 70, 71–74, 75–76, 83–87, 89, 95–96, 157, 158. *See also* Interpretation, academic; Sirk criticism; Film reviews
Captain Lightfoot, 98
"The Carol Burnett Show," 133, 138
Casablanca (Curtiz), 140, 149
Cat Ballou (Silverstein), 138
Cat on a Hot Tin Roof (Brooks), 40, 75, 112
Catholic Legion of Decency, 40, 75
Catholic World, 71, 78
Clift, Montgomery, 104
Cobweb (Minnelli), 56
Cold War, 52, 54, 64–65, 109, 112–115, 116, 117
Come Back, Little Sheba (Inge), 72
Coming Home (Ashby), 87
Commonweal, 71, 75, 76, 78
Comolli, Jean-Louis, 7–8; and Jean Narboni, 14, 15, 17, 33, 69, 159
Confidential, 53, 54, 56
Core, Philip, 132n1, 136, 141
Cory, Donald Webster, 112
Crowther, Bosley, 72–78 passim

Davidson, Sara, 125
Day, Doris, 101, 115, 119, 128

De Cordova, Richard, 98
Dean, James, 104, 105–106, 109, 115, 116
Death of a Salesman (Benedek), 72, 73
Dee, Sandra, 151
Defiant Ones (Kramer), 72
D'Emilio, John, 52, 53, 112
Demonsablon, Philippe, 4
DePalma, Brian, 87
Detective Story (Wyler), 38
Doane, Mary Ann, 28, 67
"The Donna Reed Show," 140, 141
Douglas Sirk, 6
Dyer, Richard, 51, 104, 126
"Dynasty," 123, 128, 135, 142

Easthope, Antony, 7, 14
Eckert, Charles, 126
Ehrenstein, David, 87
Eisner, Lotte, 141
Electric Horseman (Pollack), 86–87
Elsaesser, Thomas, xii, xiii, 6, 13, 15–17,
    18–25 passim, 29, 51, 92
Embryo (Nelson), 119
Evans, Linda, 123, 128

Fassbinder, Rainer Werner, 90, 93, 166n33,
    180n2
Fatal Attraction (Lyne), 148, 153
"Father Knows Best," 38, 54, 65
Faulkner, William, 80
Fernsehen und Film, 6
Film Comment, 18, 86, 87, 90
Film Culture, 3, 5
Film historiography: and textual meaning,
    xii–xiii, xvi–xx passim, 34–35, 51, 56,
    66–68, 117–118, 128–129, 154–156,
    158–160; in comparison to close analysis,
    xiii–xiv, xx, 33–35, 36–37, 51, 55–57,
    67–68, 129, 159–161; and reception, xvi–
    xvii, xix–xx, 34–35, 67–68, 117–118,
    128–129, 158–161; limitations of, xvii,
    xix–xx
Film reviews: importance of to contempo-
    rary historians, 69–70; relation to recep-
    tion, 69–70, 157–158, 173n3; methods
    of creating popular canons, 70, 71–74,
    75–76; and tastemaking functions, 70,
    79, 83–84, 85–87, 89, 95–96, 157–158
—in the 1950s: and the adult melodrama,
    74–76; and the realist canon, 70, 71–74,
    75–76, 79, 83, 157; and the New York

Film Critics, 71, 72, 93; and Cold War
    attitudes toward mass culture, 70, 80–84,
    157; and Sirk reviews, 76–80, 83; and
    attitudes toward the female audience, 77–
    78, 80, 82–84, 157
—in the 1970s: and the nostalgic canon,
    70, 84–89, 94–96, 158; connections to
    auteurism, 70, 85, 89–94; and Sirk re-
    views, 84, 87, 89–94, 95–96, 158; and
    the alternative press, 84, 91; and retro-
    spectives, 84, 91, 92, 93; and the politics
    of the 1970s, 88–89; and camp, 92–94.
    See also Canon-formation; Camp
Final Chord (Sirk), 91
The First Legion (Sirk), 11
Fischer, Lucy, 31, 163n9, 169n77
Fletcher, John, 30, 33, 34
Four Aces, 50
Frankenheimer, John, 119
Freedman, Estelle, 52, 53
French, Brandon, 168n60
Fried Green Tomatoes, 148, 153
Freud, Sigmund, 16, 17, 18, 19, 25, 112, 114
Friedan, Betty, 65–66
From Here to Eternity (Jones), 40, 53
From Here to Eternity (Zinneman), 39–40,
    72
From Reverence to Rape, 6
Fuller, Samuel, 3, 29, 31

Gaines, Jane, 57
Garland, Judy, xix, 127, 135
Gates, Phyllis, 102–103
Gavin, John, 151
Gays and Film, 135
"Get Smart," 138
Giant (Stevens), 40, 47, 99, 100, 109, 119
Ginsberg, Allen, 52, 112
Gledhill, Christine, xii, 19, 29
Godard, Jean-Luc, 3, 4, 90, 94
Gomery, Douglas, 70
Goodman, Walter, 87
Grant, Cary, 99, 126
Great Films, 74
Griffith, D. W., 143
Grosz, David, 11

La Habanera (Sirk), 91
Halliday, Jon, 6, 7–9, 10, 12–13, 17–21 pas-
    sim, 32, 92, 93
Hansen, Miriam, 118

Harvey, James, 132, 176n60
Has Anybody Seen My Gal? (Sirk), 91, 98
Haskell, Molly, 6, 17, 95, 96, 167n46
Hawks, Howard, 3, 29, 31
Heath, Stephen, 19, 22
Herrnstein-Smith, Barbara, 27
Heung, Marina, 30, 33, 34
High Anxiety (Brooks), 138, 139
High Noon (Zinneman), 72
Hitchcock, Alfred, 3, 9, 27, 87, 138
Hitler's Madman (Sirk), 91
Hoberman, J., 93–94, 133, 148
Hollywood Genres, 27
Home from the Hill (Minnelli), xii, 16, 56
Home Is Where the Heart Is, 29
Homosexuality: in the post-WWII era, 51–
52, 54, 99, 109, 112–114; and Rock
Hudson's image, 98, 109, 114–116, 120–
129, 158; and AIDS, 120–124, 126, 128;
and camp, 127–129, 135, 136, 137, 140,
149, 151. See also Camp; Hudson, Rock;
The 1950s
Homosexuality in America, 112
Horkheimer, Max, 81, 82, 95
Horrigan, William, 6, 165n9
Howl, 52, 112
Hudson, Rock, xviii, 46, 50, 58, 60, 78,
98; as an icon of "normal" masculinity,
xv, 99–103 passim, 104–106, 109, 112,
114–118, 126, 129, 157, *illustrations of*,
107, 108, 110, 111; impact on the reception of Sirk's films, xv, xix, 116–118, 127–
129, 149, 151, 157, 158; popularity, 98,
99, 101, 118–120; as representing AIDS
contamination, xv, 122–124, 128–129,
179n57, *illustration*, 124; revelations about
his homosexuality, xv, 98, 120–129, 158,
179n66; types of roles, 99–100, 109,
115–116, 119; biography, 101–102, 125;
as representing tragic AIDS hero, 121–
122, 124, 127; and camp, 127–129, 145,
149, 151, 156. Filmography, 129–130.
See also Camp; Homosexuality
Hunter, Tim, 11, 20
Huston, John, 87, 89
Hyams, Joe, 102–103, 105

Ice Station Zebra, 119
I'll Cry Tomorrow (Mann), 40, 75, 76, *illustration*, 43

I'll Cry Tomorrow (Roth), 40
Imitation of Life (Sirk), xi, xviii, 11, 21, 80;
academic criticism and, 30, 33; reviews
of, 77, 78–79; and camp, 148, 151; and
Universal Pictures, 170–171nn12,15
The Immediate Experience, 71
Inge, William, 40, 80
Interpretation, academic: and auteurism, 3,
6–7, 9–10, 17; and canon-formation,
xviii, 27–29, 31, 32–35, 158, 169n79; as
a kind of meaning-production, xviii, 1–2,
17–18, 25, 28, 31; impact of "textual
politics" paradigm on, 10, 12, 18, 20–21,
24–25, 32–34; interpretive consensus in,
21, 24–25, 26–28, 32–33; institutionalization of, 6–7, 10, 169n79; influence of
new theories on, 13–14, 18–21, 24–26,
29–30, 31; problems with formal emphasis in, 33–35, 67–68. See also Canon-formation; Progressive text; Sirk criticism
Intimate Matters, 52
Iron Man (Pevney), 100

Jacobs, Lea, xiv
Jagger, Mick, 136, 138

Kanin, Garson, 86
Kapsis, Robert, xiii, 9, 164nn14,15
Kazan, Elia, 72, 75
Keneshea, Ellen, 17, 167n46
Kinsella, James, 121
Kinsey, Alfred, 51, 53, 112, 114
Kiss Me Deadly (Aldrich), 114
Kleinhans, Chuck, 168n66
Knight, Arthur, 71, 75, 77
Kramer, Stanley, 72

Lacan, Jacques, 13, 19
Lang, Fritz, 8, 33, 89, 91
LaPlace, Maria, xiv
The Last Sunset (Aldrich), 109
Lazarsfeld, Paul, 83
Lean, David, 72, 86, 87
"Leave It to Beaver," 38, 51, 65
Lichtenstein, Roy, 138
Lipsitz, George, 65
The Lonely Crowd, 113
The Lost Weekend (Wilder), 37, *illustration*,
42
Love Me or Leave Me (Vidor), 38

Lover Come Back (Seiter), 101, 109
Lucas, George, 94, 95

MacDonald, Dwight, 81
Magnificent Obsession (Sirk), xi, xviii, 80;
    academic criticism of, 4, 21; reviews of,
    77, 78, 79; and Rock Hudson, 98, 99,
    100, 102, 109, 125; and camp, 143, 145,
    149; and Universal Pictures, 170–171*n*12
Maland, Charles, xiii, 164*n*4
Malone, Dorothy, 98
—in *Written on the Wind*, 41, 50; and
    "Temptation Dance" in, 25, 26, 27, 46–
    47, 87; 93, *illustrations of*, 48–49; aca-
    demic criticism and, 26, 27, 117; as sex-
    ual spectacle in, 46–47, 55, 60, 61, 151;
    as fashion prototype in, 59; academic
    and industry meanings for contrasted, 57;
    and camp, 143, 149
—in *Tarnished Angels*, 151. See also *Writ-
    ten on the Wind*
Man in the Gray Flannel Suit, 113
The Man with the Golden Arm (Algren), 53
The Man with the Golden Arm (Hamilton),
    39, 40, 76
Mann, Anthony, 99
Mann, Delbert, 72
Mansfield, Jayne, 53, 54, 127
Marcorelles, Louis, 4, 5, 25
Marty (Mann), 72
"Mary Hartman, Mary Hartman," 142
May, Elaine Tyler, 52, 113
McCarten, John, 79
"McMillan and Wife," 119, 120
Meet Me at the Fair (Sirk), 21
The Merchant of Four Seasons (Fassbinder),
    90
Merton, Robert, 83
Metalious, Grace, 40, 75
Metz, Christian, 19
Minnelli, Vincente, xii, 5, 15, 16, 22, 23,
    26, 36, 56, 160
The Miracle (Rossellini), 39
The Mirror Crack'd (Hamilton), 119
Mitchell, Juliet, 19
Monogram, 6, 92
Monroe, Marilyn, 46, 51–55 passim, 98–
    99, 137
Monthly Film Bulletin, 71, 78
The Moon Is Blue (Preminger), 38, 39

Morin, Edgar, 97
Morley, David, xvi
Morris, George, 91–92
Moullet, Luc, 4, 5
Movie, 7, 18
MPAA (The Motion Picture Association of
    America), 38–39, 40
Mulvey, Laura, 6, 19, 20, 22, 23, 29
My Son John (McCarey), 114
"Mystery Science Theater 3000," 133

Nabors, Jim, 120
The National Enquirer, 123, 136
Neale, Steve, 24, 30, 34, 38
New American Cinema, 84, 85–87, 89–91,
    94, 95, 158
New German Cinema, 90, 94
The New Left Review, 7, 12, 13
New York, New York (Scorcese), 95
The New Yorker Magazine, 71, 75, 79
The New York Times, 71, 72
Newsweek, 71, 75, 78
The 1950s: and the repressive label, 36, 51,
    68; and television, 38, 65; and gay sub-
    culture, 51–52, 54; and the sexual dis-
    play, 51–54, 68, 157; and the Cold War,
    52, 54, 64–65, 109, 112–115, 116, 117;
    and the ideology of affluence, 64–66,
    68, 157; and the female consumer, 65–
    66; growth of mass culture during, 80–
    81; and Cold War intellectuals, 80–83,
    84, 96, 157; and conceptions of masculin-
    ity, 99, 104–106, 109, 112–114, 116–
    118; and fears of homosexuality, 99, 109,
    112–115. See also Homosexuality
Nowell-Smith, Geoffrey, 23–24, 29
The Nun's Story (Zinneman), 72

Obsession (DePalma), 87
On the Waterfront (Kazan), 72
Open City (Rossellini), 72
Ophuls, Max, 8, 20, 33, 89
Orr, Christopher, 26–27
The Outlaw, 39

Patton, Cindy, 122
Pells, Richard, 80
Pennies from Heaven (Ross), 95
Peyton Place (Metalious), 40
Peyton Place (Robson), 53, 75

Picnic (Inge), 40
Picnic (Logan), 76
Pillow Talk (Gordon), 99, 101, 115
The Pink Panther (Edwards), 85, 87
Place, Janie, and Julianne Burton, 168n60
Playboy, 53–54, 56, 115–116
Polanski, Roman, 90
Positif, 6, 18
Preminger, Otto, 5, 8, 91
Presley, Elvis, 46, 99
Progressive text, xii, xiv–xv, 14, 17, 19–20, 24, 32, 33–35; the text/ideology relation reconsidered, 36–37, 51, 55–57, 66–68, 116–118, 129, 154–156, 159–161. *See also* Sirk criticism
Prokosh, Mike, 6, 11, 20
Psychoanalysis and Feminism, 19

Queen Christina (Mamoulian), 148

Radway, Janice, xvi
Randall, Tony, 109, 115
Ray, Nicholas, xii, 3, 5, 15–16, 36, 56, 76, 89, 160
Ray, Robert, 9, 31, 85, 138
Rebecca (Hitchcock), 28
Rebel without a Cause (Ray), 16, 56, 75, 76
Renov, Michael, 173n55
Riesman, David, 113, 114
Rock Hudson: His Story, 125
Rodowick, David, 26–27, 29, 165n5
Rogow, Lee, 77
Rohdie, Sam, 7, 13, 166n29
La Ronde (Ophuls), 38
Rope (Hitchcock), 112
The Rose Tatoo (Mann), 39
The Rose Tatoo (Williams), 40
Rosenbaum, Jonathan, 92–93, 132–133
Rosenberg, Bernard, 82–83
Ross, Andrew, 81, 135, 136, 137, 140
Russo, Vito, 115

St. James, Susan, 119
Sarris, Andrew, 1, 3, 5, 9, 87, 91, 92, 94, 132, 174n7, 176n69
"Saturday Night Live," 133, 138
The Saturday Review, 71, 75, 77, 81–82
Schatz, Thomas, 27
Screen, xiii, 5, 6, 7, 11, 13, 18–22 passim, 33, 91, 92
The Searchers (Ford), 38, 105

"Second City TV," 133
Seconds (Frankenheimer), 119
Seldes, Gilbert, 71, 82, 83
Selig, Michael, 30
Send Me No Flowers (Jewison), 101
The Shanghai Express (Von Sternberg), 148
Shawn, Dick, 115
Sign of the Pagan (Sirk), 91
Sindlinger, Albert, 47
Sirk criticism: problems in, xii, xiv–xv, 2, 32, 33–35, 51; impact on melodrama theory and criticism, xii, xiii, 1, 22, 29; importance of historical research to, xii–xviii, 35–37, 51, 55–57, 67–68, 117–118, 128–129, 154–156, 158–161; and *Cahiers du cinéma*, 1, 2–5, 7–8, 11, 14, 32; and Andrew Sarris, 1, 5, 9, 91, 92, 94; and feminism, 1, 16, 17, 19, 23, 26, 28, 30, 31; and cultural studies, 1, 28, 30–31, 32, 33, 34; and canon-formation, 2, 27–28, 29, 31, 32–35, 158; and Marxism, 5, 7, 10, 12–18, 24–25, 26, 91–94; and impact of author's intentions on, 9–10, 17, 154–156, 158–159, 166n28; and traditional auteurism, 11–12, 18, 91, 92; and the concept of the progressive text, 14, 17, 20, 24, 25, 32, 33–37, 51, 55–57, 66–68, 90, 91–94, 96, 117; and psychoanalysis, 16, 18–25, 26, 32; role of interviews in, 7–10, 14, 15, 18, 21, 32, 91. *See also* Canon-formation; Film historiography; Progressive text
Sirk, Douglas: as a subversive auteur, xi, xii, xiv–xv, 12–17, 19–20, 26, 28, 32, 33, 154–156, 158; biography, xi, 78, 163n2; interviews with, 6, 7–10; retrospectives of work, 6, 7, 18, 84, 91, 92, 93; and the political canon, 12, 32, 33–35; his artistic reputation reconsidered, xiii, 58–59, 168n62. Filmography, 181
Sirk's melodramas: and the Eisenhower era, xii–xiv, 8, 9, 12–16 passim, 21, 24, 36, 51, 57, 68, 90, 91; as subversive, xi, xv, xviii, 14–17, 19–26 passim, 36, 51, 55, 68, 91, 158; as adult, xv, xviii, 40–41, 46–51, 54–57, 66, 67–68, 157, 158, 159; and masculinity, xv, xviii–xix, 23, 98, 99, 100, 104, 109, 116–118, 127–129, 149, 151, 157, 158; as camp, xv, xix, 92–93, 127–129, 143, 145, 148–149, 151, 154–156, 158; discussions of

style, 4–5, 8–12 passim, 15, 16–17, 22–
27 passim, 30, 34, 57–63, 66–68, 90–
94, 148, 154–156; and the political
canon, 12, 18, 20, 26, 27–28, 29, 31,
32–35, 158; and female sexuality, 19, 25,
26, 27, 46–47, 55, 60–63 passim, 67–
68, 93, 151. See also Camp; Canon-for-
mation; Hudson, Rock; Progressive text
Sirk on Sirk, 6, 7–9, 10, 15, 24, 32
Slander (Rowland), 37
Sleep, My Love (Sirk), 21, 91
Slightly French (Sirk), 21
Smiles of a Summer Night (Bergman), 38
"Soap," 142
The Soho Weekly News, 84, 91, 132
Some Came Running (Minnelli), 56
Sontag, Susan, 134, 135–136, 137, 140
Spillane, Mickey, 53, 113
Spoto, Donald, 9
St. James, Susan, 119
Stack, Robert, 41, 46, 47, 50, 58, 60, 87,
98; Sirk roles and sexuality, 16, 23; roles
compared to Rock Hudson's, 109, 115; as
a "split character," 117
Staiger, Janet, xvi–xvii, 33, 164n12,
164n14, 174n8
Star Wars (Lucas), 85, 87, 94, 141
Stars: impact on reception, xv, xix, 98, 116–
118, 126–129, 149, 151; semiotics of, 97–
98, 126–127
Les Stars, 97
Stella Dallas (Vidor), 28
Stern, Michael, 25, 167n56
The Strange One (Garfein), 112
A Streetcar Named Desire (Kazan), 72, 73
A Streetcar Named Desire (Williams), 40, 72
Summer Storm (Sirk), 21, 77
Summer with Monika (Bergman), 38
Sweezy, Paul, 64

Tarnished Angels, xi, xviii–xix; Cahiers du
cinéma, 4, 5; and academic criticism, 21;
and reviews of, 77, 80; and Rock Hudson, 98, 100; and camp, 151; and Universal Pictures, 170–171n12
Taylor, Elizabeth, 119, 122
Taza, Son of Cochise (Sirk), 98, 100, 120
Tea and Sympathy (Anderson), 40
Tea and Sympathy (Minnelli), 47, 56, 112; Illustration, 44
Temple, Shirley, 98

Terms of Endearment (Brooks), 141, 153
Thunder on the Hill (Sirk), 91
Time, 71, 77
A Time to Love and a Time to Die (Sirk), 4
To Have and Have Not (Hawks), 97
Tobruk (Hiller), 119
Tompkins, Jane, xiii, 1–2
"The Tonight Show," 133
Touch of Evil (Welles), 19, 22
Trapeze (Reed), 40
True Confessions, 54, 56
Truffaut, François, 3, 4
Turner, Lana, 79, 98, 120, 148, 151

The Undefeated (McLaglen), 119
Universal Pictures, 37, 148; and Written on
the Wind, 40, 41, 47, 50, 54, 57–63 passim, 66; and Rock Hudson, 98, 99, 106,
125

Valentino, Rudolph, 104, 118
A Very Special Favor (Gordon), 115
The Village Voice, 84, 87, 93, 94
Von Sternberg, Josef, 148

Waldman, Diane, 57
Warhol, Andy, 136, 137
Warshow, Robert, 71, 81
Way Down East (Griffith), 143
Wilder, Billy, 8
Willemen, Paul, xiv, 6, 13, 14–15, 17–25
passim, 92, 132, 166n41, 168n70
Williams, Linda, 28
Williams, Tennessee, 40, 72, 80
Willson, Henry, 102, 125
Wilson, Sloan, 113
Woollacott, Janet, 55
Women and Film, 6
Written on the Wind (Sirk), xi; academic
criticism and, xii, 4, 5, 15, 16, 21, 23,
25, 26; as box-office success, xviii; aca-
demic and industry meanings for com-
pared, 36–37, 51, 56–57, 67–68; reviews of, 78, 87, 90, 92, 93–94; and
Rock Hudson's roles in, 98, 100, 109,
117, 129; and camp, 133, 143, 148, 149
—and Universal Pictures: censorship ratings
for, 40; and trade press reviews, 40–41,
46, 48; advertising as adult, 40–41, 46–
47, 50–51; posters for, 41, 46, illustration, 45; trailer for, 41–42; and market re-

Written on the Wind (continued)
  search for, 47; and the sexual display, 54–
  57; strategies directed at a female audience, 47, 50, 58, 59, 61, 63, 66, 67,
  172n31; use of the female body to sell,
  46–47, 55, 57, 59–60, 61, 62, 63, 67;
  selling as romance, 47, 50; advertising
  strategies related to social context, 51–57,
  64–68; and press books, 58–60; appeals
to class, 57, 58, 61–63, 66, 67; scale of
  ad campaign, 170n2
Wyman, Jane, 98, 100, 145, 149, 151

Young, Gig, 115
Young Mr. Lincoln (Ford), 17, 22

Zinneman, Fred, 72
Zu Neuen Ufern, 11